James Rajotte 2003

About the Fraser Institute

The **Fraser Institute** is an independent Canadian economic and social research and educational organization. It has as its objective the redirection of public attention to the role of competitive markets in providing for the well-being of Canadians. Where markets work, the Institute's interest lies in trying to discover prospects for improvement. Where markets do not work, its interest lies in finding the reasons. Where competitive markets have been replaced by government control, the interest of the Institute lies in documenting objectively the nature of the improvement or deterioration resulting from government intervention.

The **Fraser Institute** is a national, federally-chartered, non-profit organization financed by the sale of its publications and the tax-deductible contributions of its members, foundations, and other supporters; it receives no government funding.

Director, Publication Production, J. Kristin McCahon
Events Coordinator, Leah Costello
Coordinator, Student Programs, Vanessa Schneider

Research

Director, Fiscal and Non-Profit Studies, Jason Clemens
Director, School Performance Studies, Peter Cowley
Director, Pharmaceutical Policy Research, John R. Graham
Director, Centre for Studies in Risk, Regulation, and Environment, Kenneth Green
Director, Centre for Trade and Globalization Studies, Fred McMahon
Director, Education Policy, Claudia Rebanks Hepburn
Senior Research Economist, Niels Veldhuis

Ordering publications

To order additional copies of this book, any of our other publications, or a catalogue of the Institute's publications, please contact the book-sales coordinator: via our **toll-free order line: 1.800.665.3558, ext. 580;** via telephone: 604.688.0221, ext. 580; via fax: 604.688.8539; via e-mail: sales@fraserinstitute.ca.

Media

For media information, please contact Suzanne Walters, Director of Communications: via telephone: 604.714.4582 3 or, from Toronto, 416.363.6575, ext. 582; via e-mail: suzannew@fraserinstitute.ca

Website

To learn more about the Institute and to read our publications on line, please visit our web site at www.fraserinstitute.ca.

Membership

For information about membership in The Fraser Institute, please contact the Development Department: The Fraser Institute, 4th Floor, 1770 Burrard Street, Vancouver, BC, V6J 3G7; or via telephone: 604.688.0221 ext. 586; via fax: 604.688.8539; via e-mail: membership@fraserinstitute.ca.

In **Calgary**, please contact us via telephone: 403.216.7175; via fax 403.234.9010; via e-mail: barrym@fraserinstitute.ca.

In **Toronto**, please contact us via telephone: 416.363.6575; via fax: 416.601.7322.

Publication

Editing and design by Kristin McCahon and Lindsey Thomas Martin
Cover design by Brian Creswick @ GoggleBox.

Tax Reform in Canada
Our Path to Greater Prosperity

Tax Reform in Canada

Our Path to Greater Prosperity

Edited by Herbert G. Grubel

THE FRASER INSTITUTE

The Fraser Institute

Vancouver British Columbia Canada

2003

The authors of this book have worked independently and opinions expressed by them are, therefore, their own, and do not necessarily reflect the opinions of the members or the trustees of The Fraser Institute.

Printed in Canada.

National Library of Canada Cataloguing in Publication Data

Main entry under title:
Tax reform in Canada : our path to greater prosperity /
edited by Herbert G. Grubel

"The papers in this volume were presented at a conference in Toronto, Ontario, October 11, 2001"--Pref.

Includes bibliographical references.

ISBN 0-88975-199-4

1. Taxation--Canada--Congresses. 2. Tax incidence--Canada--Congresses. I. Grubel, Herbert G., 1934- II. Fraser Institute (Vancouver, B.C.)

HJ2449.T39 2003 336.2'00971 C2002-911546-9

Contents

About the authors

Jason Clemens is the Director of Fiscal and Non-Profit Studies at The Fraser Institute. He has an Honours BA in Commerce and an MA in Business Administration from the University of Windsor as well as a post-Baccalaureate Degree in Economics from Simon Fraser University. His publications and co-publications for The Fraser Institute include *Canada's All Government Debt* (1996), *Bank Mergers: The Rational Consolidation of Banking in Canada* (1998), the 1998, 1999, 2000 and 2001 *Non-Profit Performance Report, The 20% Foreign Property Rule: Decreasing Returns and Increasing Risk for RRSPs and RPPs* (1999), *Preserving Independence* (1999), *Returning British Columbia to Prosperity* (2001), *Flat Tax: Issues and Principles* (2001), *Surveying US and Canadian Welfare Reform* (2001), and *Corporate Capital Tax: Canada's Most Damaging Tax* (2002). His articles have appeared in the *Wall Street Journal*, the *National Post*, the *Globe and Mail*, the *Vancouver Sun*, the *Calgary Herald*, the *Winnipeg Free Press*, the *Ottawa Citizen*, the *Montreal Gazette*, *La Presse*, and other newspapers.

Bev Dahlby has been a professor in the Department of Economics at the University of Alberta since 1978. He was born at Beechy, grew up on a farm near Star City, Saskatchewan and attended the University of Saskatchewan, Queen's University, and the London School of Economics. He has published extensively on tax policy and fiscal federalism and was a member of the Technical Committee on Business Taxation, which issued its report on reforming business taxation in April 1998. He has also served as a policy advisor to the Alberta government, worked on tax reform projects at the Thailand Development Research Institute in Bangkok, and served as a technical advisor on an International Monetary Fund mission to Malawi. In 1998/1999, he held a McCalla Research Professorship at the University of Alberta.

Joel Emes is a Senior Analyst with the BC Progress Board. From 1996 to 2002, he was senior research economist at The Fraser Institute, where he was the primary researcher for Tax Freedom Day and the Institute's provincial and state-provincial fiscal comparisons, the Budget Performance Index and the Fiscal Performance Index. He was also a regular contributor to the Fraser Institute's monthly magazine, Fraser Forum. He was co-author of Tax Facts 10, 11, and 12, and Canada's All Government Debt (1996, 1998, and 1999 editions). His articles have appeared in the National Post, the Globe and Mail, the Calgary Herald, the Vancouver Sun and the London Free Press. He received his M.A. in Economics from Simon Fraser University in 1995.

Herbert G. Grubel is Professor of Economics (Emeritus) at Simon Fraser University and a Senior Fellow at the Fraser Institute (Vancouver, Canada), where he holds the David Somerville Chair in Fiscal Studies. He has a B.A. from Rutgers University and a Ph.D. in economics from Yale University (1963). He has taught full-time at Stanford University, the University of Chicago, and the University of Pennsylvania and has held temporary appointments at universities in Berlin, Singapore, Cape Town, Nairobi, Oxford, and Canberra. Herbert Grubel was an elected member of the Parliament of Canada from 1993 to 1997 and served as the Minister of Finance in his party's shadow cabinet. He has published many books and articles on economics and finance.

Kenneth J. McKenzie is Professor in the Department of Economics, University of Calgary and specializes in public finance, in particular tax policy and political economy. He has published widely in these areas and has won several awards for his research, including the Harry Johnson award for the best article in the *Canadian Journal of Economics,* the Doug Purvis Prize for research in public policy, and the Faculty of Social Sciences Research Achievement Award at the University of Calgary. He is a fellow of both the Fraser Institute and the C.D. Howe Institute, where he delivered the 2001 Benefactor's Lecture.

Jack M. Mintz is the President and CEO of the C.D. Howe Institute. and Professor of Taxation, J.L. Rotman School of Management, University of Toronto. He has published over 180 books and articles on public economics and his book, *Most Favored Nation,* was awarded the 2002 Purvis prize for best writing in economic policy and was runner-up for the Donner book prize. Mr Mintz has served as Clifford Clark Visiting Economist at Finance Canada, 1996/1997, and headed the Technical Committee on Business Taxation. He serves on numerous boards and is the founding editor-in-chief of *International Tax and Public Finance,* a leading public economics journal.

Finn Poschmann is Senior Policy Analyst at the C.D. Howe Institute, where he has worked since 1998. For more than a decade previous to 1998, he was at the Parliamentary Research Branch in Ottawa, where he held a number of research positions principally involved with providing economic analysis and advice to Parliamentarians and Standing Committees. He has worked in numerous areas within the field of economics but his prime concern has been with public finance and taxation and relation between federal and provincial governments. He is particularly interested in the distributional impact of taxation and in the use of microsimulation tools in the design of tax policy but his work also has taken him into monetary policy and other areas of Canadian public policy. Recent publications dealt with the international monetary system and the tax treatment of retirement savings.

William B.P. Robson is Vice President and Director of Research at the C.D. Howe Institute. He specializes in Canadian fiscal and monetary policy. He has written extensively on government budgets and their economics effects, on pension policy, and on the Bank of Canada and inflation. He also wrote, with co-author David Laidler, the prize-winning *The Great Canadian Disinflation*. Mr. Robson is a familiar commentator on economic issues in the media.

Rodger Scott was a Fiscal Policy research intern at The Fraser Institute during the summer of 2001. He holds a BA (Hons) in Economics from Queen's University and an MA in Economics from York University. He is currently employed by the Personal Income Tax section, Federal Department of Finance.

Michael A. Walker is Executive Director of The Fraser Institute (Vancouver, Canada). He writes regularly for daily newspapers and financial periodicals. His articles have also appeared in technical journals in Canada, the United States, and Europe, including *The American Economic Review*, the *Canadian Journal of Economics, Canadian Public Policy, Health Affairs* and the *Canadian Tax Journal*. He has written or edited 40 books on economic matters. Born in Newfoundland in 1945, he received his B.A. (summa) at St. Francis Xavier University in 1966 and completed the work for his Ph.D. in Economics at the University of Western Ontario in 1969.

Brendan Walsh has been Professor of National Economics at University College, Dublin since 1980. He graduated from University College, Dublin in 1961, obtained a doctorate in economics from Boston College in 1966 and taught in several American universities before returning to Ireland to take up a post at the Economic and Social Research Institute in 1969. He has served overseas—in Iran in 1975/1976 and in The Gambia from 1989 to 1991—as an economic advisor with the Harvard Institute for International Development. He has written widely on the Irish economy and has acted as a consultant to bodies such as the ECD and the Commission of the EU. He is a member of the Royal Irish Academy.

Thomas A. Wilson is the Director of the Policy and Economic Analysis Program at the Institute for Policy Analysis, University of Toronto. He is also the Area Coordinator for Business Economics at the Faculty of Management. Professor Wilson's research interests include fiscal and tax policy, applied macro-economic modelling, and industrial organization. He has published numerous research papers in each of these areas. He has also been the co-author or co-editor of 15 books, including the recent volumes, *Fiscal Policy in Canada* (with P. Dungan), *Fiscal Targets and Economic Growth* (with T. Courchene), *The Electronic Village: Policy Issues of the Information Economy* (with Dale Orr), *Rationality in Public Policy: Retrospect and Prospect, A Tribute to Douglas G. Hartle* (with R. Bird and M. Trebilcock), and *The 2000 Federal Budget: Retrospect and Prospect* (with Paul A. R. Hobson). His consulting work has included economic forecasting, fiscal and tax policy analysis, regulation of telecommunications, and competition policy. He received his Ph.D. and A.M.in Economics from Harvard University and his B.A. in Economics from the University of British Columbia.

Preface

The papers in this volume were presented at a conference in Toronto, October 11, 2001. The audience included a number of taxation experts from the private and public sector. Their valuable questions and comments are reflected in the revised papers in this book.

This volume is the fourth in a series concerned with fiscal and taxation issues facing Canada. The preceding three volumes, also edited by Herbert Grubel and published by The Fraser Institute, are: (1) *How to Use the Fiscal Surplus: What is the Optimal Size of Government* (1998); (2) *Unlocking Canadian Capital: The Case for Capital Gains Tax Reform* (2000); (3) *International Evidence on the Effects of Having No Capital Gains Taxes* (2001)

The projects have been financed by a grant from the John Dobson Foundation of Montreal. John Dobson attended the conferences and made valuable contributions based on his long experience as the manager of *Formula Growth*. This private investment fund has enjoyed the highest long-run rates of return of all Canadian funds for which data are published.

My thanks go to John Dobson; Michael Walker, the Executive Director of The Fraser Institute; its production staff, Kristin McCahon and Lindsey Thomas Martin; Lorena Baran and the staff of the events department; and, of course, the authors of the papers included in this volume for their contributions to the success of this project. The authors' cooperation in returning their revised papers promptly is especially appreciated. I also thank Jason Clemens, Joel Emes and Rodger Scott for allowing the inclusion of their study on the capital tax, which was not delivered at the Toronto conference.

Herbert G. Grubel, Vancouver, April 2002

Tax Reform in Canada
Our Path to Greater Prosperity

Introduction

Herbert Grubel

This introduction consists of three parts. The first outlines conditions that make tax reform possible and desirable. It is argued that these conditions exist in Canada at the beginning of the new millennium. The second part provides very short summaries of the papers included in this volume. The final part presents a simplified agenda for tax reform that emerged from the conference.

Conditions for tax reform

Major tax reform is needed and possible when three conditions are met. First, the existing tax code has become so cumbersome and complex that its operation is excessively expensive. Second, changes in the economic environment have made obsolete policies that were designed to deal with once pressing economic and political issues. Third, new theoretical and empirical knowledge has accumulated and shows that the costs of the existing tax structure are unnecessarily high relative to available alternatives.

The complexity of the present tax system

Most Canadians, especially after they have filed their annual personal income-tax returns every spring, are convinced that the Canadian tax code is too complex and costly to comply with. Revenue

Canada, now the Canadian Customs and Revenue Agency, has been adding directives to the existing code almost daily for decades so that the rules in force now occupy several feet of space on the shelves of libraries, accountants, and tax lawyers. One professional tax adviser working for one of the world's largest consulting firms once told me that, when he travels abroad to consult with foreign governments, he feels that his knowledge is obsolete upon his return to Canada one month later. That reflects how many CCRA bulletins and regulations he has missed and discussions and interpretations he has failed to share with his colleagues.

There are good reasons why Canada's tax code has become increasingly complex. The tax collectors, pushed by politicians, want the system to be fair in the sense that it responds to the special circumstances of individual taxpayers that are not covered by existing regulations. An employee of the Department of Finance in 1996 told the Finance Committee of the House of Commons (on which I served as the representative of the Reform Party) that the original legislation setting up the Registered Retirement Savings Account system covered one paragraph. The code has been amended ever since by many bulletins and it now covers many pages. These amendments were the response to demands by Canadians who were able to show that their individual circumstances made the existing code highly unfair. Often, their personal financial affairs, arranged a long time before the creation of the latest law, would result in costly consequences that were not intended by the legislation. I believe that the government is acting properly in taking account of such special personal circumstances and most Canadians would agree.

The complexities of the tax code also arise as a result of the desire of politicians to provide benefits to special-interest groups in the economy. For example, investment in the film industry is guided by many special tax rules designed to subsidize this activity. These rules favour certain types of workers and firms. They are designed to create a national capacity to make films and encourage an entertainment industry that promotes Canadian culture and values. These policies bring politicians support at the ballot box from those in one industry or another who benefit directly and from cultural nationalists driven by their own agenda. The cost of the rules in the form of higher other taxes or complexity of the tax code are relatively small for other Canadians and politicians do not face punishment from them at the ballot box.

As another example of unjustifiable complexity, consider the special treatment of broader industry classes. As discussed at length in Tom Wilson's paper, Canadian manufacturing industries benefit from preferential rates of taxation, certain resource industries are favoured by special allowances and deductions, and small, Canadian-controlled, private companies enjoy special low rates of taxation. Such differences in taxation levels cannot be justified on grounds of economic efficiency or equity. Their defenders, of course, justify the special privileges, on the grounds that they bring substantial, but largely immeasurable, non-market benefits to society. The technical Committee on Business Taxation (1997), also known as The Mintz Commission, recommended that the government should reform business taxation to correct the existing flaws. Wilson's paper provides useful perspectives on these flaws and what the government has done to fix them.

Changes in the economic environment

Economic development policies for Western Canada during the last half of the nineteenth century involved the encouragement of agriculture in the prairies. In the pursuit of this objective, the government made a deal with the Canadian Pacific Railroad. It granted the railroad rights of way and strips of land for development, and required that it bind itself to the shipment of grains across the Rockies at a fee that was fixed in perpetuity. The resultant "Crow rate" (after the Crow's Nest Pass on the border betweenAlberta and British Columbia) has long represented an inefficient subsidy to Canadian grain farmers in the prairies.

Initially, the low, fixed tariff encouraged farming and grain exports. However, eventually the main effect of the subsidy was to raise the value of agricultural land and every new generation of farmers that bought the more expensive land faced the same eternal economic struggle with low prices for their output and high prices for their inputs. The subsidy did not help. In addition, the subsidy encouraged the shipment of grain when it would have been more rational to ship beef and hogs fed with the grain in the prairies. The railroad suffered increasing deficits on the Crow's Nest route as inflation raised the costs of operation while the price charged to farmers was fixed in nominal dollars. The Crow rate was removed, after nearly a century, in the middle of the 1990s and only after many studies had shown the real economic costs they had imposed on the entire economy and the limited benefits it provided present farmers.

There are other examples of tax rules and subsidies that once could be justified but that are no longer rational as economic circumstances have changed. Thus, exploitation of natural resources through farming, mining, fishing, and forestry once was the primary source of strength for the Canadian economy. However, at an increasing rate during the twentieth century, economic wealth in the world came to be created through manufacturing. For most of the century, the conventional wisdom was that autarky in manufacturing was desirable for national security and pride and, so, the government of Canada offered preferential rates of taxation to foster manufacturing. Now that Canada has a prosperous manufacturing sector and free trade has replaced autarky as the best road to prosperity, it is time to end the preferential tax treatment of that sector.

For another example of the use of taxation to foster the development of special industries and of the effect of changing conditions, consider the energy sector. The OPEC crisis of the 1970s resulted in increased subsidies to the discovery and production of oil and gas and the development of alternative energy resources like the Alberta tar sands and wind and solar power. These ongoing subsidies result in the over-production of energy for both domestic use and export. There is no rational economic case for the continuation of these subsidies in a world awash with energy and fully integrated globally.

Finally, the capital gains tax has become an increasingly costly burden because, during the last 20 years, the world's capital markets have become increasingly integrated. Investors have become much more responsive to small differences in expected rates of return, the safety of their property rights and political stability. Canadian wealth-holders are important players in these global capital markets. As a result of these developments, rules of taxation that impose higher costs on investment in Canada than exist abroad, result in the loss of capital in Canada until the after-tax rates of return are raised and again equal those abroad. As I argue in my own paper in this book, this new and stronger international tax arbitrage has made it likely that the capital gains tax in Canada has lowered tax revenue from other sources by more than is raised by the tax itself.

All of the negative aspects of the capital gains tax apply to the corporate capital tax. In addition, this tax has the disadvantage that it is payable whether or not a firm is profitable. Corporations find this feature to be especially burdensome since it results in cash-flow problems at times when business activity is depressed and profits are down. Jason Clemens, Joel Emes and Rodger Scott discuss various other damaging effects of this tax in their second contribution to this volume. (The paper was not delivered at the Toronto conference because of time limitations. It is a shortened version of a longer study published separately by The Fraser Institute.)

New knowledge about taxation

Canada's last major tax reform in the early 1970s was based to a considerable degree on the best knowledge about the nature and effects of taxation existing at the time. It was also based on the popular ideology that the fairness of the tax system and distribution of income were more important than efficiency and economic growth.

Since the 1970s, much has changed that impinges on the merit of the tax system created then. Communist, socialist and even social-democratic policies for taxation, income distribution, and economic management lost much of their appeal as the Russian empire disintegrated and the United States flourished under a regime favouring free markets. In Canada, the relative decline of per-capita income has prompted a debate over its causes that has pointed to the obsolete taxation system as a major factor.

More important for this study, research by economists, financial experts, and taxation specialists has produced much new knowledge about the nature and effects of taxation. There are two types of such research. The first involves theoretical modeling of economic processes and human behaviour and empirical estimates based on micro- and macro-economic data. Second, researchers compare the experiences of different countries that have different tax regimes or have gone through major tax reforms.

Induced changes in human behaviour

History provides an outstanding example of how taxation induces changes in human behaviour designed to avoid the payment of taxes: the taxation of property based on the number of windows in a house. This tax base is ideal from the point of view of tax collectors. It cannot be avoided by illegally designed transactions. It also cannot be evaded because it costs too much to redesign houses. However, as history has shown, although the evasion of the tax may have been impossible in the short run, in the longer run houses were rebuilt and new ones designed with ever fewer windows. It is important to note that the new designs of houses were accompanied by costs. Obviously, esthetically, homeowners had preferred more windows per house before the government induced them to have fewer. Less obvious, perhaps, are the implications for hygiene resulting from less ventilation and for the cost of lighting the houses. In sum, taxation not only resulted in a shrinking of its base, it also resulted in the misallocation of resources that lowered real incomes.

Economists in recent decades have developed the concepts of optimum taxation and the related marginal efficiency cost of taxation or marginal cost of public funds. These concepts formally incorporate and measure the costs created by changes in human behaviour caused by the imposition of a given tax. As one would expect, these costs depend on a host of conditions but, especially, the ease with which taxpayers can avoid a given tax, known formally as the elasticity of response.

It does not come as a surprise that the marginal efficiency costs are different for different taxes, both in the short run and in the longer run. Direct taxes on work, investment, and risk taking have the highest costs since individuals can easily change their behavior to avoid the tax. The growth of the underground economy reflects the shift of labour from the formal and taxed into the informal and untaxed markets. In addition, workers can avoid the payment of taxes by enjoying more leisure or using their time to do their own home and car repairs and engage in similar productive activities that legally escape taxation.

Taxes on capital and risk taking similarly can be avoided easily. People shift their investments abroad or, more important, consume rather than invest their money. They avoid risky investments in favour of government securities that are safer but have a lower return.

The lowest marginal efficiency costs are found for direct taxes on consumption, be they sales, excise, or value-added taxes. These taxes cannot be avoided since everyone has to buy goods and services to sustain and enjoy life.

In recent years, economists have made numerous studies to measure the marginal efficiency cost of taxation. Even the Department of Finance has produced research on the subject, which in turn appeared in a publication by the OECD. Bev Dahlby in his contribution below reviews these empirical studies, which confirm the theoretical expectations noted above.

The theory and empirical studies have some very important implications for tax policy in Canada. Dahlby argues that the substitution of direct for indirect taxes would reduce substantially the drag on efficiency due to the overall system of taxation. Increases in the GST and the provincial sales taxes and the lowering of taxes on personal and capital income would bring gains in efficiency in the short run as well as increases in productivity and labour income over the longer run.

One way in which the tax on work can be made less distorting is through the introduction of a tax that does not have progressive marginal rates. Jason Clemens and Joel Emes in their paper suggest that lost revenue can easily be made up by the elimination of existing tax exemptions and exceptions.

Given the importance of investment for productivity, living standards, and economic growth, several papers in this volume lament the multiple taxation of capital income under the present tax system. As it stands, businesses pay the corporate income tax on their profits. The dividends paid out of this after-tax business income are then subject to taxation in the personal returns of the recipients. Capital gains from the sale of the business are subject to capital gains taxation.

There is no doubt that such multiple taxation is unfair and results in lower investment. This fact has implicitly been acknowledged in the Canadian tax code, which in principle allows individuals to eliminate the double taxation of dividends. However, the system used is deficient in several ways stressed by Tom Wilson in his paper. There is a complicated system of grossing up of dividend income and a deduction from taxes owed, which most taxpayers do not understand. Dominant in the filing process appears to be the need to report dividends as taxable income in the first place.

In addition, the rates used for gross-up and deductions do not eliminate double taxation completely. This failure is due to the fact that the rates were set to assure the elimination of the double taxation of income from small business, which is lower than that for most corporations. Wilson argues that the preferential rates for small business should be eliminated for the sake of efficiency. If this were done, it would be possible to eliminate double taxation of business income very easily and clearly by a simple credit for the taxes already paid by the business.

The taxation of capital gains has similarly been studied and shown to result in larger losses in efficiency and smaller effects on the equality of income than had been known before. Grubel in his contribution argues that the new information makes a good case for the abolition of the capital gains tax.

International evidence

Unfortunately, it is not possible to engage in empirical tests of the validity of most of the policy conclusions that have emerged from new theoretical insights and the indirect empirical evidence assembled to measure the effects of different tax policies. Many of the favourable developments from changes in the mix of taxes will come about only slowly and are likely to be dominated by a host of other changes taking place in the economy.

However, the experience of other countries with tax changes is relevant to questions about the likely effect of proposed similar changes in Canada. One of the most widely studied set of tax changes took place in the United States under the leadership of President Ronald Reagan. The cuts had been inspired by research known as supply-side economics and associated with the names of Arthur Laffer and Robert Mundell.

Not all economists agree with the theory and empirical evidence on the effect of tax and spending cuts on economic growth. However, many are convinced by, and have successfully advocated policies such as those introduced in Margaret Thatcher's Britain. The tax cuts undertaken under President George W. Bush in 2001 are based on this empirical evidence.

Ireland has been the poor cousin of its more prosperous neighbour Britain and continental Europe for many years. In the early 1990s, Ireland changed its economic policies. Since then, its economy has grown very rapidly. Ten years after the reforms, Ireland's per-capita income exceeds that of most of its neighbouring countries. How important were changes in the level and structure of taxation in this Irish success story?

The paper by Brendan Walsh in this volume examines this question and concludes that taxation reforms have been important but that there have been a host of other changes that contributed to the superior economic growth record. The removal of rigidities in the labour market, the adoption of the euro, and some subsidies from the European Community are shown to have played major roles in Ireland's economic renaissance.

The paper by Michael Walker introduces more evidence on the beneficial effects of taxation on economic growth. He draws on data from a large number of countries with widely different tax levels and concludes that indeed taxation is an important determinant of economic growth.

Conclusions

In my view, the studies found in this volume imply strongly that Canadians could gain much from lower levels of taxation and some important structural tax reforms. The theoretical insights developed since Canada's last major tax reform and the empirical evidence validating the theories, back up this recommendation.

All tax reforms produce some winners and some losers. That is one reason why reforms are so difficult and take place so infrequently. The losers tend to protest loudly and cause much political turbulence while the winners enjoy their higher incomes quietly. However, at the beginning of the new millenium there are large fiscal surpluses generated by rapid economic growth and caps on spending increases. These surpluses offer a rare window of opportunity to have tax reforms that lower the after-tax income of no one interest group. The government of Canada would be wise not to let this opportunity slip away.

Summary of papers included in this volume

The first two papers were presented to a general audience after lunch on the day of the conference. The speakers are the heads of the two leading economic think tanks in Canada, Michael Walker of the Fraser Institute and Jack Mintz of the CD Howe Institute. These authors set out in general terms the two different, but related, issues facing Canada's fiscal policy makers, the need to reduce the overall level of government taxation and spending and Canada's tax structure in need of reform, whatever the level of spending and taxation.

The level of government spending matters most
Michael A. Walker

The Economic Freedom Index published by The Fraser Institute in the annual reports, *Economic Freedom of the World,* shows that the level and growth rate of income in various countries are an increasing function of economic freedom—the level of taxation, regulation, and a host of other measurable determinants of economic incentives. Walker discusses Canada's world ranking in a number of areas. He concludes that the country's economic growth would increase substantially if the size of government were decreased to its optimum level.

Taxation with the least pain—a new tax structure for Canada
Jack Mintz

The author sets the stage for the rest of the papers found in this book by stressing that the structure of taxes is important for incentives and, therefore, for economic growth and the well-being of Canadians. He then makes the case for replacing income tax with an expenditure tax. This goal can be achieved under the present personal income-tax regime if all savings and income from capital are exempted from taxation. He believes that this recommended tax structure would not only create powerful, growth-enhancing incentives but would also help in dealing with some important future problems like the aging of Canada's population and the strain it will put on fiscal resources, as well as the challenges created by the recent slow growth in productivity and competitiveness.

The flat tax—a model for personal and business tax reform
Jason Clemens and Joel Emes with Rodger Scott

Many economists and politicians in the United States and Canada have recommended the flat personal income tax to simplify the filing of returns and to eliminate the disincentive effects that are the result of the existing system. The authors of this paper consider the steps needed to introduce such a tax in Canada and provide empirical estimates of the rate of flat tax needed to raise the same revenue as raised by the present tax. They consider the incidence of the tax and the sensitivity of their results to changed assumptions about the size of the basic personal exemption and of different exemptions for families with children and contributions to charity.

Restructuring the Canadian Tax System by changing the mix of direct and indirect taxes
Bev Dahlby

Direct taxes like the personal and business taxes have much stronger disincentive effects than indirect taxes like sales and value-added taxes. For this reason, many economists believe that Canada's tax system should be reformed by changing the present mix of direct and indirect taxes. Dahlby expands on this recommendation by a review of the estimates of the available gains found in the literature. He concludes that the proposed new tax structure would have small but significant effects on Canada's rate of economic growth and future living standards.

An evaluation of business taxes
Thomas Wilson

The author was a member of the team of experts that produced the Mintz Report on Business Taxation. This report recommended to the Minister of Finance a number of important changes to the existing system of business taxation that would increase its efficiency and equity. Wilson reviews these recommendations and examines what policy changes have taken place since they were made. He found that most of the recommendations have been ignored. The author the goes on to analyze the merit of a more transparent and complete integration of the corporate and personal income taxation.

Why there should be no capital gains tax
Herbert Grubel

Drawing on much new empirical evidence, the author makes the case that the capital gains tax brings more harm than benefits. The tax has a substantial negative impact on economic growth while it raises little revenue and falls on those earning low and moderate incomes as much as on the rich. Canada should abandon the capital gains tax and deal with problems of tax arbitrage in the way Hong Kong does.

The corporate capital tax—Canada's most damaging tax
Jason Clemens and Joel Emes with Rodger Scott

The authors describe the nature of the corporate capital tax, which imposes a levy on business whether it is profitable or not. This newest Canadian tax is very damaging to investment incentives, is costly to administer, and raises very little revenue. The elimination of this tax should be high on the agenda of any policy makers interested in raising Canada's productivity and economic growth.

Interprovincial fiscal competition in Canada—theory, facts and options
Finn Poschman and William B.P. Robson

There is a widespread belief that provincial policies that lower taxes induce a competitive race to the bottom that leads to a less than efficient and equitable level of government spending. The authors examine this belief critically and come to the conclusion that such a race to the bottom is unlikely. The decisions to locate and invest in a given province are based on both the levels of taxation and the services provided with the revenue. Provinces that provide good and wanted services will attract immigrants and capital even though they have higher taxes than other provinces. Competition among jurisdictions to provide the best level and mix of government services for any level of taxation is beneficial for Canada.

Taxation and foreign direct investment in Ireland
Brendan Walsh

Advocates for lower and better taxes consider Ireland's recent, stellar growth performance as a powerful example of the merit of their policy recommendations. Walsh shows that tax reforms and spending propensities in Ireland indeed contributed significantly to Ireland's recent success but he also points out the importance of other policy changes, like reform of the labour market, targeted tax subsidies, the adoption of the euro and transfers from the European Economic Community.

A tale of two provinces—tax policy in Alberta and Ontario
Kenneth McKenzie

The governments of Alberta and Ontario in recent years have cut spending and lowered taxes. The author examines the nature of the tax changes in both provinces and discusses the impact they have had on labour and capital markets and how they can explain the bursts in economic growth enjoyed by these two provinces.

Outline of proposed tax reforms

The following is an outline, simplified and without attribution, of the proposals for tax reform that emerged from the conference and are reflected in the papers in this book.

1 The taxation of income from work, investment, and risk-taking should be eliminated or, at least, reduced significantly. The taxation of consumption should be increased correspondingly. These basic objectives can be attained by two different approaches:

a Turning the current income tax into an expenditure tax by exempting from taxation all savings. This goal can be achieved by the removal of all limits to tax-free contributions to RRSPs.

b Raising the rates on indirect taxes like the GST, sales and excise taxes and lowering correspondingly the rates on direct taxes like personal, business and capital income.

2 The multiple taxation of income from investment should be eliminated. To attain these objectives it is necessary to consider the following policies.

a The tax regimes for personal and business income should be integrated so that taxes on profits paid by business can be used to reduce personal income taxes due on dividends.

b The taxation on capital gains should be eliminated.

c The capital tax paid by business should be eliminated.

3 The personal income-tax system should be simplified and disincentives to work, investment, and risk taking should be eliminated by the following measures.

a Progressive income-tax rates should be replaced by constant marginal rates.

b Most deductions from the personal income-tax base should be eliminated.

c The personal and business income taxes should be fully integrated.

The level of government spending matters most

Michael Walker

This chapter considers how the size of government affects Canada's ability to achieve high levels of productivity and sustained economic growth. The departure point is a consideration of the international evidence on why some countries succeed and other countries fail to attain these economic objectives. The discovery that a government's policy regime plays a crucial role in determining whether countries succeed or fail leads to an examination of how Canada's policies compare with global best practices. Finally, the chapter considers what Canada needs to do to improve its record of productivity growth and economic development.

Why do some countries succeed and others fail?

The Economist magazine in its end-of-the-millennium edition (December 11, 1999) engaged in reflections on the twentieth century. One of the questions asked in this special edition was: Why do some countries succeed and others fail? *The Economist* considered a number of answers to this question. The answer they preferred derived from the Economic Freedom Index, published by The Fraser Institute in the annual reports, *Economic Freedom of the World*

(Gwartney and Lawson 2000, 2001). This Index catalogs 21 different policies of government from 1970 to the present time. It is, in effect, a measure of governmental competence. It is constructed through the use of published, objective data that reflect the conduct of government policy and of surveys that have been created by third parties for different purposes. The data used in the construction of the Index include measures of the following:

- the size of government and levels of taxation
- public versus private ownership of resources and the means of production
- the existence and extent of private property and the rule of law
- the extent of trade regulation and taxes and tariffs on trade
- the conduct of domestic monetary policy
- the ability of citizens to exchange their currency freely for foreign currencies
- the extent to which government has maintained a non-inflationary environment
- controls on sales of assets to foreigners and other interferences with capital markets
- the right of domestic citizens to engage in commerce with residents of other countries.

The Index is constructed in such a way that highest values for these measures are given when government interference is smallest and therefore, by assumption, economic freedom is the highest. The measures are designed to reflect the actions of governments, not the outcome. As a result, it is possible that the Index is correlated either positively or negatively with the economic performance of countries through time or in comparison with other countries.

The Index uses 21 variables and is constructed for up to 123 countries over the period from 1970 to 1999. The details and methodology of the construction of the Index are complicated and readers interested in more detail can consult the book, *Economic Freedom of the World 2001* (Gwartney and Lawson 2001), which is in print and can be found in its entirety on the Fraser Institute website (www.fraserinstitute.ca). Suffice it to note that the weights given to each component of the Index for every country are determined through the use of a transparent, reproducible statistical technique involving first-principle components.

The Economist concluded that the policy regimes adopted by governments and as measured by the Index are a reliable and powerful explanation for the success and failure of economies. Economies in which governments permitted more economic freedom did better than countries that permitted less.

The ten best and worst performers

Figure 1 shows the top ten ranked countries in 1999 and the path by which they got to their current position. As can be clearly seen, countries like Hong Kong have always enjoyed a very high rank whereas other countries enjoying a very high rank, such as New Zealand, Ireland, and the United Kingdom, came to that position after dramatic change in their policy regimes. The experiences of these latter countries are of special interest since they permit a study of the impact of variations in the level of economic freedom on economic performance through time.

Impact on economic growth and development

In a technical analysis of the relationship between income growth and economic freedom published in the *American Economic Review* in May 1997, my colleague Stephen Easton and I (Easton and Walker 1997) were able to show that the level of economic freedom has a statistically significant impact on the level of income and its rate of growth. Economic freedom was a significant variable in the context

Figure 1: The top ten and how they got there

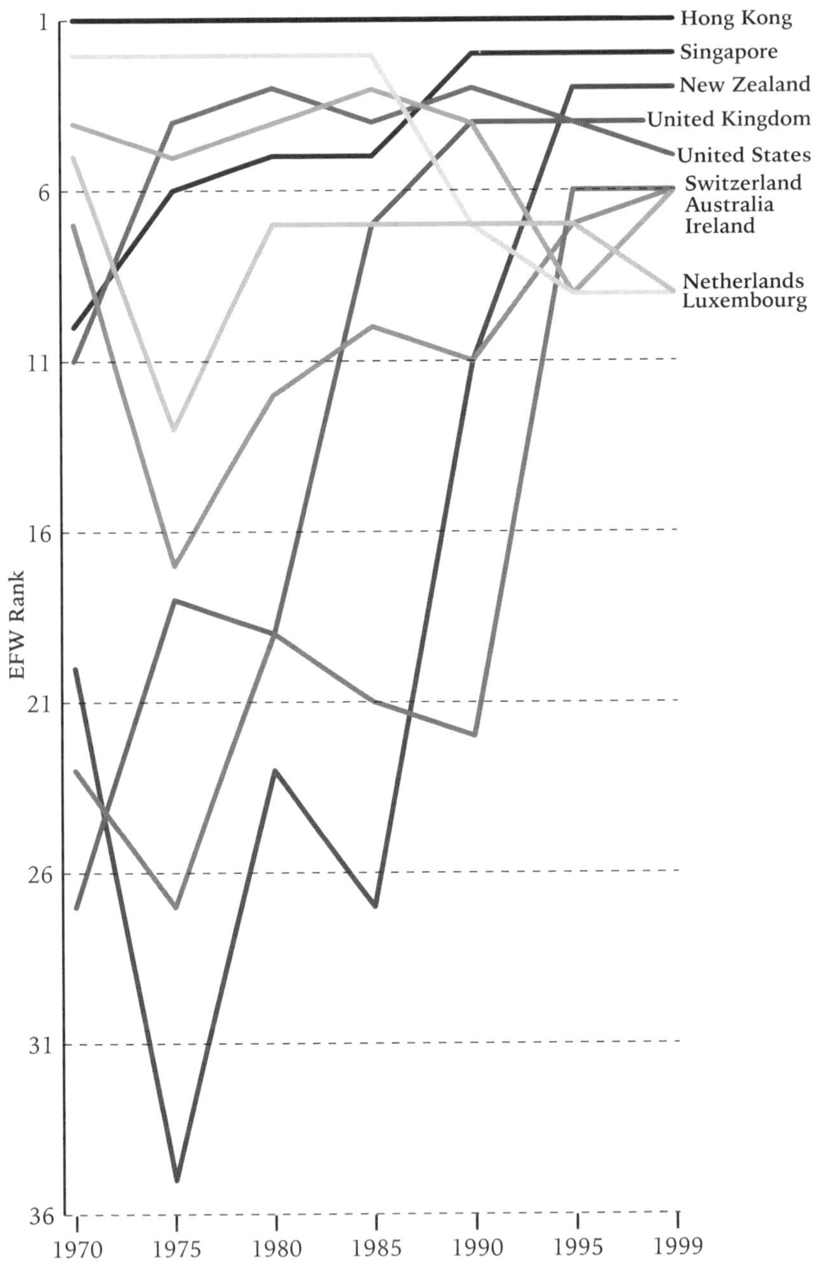

Source: Gwartney and Lawson 2001

of a standard neoclassic growth model that allows for differences in population growth, human capital, and investment. While that technical analysis shows that economic freedom is an important contributing factor to economic performance, it is difficult using that sort of analysis to depict the impact conveniently.

In order to make information about the impact of economic freedom more accessible, this section presents a number of charts that show the correlation between economic freedom and a variety of economic indicators by using quintile analysis. In this analysis, the countries of the world are arranged in ascending order of economic freedom and then grouped according into quintiles from the least to the most free. The average levels of income per capita are then calculated for the countries in each quintile. Figure 2 uses these data and shows clearly that per-capita income is an increasing function of economic freedom.

This same relationship also shows up in Figure 3, which uses a scatter diagram based on all countries used to construct the quintiles presented in figure 2. The level of economic freedom explains

Figure 2: Per-capita income and economic freedom quintile

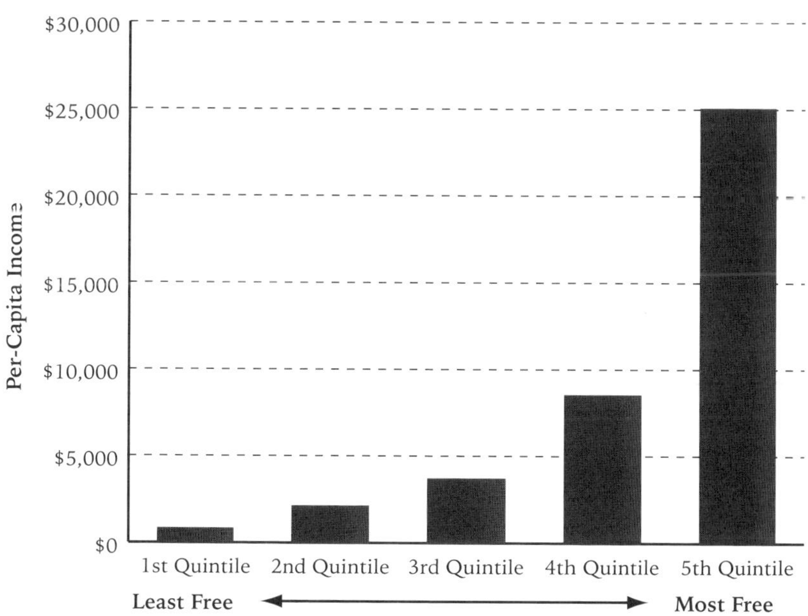

Source: Gwartney and Lawson 2001

Figure 3: Economic freedom and affluence

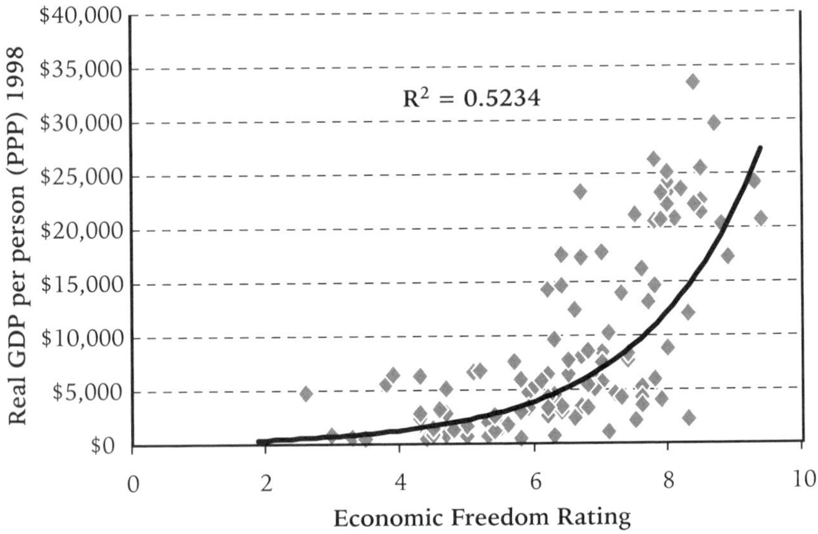

Source: Gwartney and Lawson 2001

52% of the variation in the level of per-capita income amongst the 123 countries studied. The non-linear, best-fit curve in the chart shows the elasticity of the relationship, which is greater, the higher the level of per-capita income.

Figure 4 shows the relationship between growth in real GDP per capita and economic freedom. The correlation is not as strong as that found in figure 2 but it still supports strongly the earlier finding that economic success is an increasing function of economic freedom. It is interesting, but not surprising, that the extreme lack of economic freedom can actually result in negative economic growth.

Canada's level of economic freedom

Figure 5 shows the scores for seven major subcomponents in the Economic Freedom Index for Canada, the United States, and Mexico. There are few surprises in this comparison. Canada and the United States have similar, high scores and Mexico is below these two countries for most components. In two areas, the size of gov-

Figure 4: Growth in real GDP per capita in each economic freedom quintile

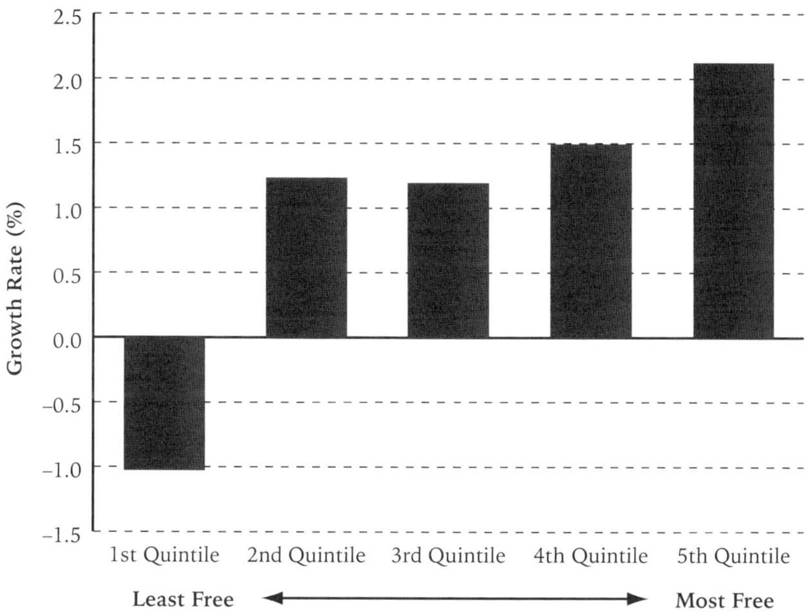

Source: Gwartney and Lawson 2001

ernment and international trade, Canada lags behind both Mexico and the United States. This result will be examined below in some more detail.

Figure 6 puts Canada's conditions in another important perspective by comparing it with the ten freest countries. It is not surprising to find that Canada scores below the average of the top ten since it does not belong in that group. Canada scores least well in comparisons involving international exchange and in the size of government, just as it did in the comparison with NAFTA countries. Comparisons of the indices for freedom of capital markets, the use of alternative currencies and the legal structure and the property rights, monetary policy, and the structure of the economy show that Canada performs quite well relative to the top ten countries. However, given the focus of this paper on the relationship between the size of government and economic growth, we find that Canada's index for the size of government scores 4.5, which is 25% lower than the score of 6 of the countries in the top ten.

Figure 5: Some measures of economic freedom for the United States, Canada, and Mexico

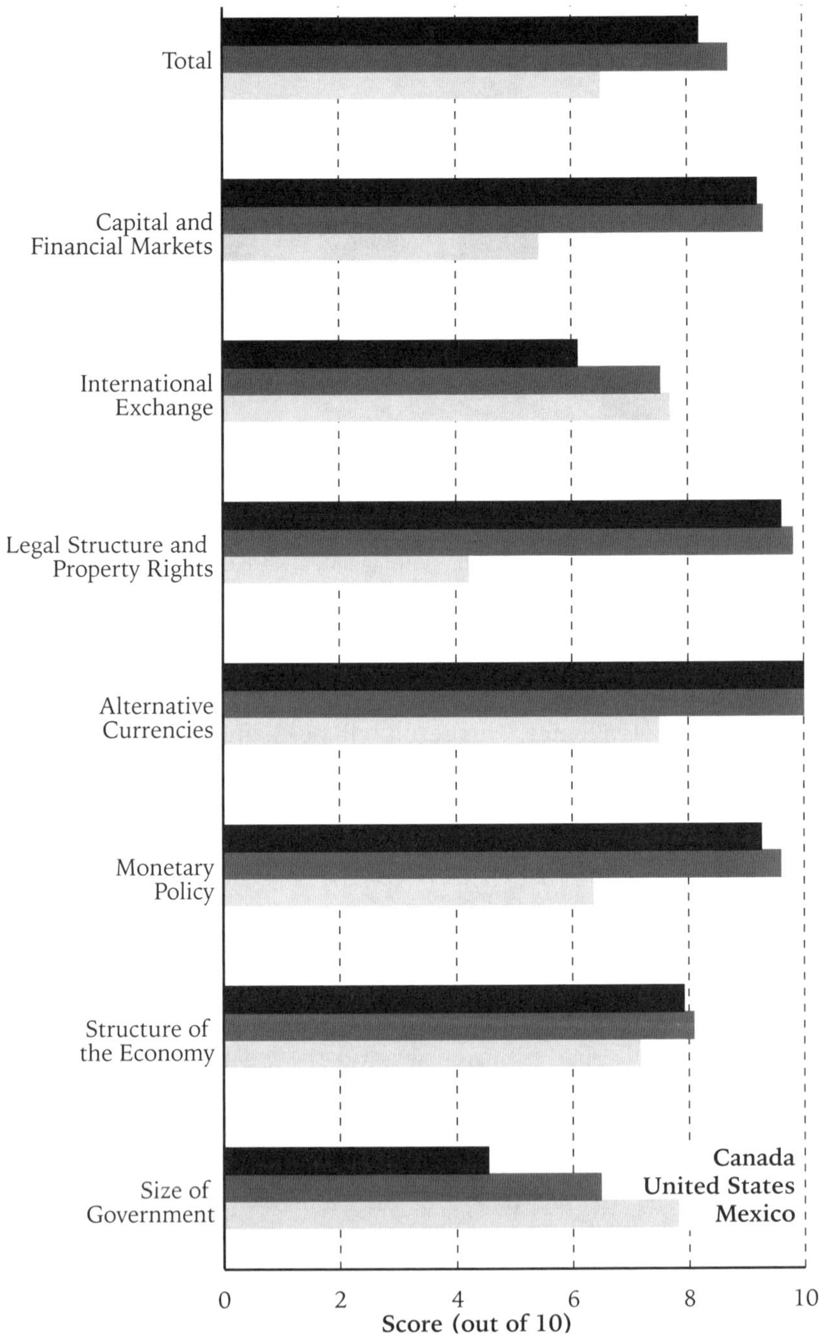

Source: Gwartney and Lawson 2001

Figure 6: Some measures of economic freedom, Canada and the average for the top ten countries

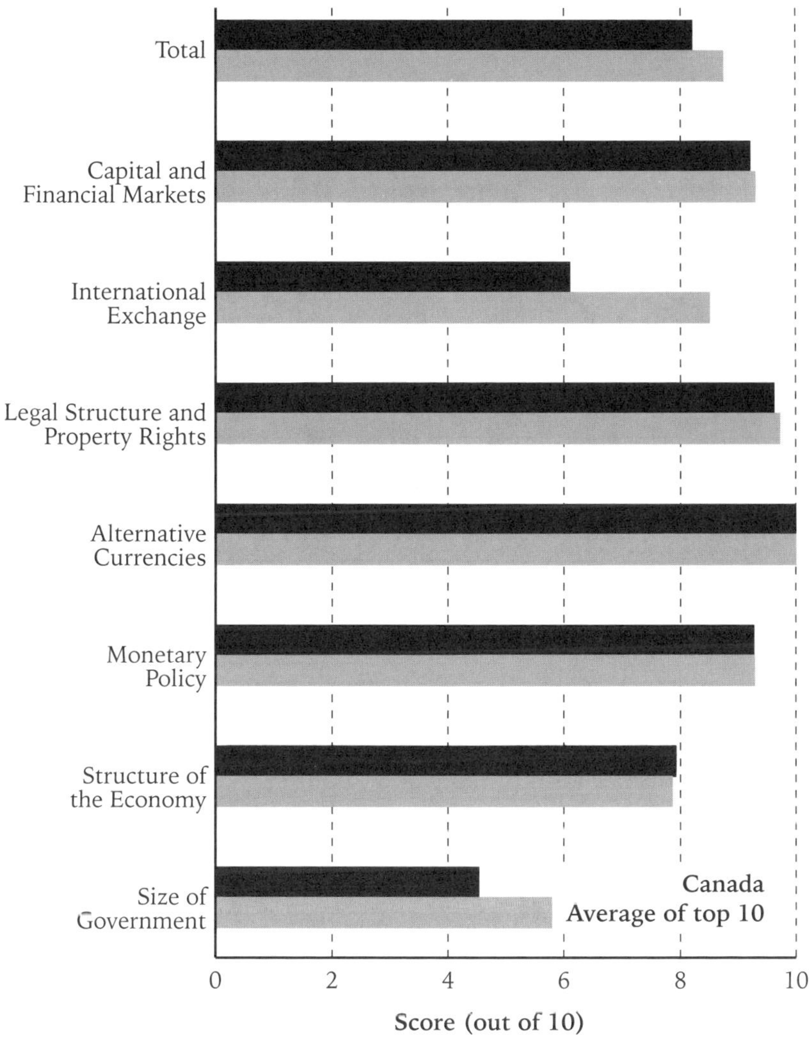

Source: Gwartney and Lawson 2001

Figure 7: Canada is falling behind

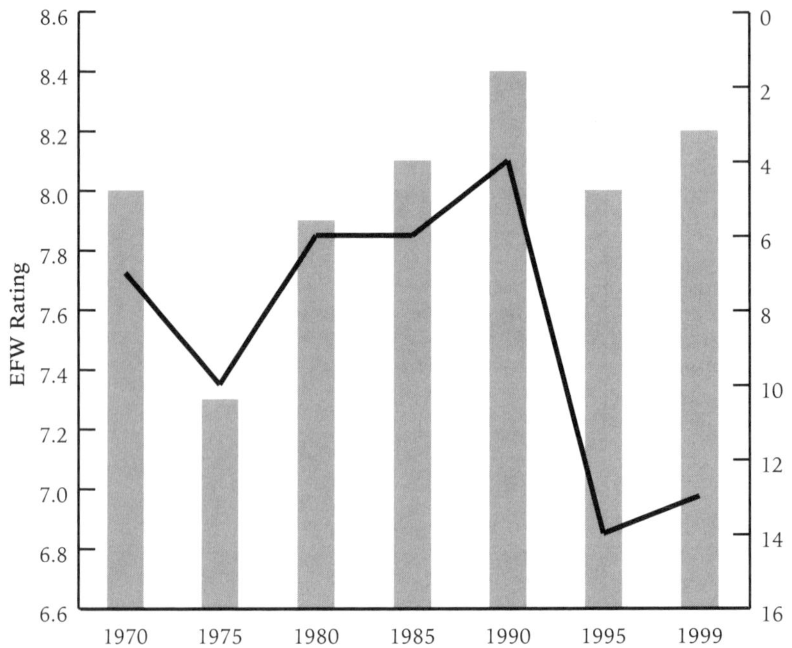

Source: Gwartney and Lawson 2001

Figure 7 traces Canada's performance from 1970 to the present. The bars show the value of Canada's overall index. The thin line shows Canada's rank in the world, given the value of its index. It is interesting to note that there is no discernible trend in the value of the index, though there were some noticeable fluctuations. But there is a strong decline in Canada's ranking from fourth in 1990 to thirteenth in 1999, which suggests that Canada has not kept up with the growth in economic freedom experienced by many other countries.

Figure 8 compares the performance of Canada, Australia, and the United States. These two countries were chosen because Australia is a key competitor for Canada in the export of natural resources and the United States is Canada's largest trading partner. It is interesting to observe that during the entire period, but in particular since the 1990s, Canada's position has deteriorated relative to both of these countries: Australia has improved its overall rank from sixteenth in 1975 to sixth in 1999. The United States contin-

Figure 8: Canada is losing ground to the United States and to Australia, a key competitor in the export of natural resources

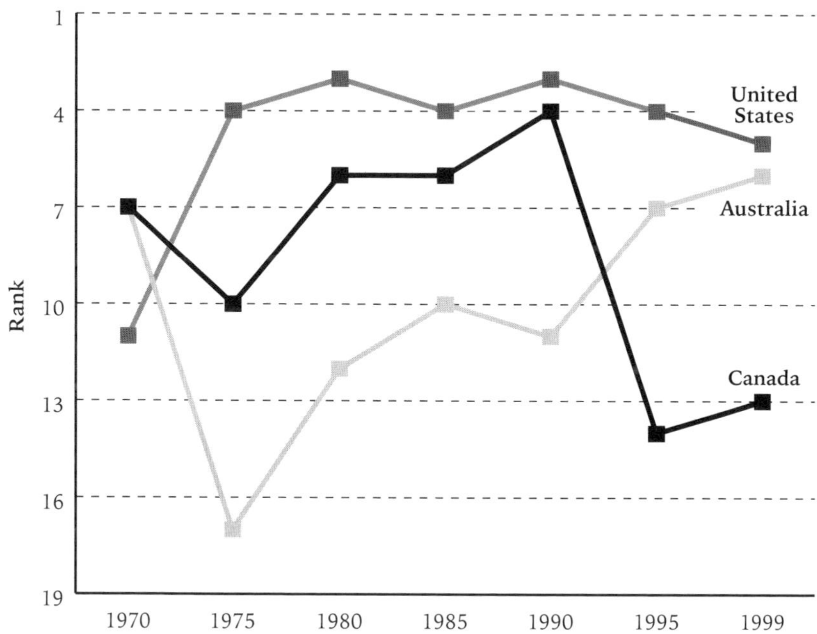

Source: Gwartney and Lawson 2001

ues to have a freer economy than Canada and, except for one year, has always been among the ten freest countries in the world.

The comparative size of the government sector

In 1999, Canada's public sector equaled 40.2% of GDP while that of the ten freest countries displayed in figure 1 was only 35.6%. This gap of 4.6 percentage points is equal to 13%. Figure 9 shows the size of government in some countries that invite comparison with Canada. It can be seen that in 1999 the public sector in Canada was nearly twice as large as that in Hong Kong. More distressing is the fact that Canada's public sector is about one third larger than that of the United States, our most important trading partner. Canada's public sector is also larger than that of Australia, which has an economy that resembles ours in several important ways and that of Ireland, a

Figure 9: Size of government in Hong Kong, the United States, Australia, Ireland, and Canada

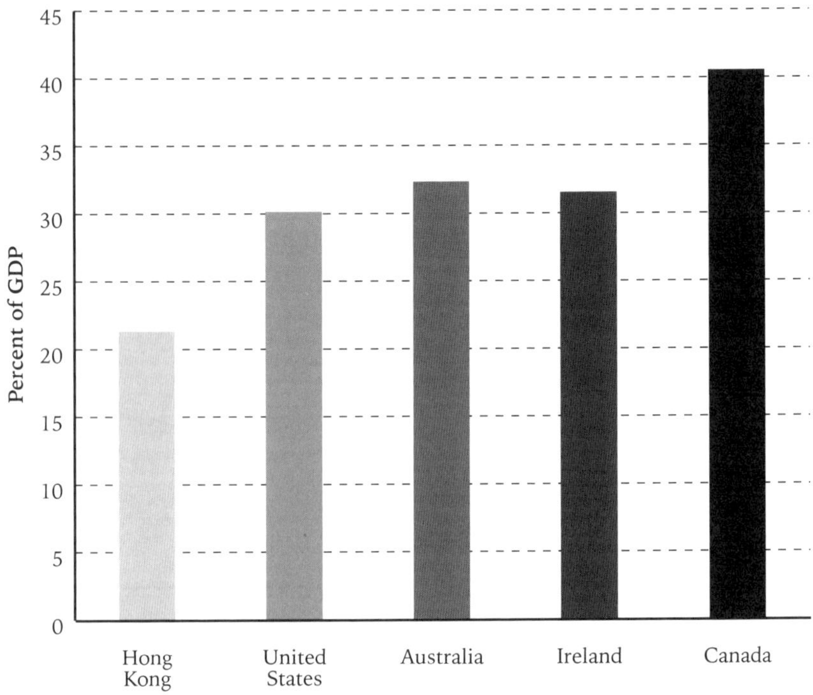

Source: Gwartney and Lawson 2001

small country that holds a position relative to the European Union much like the position Canada has vis-à-vis the United States.

Figure 10 depicts the relationship between the size of government in Canada and in the United States during the period from 1929 to 1999. The data show that the size of government in Canada and the United States was roughly the same during the Second World War and the immediate postwar years. Since about 1960, Canada's relative <correct?] size of government began to exceed that of the United States gradually until it reached a maximum gap of 15 percentage points, or 43% above the United States in 1992. Since then, the gap has narrowed to ten points or one third.

Another way of measuring the relative burden of government in Canada and the United States involves the time it takes for the average tax payers in the two countries to reach tax freedom day. At this date, conceptually taxpayers have met their obligations to their

Figure 10: Government spending as a percentage of GDP in Canada and the United States

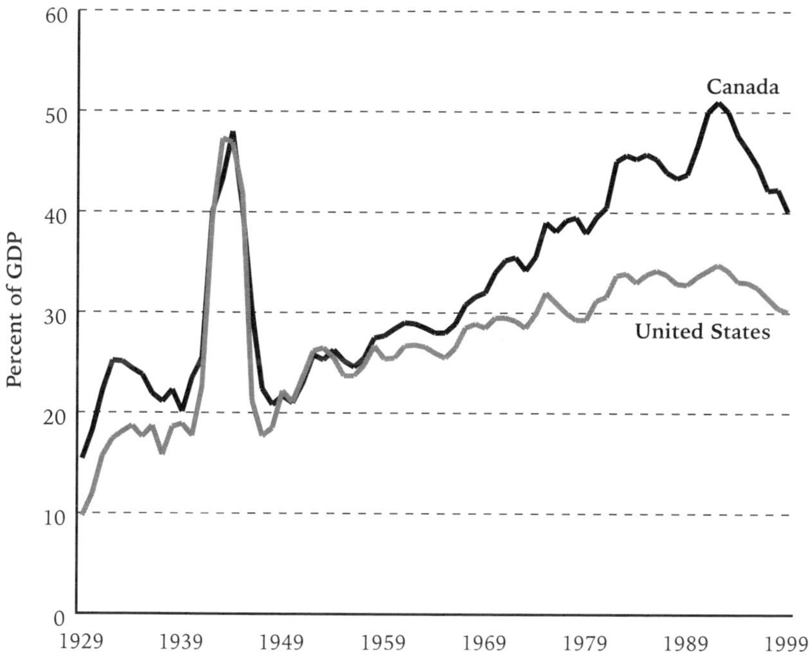

Source: Gwartney and Lawson 2001

governments and begin to keep additional earnings for their private use. Such a calculation is made annually by The Fraser Institute for Canada and by the National Tax Foundation for the United States. Figure 11 shows the tax freedom day for Canada and the United States from 1961 to 2000. As can be seen, tax freedom day in the two countries fell virtually on the same date in 1961 but, by the year 2000, tax freedom day in Canada was more than a full month later than in the United States.

It is often claimed that the main reason for the gap between the tax freedom days in the two countries is that Canada provides a tax financed public health-care system whereas the United States does not. Figure 12 shows clearly that this is not the case. In 1999, the United States government spent 6.1% of GDP on health care while the government of Canada spent 6.6%. The gap of 0.5 percentage point represents only 5% of the ten-point difference in overall taxation that year.

Figure 11: Tax Freedom Day in Canada and the United States (US methodology)

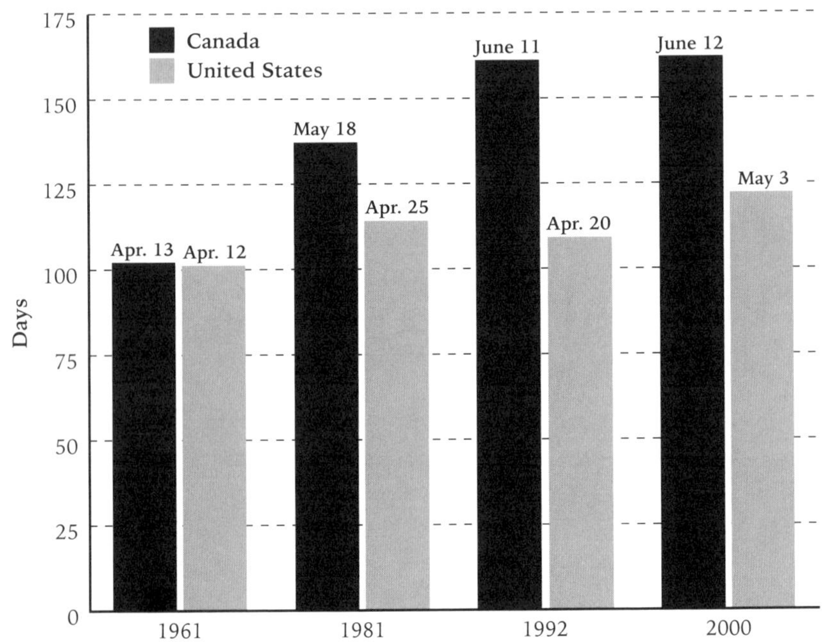

Source: Gwartney and Lawson 2001

Consequences of larger government and higher taxes

Gerald Scully (1989) showed that theoretically and empirically the size of government spending (and taxation) is an important determinant of economic growth. An application of the Scully model is found in Grubel 1998. These studies argue that at low levels of spending, economic growth is slow because the government does not provide a sufficient services to make the economy function at optimal efficiency. At high levels of spending and taxation, the government replaces efficient private spending with inefficient public spending. In addition, the inefficiencies that accompany high tax rates become a large burden on the economy. Between these two extremes lies an optimal spending level where economic growth is maximized. The research for Canada showed strong evidence of the existence of a relationship of ∩ shape between economic

Figure 12: Government health spending in Canada and the United States

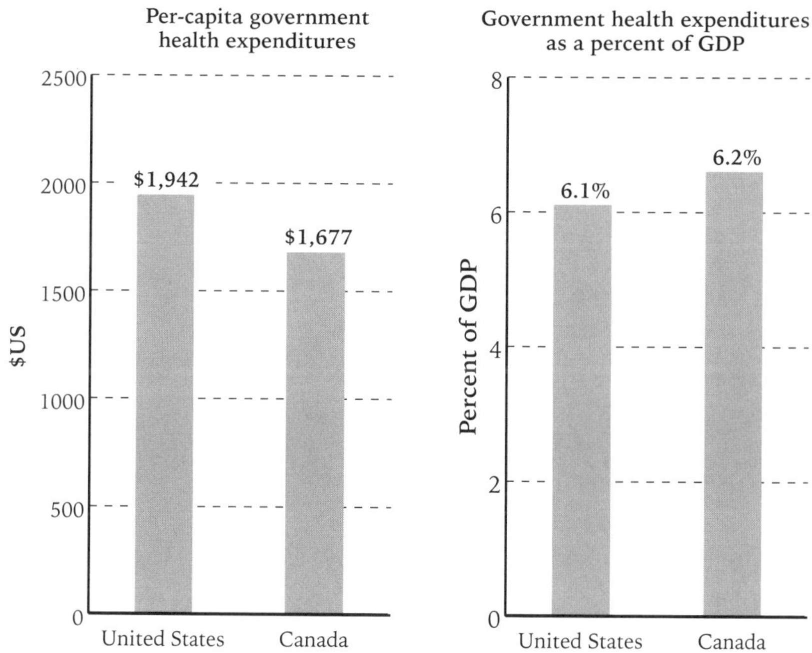

Source: Organisation for Economic Cooperation and Development 2000

growth and spending levels. The optimal level was found to be at 34% of national income.

The data on economic freedom lend themselves to the testing of the Scully model for the world as a whole. For this purpose, figure 13 shows on the vertical axis the average level of economic growth in countries contained in the five quintiles shown along the horizontal axis. In this case, the quintiles were determined on the basis of the level of government spending in a sample of 123 countries. As can be seen, the relationship has a ∩ shape predicted by Scully's theory. Countries in the fourth quintile by level of government spending have the highest rates of growth. Those with less spending grow more slowly as do those with more spending.

Figure 14 repeats figure 13 but is expanded to include information about the size of government chosen by, and the rate of economic growth of, some countries of interest to Canada. As can be seen, Hong Kong has the highest growth rate and its spending

Figure 13: Size of government and average global economic growth

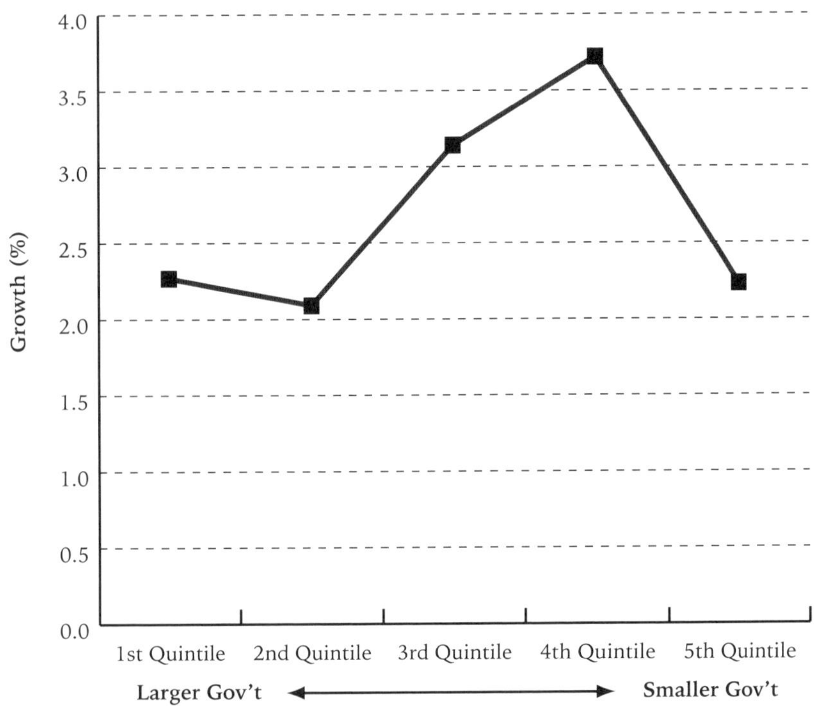

Source: Gwartney and Lawson 2001

puts it into the fourth quintile of countries by the size of government spending. Canada, in turn, has one of the lowest growth rates and is in the first quintile along with other countries that have the largest government sectors. The location of the United States and Mexico on the graph is also consistent with the Scully model.

The results in figure 14 imply that Canada can enjoy a significant improvement in its level of economic growth by perhaps as much as 2 percentage points if it reduced the size of its government to that of Hong Kong's. Such a shrinking of the size of government in Canada involves many important economic and social considerations but the data show clearly that the benefits believed to accompany the present level of government spending have exacted a very distinct growth penalty on all Canadians.

Figure 14: Size of government and economic growth in Canada, Spain, the United States, Mexico and Hong Kong

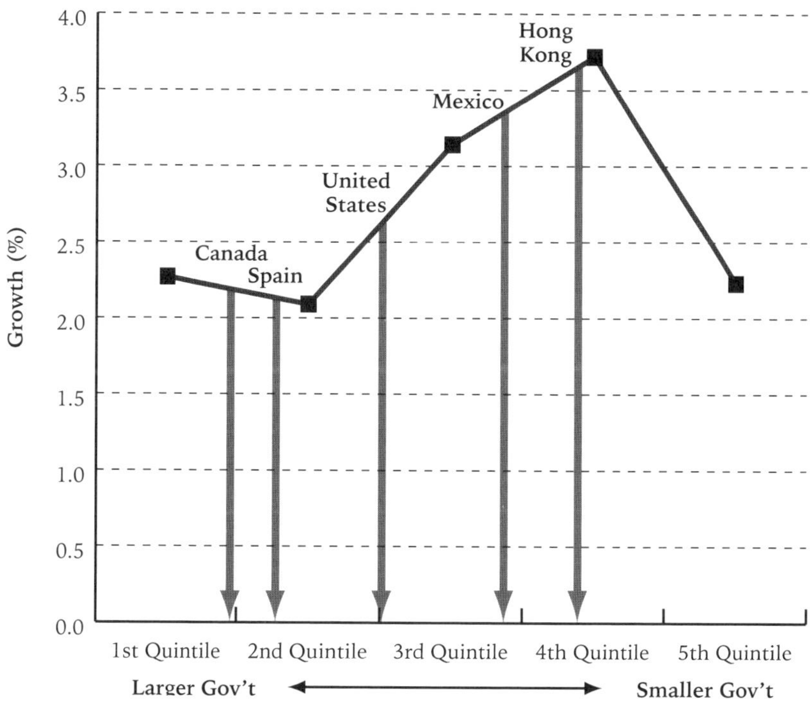

Source: Gwartney and Lawson 2001

The structure of taxation

Economic growth is also affected by the strength of the disincentives to work, investment, and risk-taking caused by the progressivity of the personal income tax rates. Figure 15 shows along the vertical axis the rate of economic growth averaged for countries found in the quintiles on the horizontal axis. These quintiles reflect the "friendliness" of the personal income tax system as measured by the level of the tax rates and the brackets at which they apply. This chart shows that the friendlier the tax system, the higher the rate of economic growth. This relation does not appear to decrease in any way as the tax system becomes more and more friendly. Figure 16 shows where on the spectrum individual countries can be found.

Figure 15: Economic growth and the "friendliness" of the personal income tax system as measured by the tax rates and the brackets at which they apply

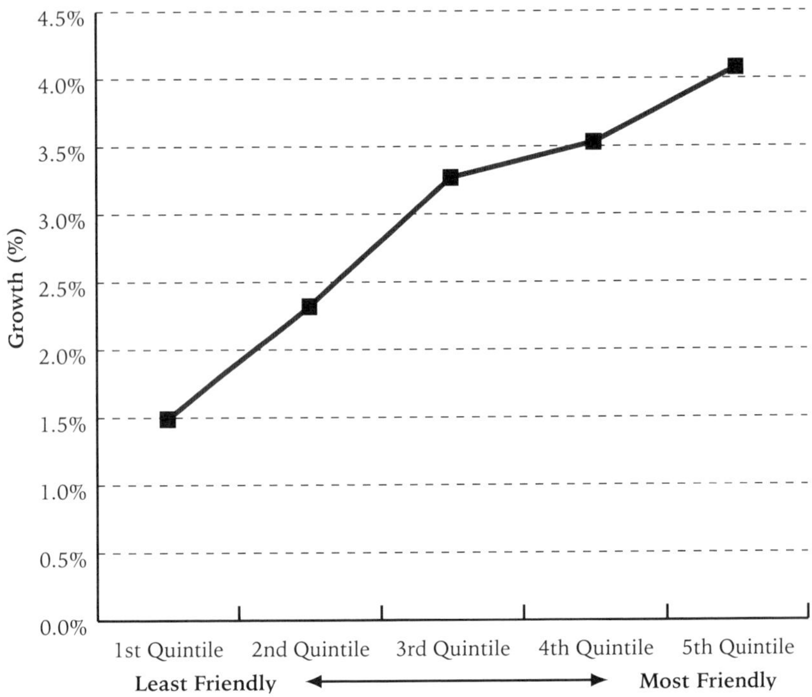

Source: Gwartney and Lawson 2001

Canada can be seen to have one of the least friendly tax systems while the United States is in the third quintile and Hong Kong in the top.

Economic growth is related not only to the level of taxation but also the mix of taxes used to collect given amounts. Consumption taxes and broad-based income taxes are the least distorting and, therefore, have the smallest effect on growth. Taxes on capital, profits, rental income, wealth, and the property of other small groups in society tend to be politically more popular than broad-based taxes but they also distort incentives the most and have the greatest negative effects on economic growth.

The capital tax has one of the most serious negative effects on incentives to invest. It is payable whether or not a company earns

Figure 16: Economic growth and the "friendliness" of the personal income tax system in Canada, China, the United States, Mexico and Hong Kong

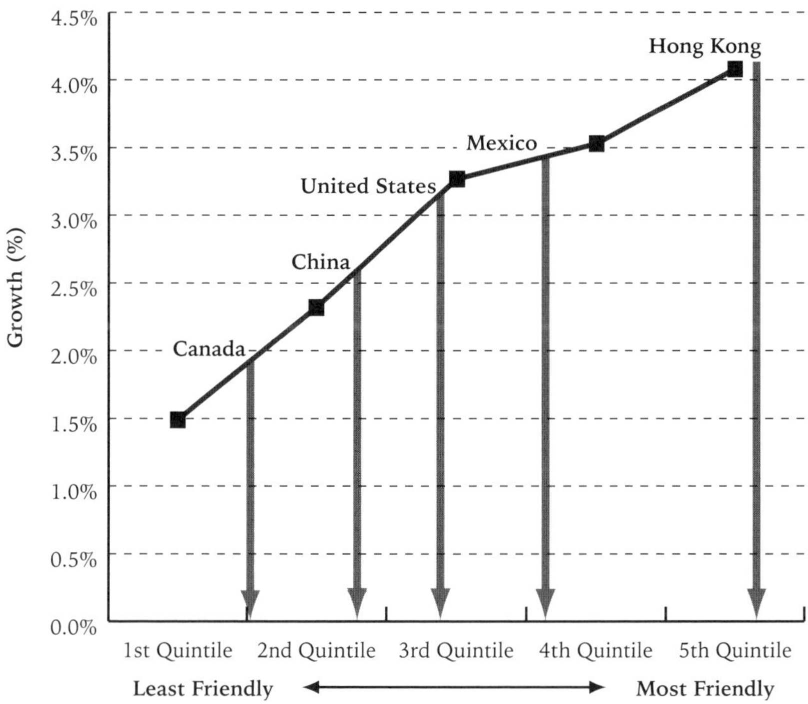

Source: Gwartney and Lawson 2001

a profit. The owners of capital show a special dislike for this tax: Canadians avoid it by investing abroad and foreigners by simply not coming to Canada. Figure 17 shows the burden of capital taxes in Canada during the period from 1989 to 1999. The burden is measured as a percentage of corporate profits for individual provinces and for Canada as a whole, where the national average is weighted by the provincial share of national corporate profits. As can be seen, over this period capital taxes as a percentage of corporate profits have trended up from about 3% to 5% of corporate profits. The level reached a peak of 11% in 1992 when the government sector in Canada as a percentage of GDP had also reached its highest level. (For a more detailed analysis of the size and effects of capital taxes, see Clemens 2002).

Figure 17: Corporate capital taxes in Canada as a percent of corporate profits*

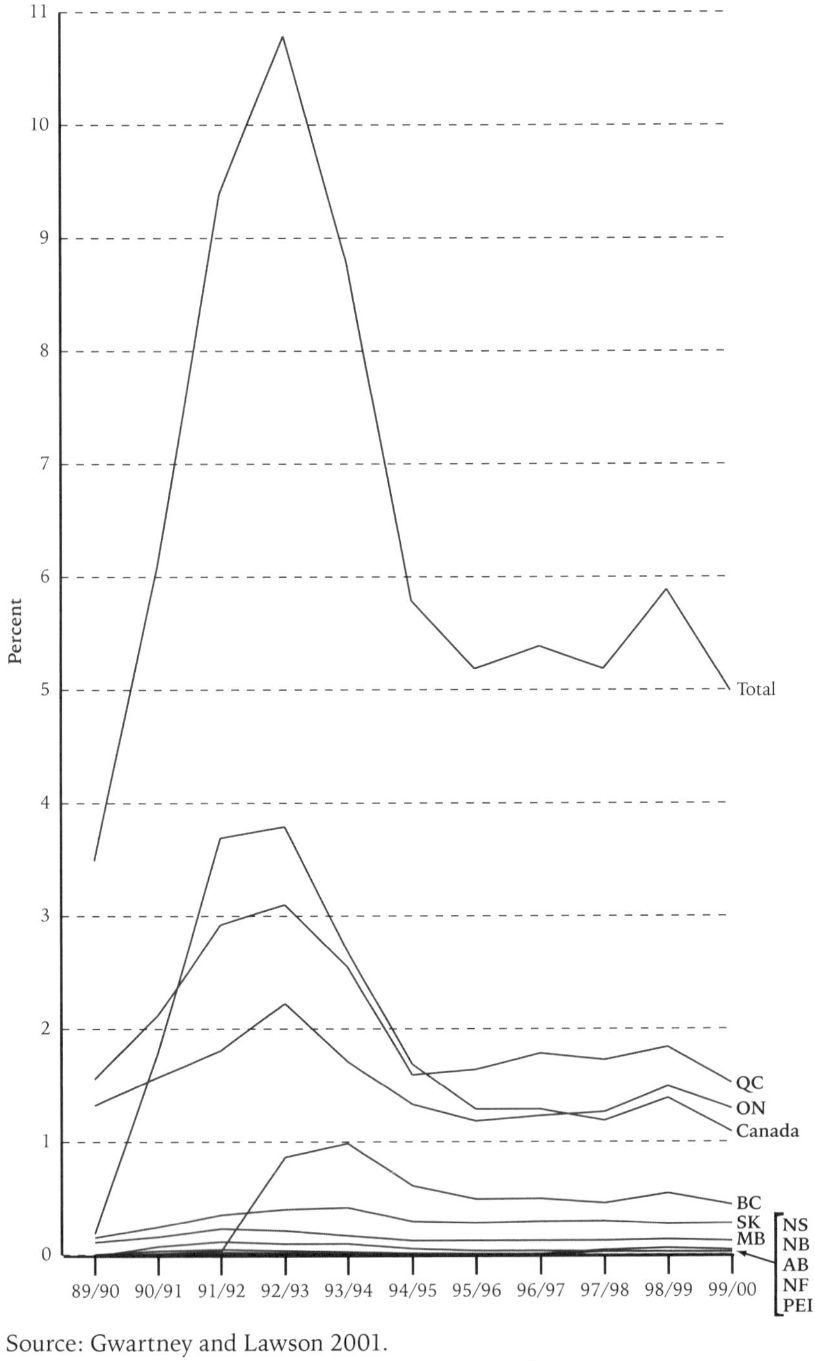

Source: Gwartney and Lawson 2001.
* weighted by provincial share of corporate profits)

Tariffs on specific products are another form of taxation that is very distortionary and has a negative impact on efficiency because it keeps labour and capital in declining industries and away from use in new, more dynamic, and profitable employment. The extent of discrimination contained in a country's tariff structure is measured by the standard deviation of rates. The greater the standard deviation, the more targeted and discriminatory is a country's tariff structure.

Figure 18 shows for different countries the average level of tariffs and the standard deviation of the rates around that average. As can be seen, Canada's standard deviation is greater than that of any other of its important trading partners in the sample. In addition, Canada also has a fairly high average level of tariffs. The combination of the average tariff rate and the standard deviation provides an index on the basis of which Canada has by far the costliest system of protection of all of its major trading partners. There is little doubt that this implicit taxation has an important effect on Canada's economic growth.

Figure 18: Tariffs and the extent to which they discriminate

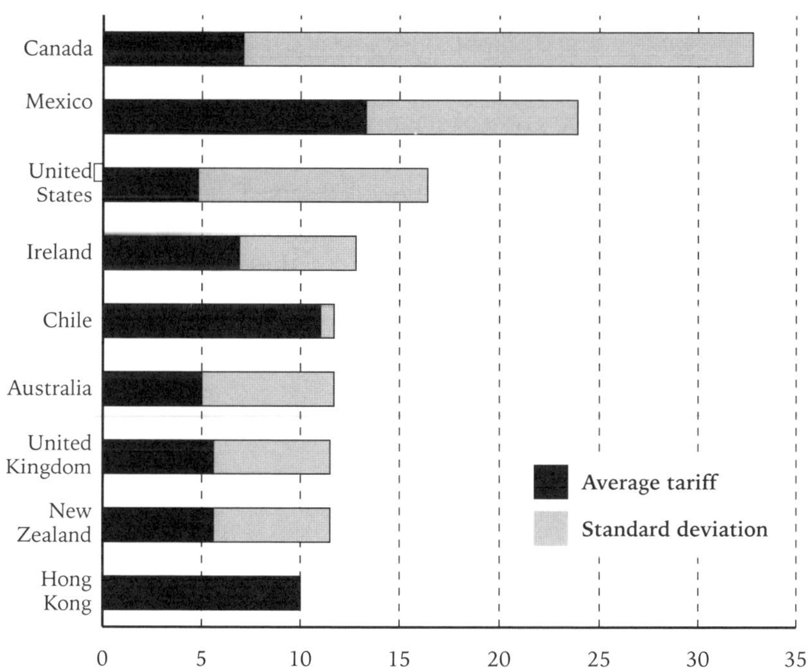

Source: Gwartney and Lawson 2001

Conclusions and policy implications

The preceding analysis shows that the economic policy of Canada's government is falling behind that of its major trading partners and other major countries with which it is in competition. Canada once had one of the highest levels of economic freedom and placed among the ten freest countries in the world. In recent years, it has fallen to thirteenth. The biggest contributors to this declining rank are the size of government and trade-sector policies relative to those of other countries important to Canada.

Empirical evidence presented above shows that economic growth is positively related to economic freedom. Canada's relatively slow economic growth in recent years, therefore, can be attributed to Canada's lower ranking on the economic freedom index. In particular, the slower growth has been associated with the size of government and taxation, which have declined very little while those of competing countries have fallen substantially.

The preceding analysis and evidence from the experience of most countries of the world has clear policy implications. If Canadians want economic growth and per-capita incomes to return to their traditional levels and improve by international standards, the size of government and the associated tax burden must be reduced. In addition, the structure of the tax system, including tariffs, must be improved.

The preceding analysis also provided some information about an appropriate level of government spending and taxation and a number of other policies needed to achieve these objectives. Needed now is the political will to act on these findings.

References

Clemens, Jason, Joel Emes, and Rodger Scott (2002). *The Corporate Capital Tax: Canada's Most Damaging Tax.* Public Policy Sources 56. Vancouver, BC: The Fraser Institute.

Easton, Stephen T., and Michael A. Walker (1997). Income Growth and Economic Freedom. *The American Economic Review* 87, 2 (May): 328–32.

Grubel, Herbert (1998). *How to Use the Fiscal Surplus: What is the Optimal Size of Government?* Vancouver, BC: The Fraser Institute.

Gwartney, James, and Robert Lawson (2000). *Economic Freedom of the World: 2000 Annual Report.* Vancouver, BC: The Fraser Institute

——— (2001). *Economic Freedom of the World: 2001 Annual Report.* Vancouver, BC: The Fraser Institute

Organisation for Economic Cooperation and Development 2000. *OECD Health Report.* Paris: OECD.

Scully, Gerald (1989). The Size of the State, Economic Growth and the Efficient Utilization of National Resources. *Public Choice* 63: 149–64.

Taxation with the least pain—a new tax structure for Canada

Jack M. Mintz

Canada's tax burden—total government revenues are now about 43% of GDP—is well above levels that existed in the past 50 years. It is substantially higher than that of many other countries, including Australia, Hong Kong, Iceland, Ireland, Japan, Korea, Spain, Switzerland, the United Kingdom, and the United States, to name but a few. Although this tax burden has been rightfully a subject of debate in Canada, little attention has been paid to another aspect of tax policy—the tax structure.

The tax structure is important. Taxes can significantly deter work effort, savings, risk taking, and investment, resulting in a smaller economic pie to support the population. Thus, even if one is reducing taxes, it is important to reduce them to remove the most objectionable tax distortions that impair economic growth and job creation.

In the light of the events of September 11, 2001, it is easy to dismiss the need to address issues surrounding the tax burden and tax structure. In fact, some experts have almost given up on long-term fiscal issues, arguing that we will have bigger governments and higher taxes to contend with in future years. However, I believe that the issue of tax reform—better tax levels and structure—should not be put on the back burner.

We ignore taxation and its structure to our peril. The problems facing Canada prior to September 11, 2001 have not disappeared: productivity, competitiveness, and an aging population continue to remain at the forefront.

How can we improve productivity and competitiveness through a better tax system? At the heart of the issue is the need for Canada to be an attractive place for skilled workers and jobs. With greater economic integration, particularly in North America, Canada will need to offer economic policies that will attract people and businesses here. Part of our economic plan should be to improve our tax structure.

Below, I outline a tax structure that I envision for Canada, one that would result in greater productivity and improved competitiveness in North America; a tax structure that is far better than that found in other countries, including the United States.

A tax structure for the twenty-first century

What kind of tax structure do I have in mind? In pursuit of both efficiency and fairness, the tax structure that best maximizes opportunities for growth and job creation is one that taxes people according to what they consume rather than what they produce. Thus, the best taxes are those based on consumption.

Tax research in the past several decades has recognized that the most important revenue source today—the annual personal income tax—discriminates against savers. If two people have the same lifetime earnings but one saves some earnings for future consumption, the saver pays more tax than the consumer does over a lifetime. The reason for this is that saver is taxed twice—once on earnings and a second time on income earned on saved earnings. On the other hand, the consumer is taxed only once—only when earnings are received since consumer does not save anything and, therefore, has no capital income. Thus, the annual income tax falls more heavily on those who wish to consume more in the future.

Yet, the Carter Report (Canada 1966), still the bible of Canadian tax policy at the Department of Finance and among practitioners,[1] argues that annual income—earnings plus income earned on investments—is the most efficient and fair base for taxation. However, the non-uniform taxation of consumption under the annual income tax is troubling. If a person's welfare depends on consumption of goods and services throughout all periods of life, what rationale is there for taxing future consumption more highly than current consumption? Taxing the return on investment does not seem efficient or fair.

Taxation of savings can impose high costs on the economy at the same time that it lowers our productivity. The economic cost of taxing savings can be quite significant, varying from 11 cents to one dollar on each dollar of revenue raised by governments (Bernheim 1999). In terms of economic output, in the year 2000, taxation of savings can result in a loss of GDP ranging from $15 billion to $140 billion per year or, per person, from $500 to up to $4500 per year.

However, these estimates of the economic gains resulting from eliminating taxes on savings fail to account for other pressing needs in the future: the demographic time bomb and competitiveness pressures.

Demographic impacts

The demographic picture for Canadian and other industrialized economies is well known. The population over 65 years of age will rise sharply over the next 50 years with very little growth in the population at working age from 2020 onwards. The impact of these projected changes on public resources will be significant (OECD 2001). While expenditures on education and child support will fall by 1.2 percentage points of GDP by 2050, expenditures on benefits for the elderly and health care shall rise by 9.4 percentage points. Further, with more people retired, who pay less tax, taxes, as a proportion of GDP, will decline by 1.2 percentage points. The net effect shall be a worsening of primary balances by 9.4 percentage points that can only be made up by major expenditure cuts, lower debt, or substantially higher taxes that will be felt by the working population.

The impact of these demographic changes on public expenditures and taxation is only part of the story. The current working population will need to accumulate sufficient wealth to cover significant private expenditures when they retire in later years. Further, to the extent that governments target public support to the elderly who most need it, these elderly will need greater resources after retirement. Thus, savings today will be important to cover the future needs. As the day of reckoning is not far away—only two decades from now—governments will have to plan carefully now to ensure that future needs shall not place immense burdens on the younger population.

Productivity and Competitiveness

After a decade of slow growth, Canada must do more to improve its standard of living. To achieve growth in the future, Canada will have to compete with other countries for human and capital resources. The past two decades has witnessed an explosion in cross-border financial transactions, intrafirm trade within multinational companies, and inbound and outbound investment. Although not disappearing, borders between countries are "thinning" (Helliwell 2000), especially between Canada and United States. The recent security measures adopted at the border between Canada and United States and difficulties this poses to businesses and travellers is a testament to how much trade matters between the two countries.

To attract investment and jobs, countries have been looking towards improving the quality of their skilled labour, infrastructure, and other factors that improve the business environment. Canada will have to make changes in these fields, just to keep up with international rivals. Coupled with the demographic changes discussed above, capital investment is critical for improvements in productivity.

Seen in this light, savings and investment play an important role in creating a better environment for economic growth. Some recent theories suggest that savings can also reduce income inequality. With additional resources, lower-income households can benefit from increased investments in capital, including the acquisition of skills and training, and reduced levels of unemployment.

Further, given the difficulties being encountered at the international level to tax income from savings, the administrative and compliance problems of levying income taxes are becoming more troublesome. I have argued elsewhere (Mintz and Chen 2000) that the corporate income tax, as we know it today, could wither in the next two decades given the problems involved with levying corporate taxes on income that can be easily shifted from one jurisdiction to another.

A dramatic departure—replace income taxes with an expenditure tax

A dramatic move that would substantially improve Canada's standard of living is to adopt a new tax structure that would replace the income taxes with expenditure taxes. This type of approach has already been proposed in the United States but, even if not adopted there, Canada could achieve a significant economic advantage by adopting a consumption tax.

Canada already has some forms of consumption taxation so it would not be difficult to expand on what is already in place. The types of consumption taxes we have at present include the following:

- federal and provincial sales and excise taxes on consumption goods
- taxes and fees that are related to the consumption of public services
- some use of the expenditure base for the personal "income" tax.

The latter type of consumption taxation—an expenditure tax for personal taxation—requires some elaboration. Under a personal expenditure tax, once a person receives earnings, the same amount of tax is paid on a present-value basis no matter whether the earnings are consumed immediately or deferred until a later time for consumption. Two approaches can be used for consumption taxation (Institute for Fiscal Studies 1978).

First, taxes could be levied on expenditure measured as the difference between earnings and savings. This type of approach is used for the tax treatment of registered pension (RPP) and retirement savings (RRSP) plans, whereby a person can deduct contributions to these plans from their base and pay tax on withdrawals of the principal and accumulated income at a later time. Thus, for a full expenditure tax, no limitations would be placed on contributions made to registered plans.

Second, consumption taxes could be imposed by simply exempting interest, dividends and capital gains earned by taxpayers (as discussed below a parallel business tax would be needed with this approach). This latter approach is referred to as the exempt-yield approach and it has been largely followed in Hong Kong, for example (see Mintz and Richardson 2002).

In Canada, we have used the expenditure approach to tax owner-occupied investments in housing. Taxpayers cannot deduct contributions to housing investments nor are they taxed on the sale of their house or on any "imputed rent" that they receive by effectively renting the house to themselves as owners.

Under the expenditure tax, deductions and credits to recognize families of different sizes, disability costs, medical costs, and so on could continue. The schedule for tax rates could be flat (same rate for all levels of income) or rising with income. Both the registered asset and exempt-yield approaches to expenditure taxes would allow taxpayers to smooth out their expenditure base over time. Such self-averaging could avoid the impact upon taxpayers who now high tax rates in some years and low rates in other years.

Business taxation is a significant issue for a regime of expenditure taxation. If there were no business tax, individuals could avoid taxes by withdrawing their earnings from businesses in the form of dividends or other forms of capital income that might escape tax under the exempt-yield approach. A business-value tax could therefore be levied, the base defined as the difference between revenues and current and capital costs. Effectively, the business-value tax would eliminate the business tax on marginal investment projects and encourage productivity and job creation.

A full-fledged approach to expenditure taxation in Canada would therefore result in the following improvements upon the current income tax:

- taxpayers would be able to deduct contributions to RRSPs and pension plans without limit
- taxpayers would be able to invest in other forms of savings without paying tax on dividends, capital gains or interest income
- corporate income and capital taxes would be replaced by business-value taxes.

The economic gains from moving to an expenditure tax approach have already been stated. One could argue that fairness is also improved by taxing savers and consumers on the same basis. Further, it would make it easier to administer taxation and would encourage compliance. Levying annual income taxes raises many problems since it is so difficult to measure components of income properly. Income should be indexed for inflation. Depreciation of assets should be based on true economic lives and obsolescence. Capital gains should be taxed on an accrued, not a realized, basis. The latter is especially difficult since accrual taxation requires periodic valuation of assets, some of which are not frequently traded, and taxes have to be assessed even if the asset is not sold (thereby raising issues of liquidity). Expenditure taxes avoid all these problems of measurement and are thus easier for taxpayers to comply with and for governments to administer.

How do we get from here to there?

Given these gains in efficiency, equity and compliance, why are Canadian governments not jumping at the opportunity of adopting an expenditure tax? Three issues are critical but none are insurmountable.

Equity

The usual argument against expenditure taxes is that they are not fair. Since savings are a larger proportion of annual income for upper-income taxpayers, critics of consumption taxes suggest that the exemption of savings results in a regressive tax (regressivity implies that taxes proportionally decline in relation to the base). Advocates of a consumption tax argue, however, that expenditure taxes can be made progressive if desired.

The reply to the argument that consumption taxes are unfair notes that savings simply defer taxes on consumption to future years. Therefore, one should calculate the present value of taxes paid on savings and add this value to current taxes to measure the total amount of taxes paid by individuals on their earnings. Calculated in this manner, a consumption tax levied at a flat rate is at least proportional to earnings, once taking into account deferred taxes on savings.

Further, the argument rests on the implementation of expenditure taxes. If a refundable tax credit or a rising rate schedule is provided, the expenditure tax is made progressive in the sense that the average tax rate rises with consumption levels (income-testing the credit will surely make the expenditure tax more progressive).

Concerns about the accumulation of wealth

Since the accumulation of savings is equal to the stock of wealth held by people, proponents of annual income taxes argue that savings should be subject to tax. Wealth provides opportunities for people to enjoy more untaxed consumption goods including leisure (the landlord's son who does not work) and political power. Therefore, it is appropriate to tax savings for these two reasons. The first argument—the consumption tax is applied on a narrower base compared to an income tax—is an important criticism since an equal-yield expenditure tax as a replacement for the income tax would result in a heavier tax on labour earnings. However, the argument does not provide a basis for an annual income tax; it is not a foregone conclusion that the return on savings should be taxed at the same rate as labour earnings.

The second argument made against consumption taxation is that the accumulation of wealth provides political power. Little research has modeled wealth as a source of political power and therefore providing special gains to certain individuals. One would need to provide an explicit model of political decision-making to understand the role of wealth, an area that should be open to greater analysis with new models of political economy that are now fashionable. Not all forms of wealth leads to greater political power: housing and retirement assets, the most significant forms of wealth for many people, unlikely play an important role in political influence. Instead, a tax on the very wealthy might be appropriate in principle, as some consumption advocates have argued. However, the wealth tax has provided very little revenue to governments since so many forms of wealth, such as housing, farming and small business investments, have been exempted .

Transition problems

Although there might be good arguments for the adoption of any major change to the tax system, any change could flounder in the midst of transition problems. By shifting from an income to consumption tax, old assets and accumulated wealth of the elderly would be subject to new levies and there would be a desire to provide some tax relief for low-income individuals. Transitional relief that would make it more politically acceptable to adopt a new form of taxation could possibly reduce some of the efficiency gains from adopting a consumption tax as a replacement for the income tax.

One very recent study (Altig et al. 2001) has modeled transitional measures for the adoption of a flat tax on consumption in the United States and found that most efficiency gains would be lost from adopting a consumption tax that provides offsets for low-income and elderly taxpayers. However, this study is based on the assumption that a move to an expenditure tax would raise the same revenue as the existing income tax. If governments are cutting taxes while changing the tax structure, it is possible to move to the desired tax base without hurting some taxpayers. Thus, for example, an expenditure tax could be easily adopted in Canada by expanding RRSP limits and introducing the exempt-yield approach over time.

The above arguments explain much of the public's ambivalence towards the full adoption of expenditure taxation in Canada. Although several points may be raised against the adoption of an expenditure tax, advocates of the expenditure tax can easily refute most of the arguments. The economic case for expenditure taxation is, therefore, pretty strong. But, in the end, political perception plays an important role in determining tax policy.

Conclusion: potential Canadian tax reforms

Given demographic pressures and increased economic integration, especially with the United States, Canada could sharply increase its standard of living and productivity by replacing the income tax with an expenditure tax. Several policies that would not be difficult to achieve include:

- a sharp increase in sales tax revenues (sales and excise) to reduce income taxes

- a major expansion of RRSP and pension limits to allow for greater accumulation of wealth to meet future contingencies of various sorts

- the introduction of an exempt-yield tax saving plan (with restrictions on contributed amounts) that would encourage saving by individuals expecting increases in future tax rates.

The adoption of an expenditure tax would certainly set Canada apart from other countries, including the United States. However, such a reform would require a careful consideration of implementation issues, including distributive impacts, transition and business level taxation. As has been recorded in studies found in the past literature, the technical issues are not insurmountable. The primary issue is to improve the tax structure to remove taxes on savings and investments and so create greater opportunities for economic growth and job creation.

Note

1 Even the tax expenditure accounts, often cited in the press and expert analysis, rely on annual income as the benchmark for evaluating the value of such expenditures.

References

Altig, David, Alan J. Auerbach, Laurence J. Kotlikoff, Kent A. Smetters and Jan Walliser (2001). Simulating Fundamental Tax Reform in the United States. *American Economic Review* 91, 3: 574–95.

Bernheim, B. Douglas (1999). *Taxation and Saving.* NBER Working Paper No. 7061, Cambridge, MA. Forthcoming in the *Handbook of Public Economics,* edited by Alan Auerbach and Martin Feldstein, North Holland, Amsterdam.

Canada (1966). *Report of the Royal Commission on Taxation* (Carter Report). Ottawa, Queen's Printer.

Helliwell, John (2000). *Globalization: Myths, Facts and Consequences.* Benefactor's Lecture, C.D. Howe Institute.

Institute for Fiscal Studies (1978). *The Structure and Reform of Direct Taxation: Report of a Committee Chaired by Professor J. E. Meade.* London: Allen and Unwin.

Mintz, Jack, and Duanjie Chen (2000). Will the Corporate Income Tax Wither? In the *World Tax Conference Report,* Canadian Tax Foundation, Toronto.

Mintz, Jack, and Stephen Richardson (2002). Taxation of Financial Intermediation Activities in Hong Kong. *Tax Notes International* 25, 7: 771–96.

The flat tax— a model for reform of personal and business taxes

Jason Clemens and Joel Emes
with Rodger Scott[1]

The flat tax is a viable model for broad-based reform of both personal and business taxes. This chapter, which is based on *Flat Tax: Principles and Issues* (Emes and Clemens 2001), a comprehensive evaluation of the flat tax, is focused on the reform of personal income taxes. There are three sections. The first summarizes where the current tax system fails when judged by traditional tax-policy criteria: efficiency, fairness, and simplicity. Also contained in the first section is a review of previous economic research on the costs of increasing marginal tax rates, one of the main problems with the current personal income tax system. The second section presents an overview of the flat-tax model developed by Professors Robert E. Hall and Alvin Rabushka (1995) of the Hoover Institution. The third section presents a number of flat-tax alternatives to the current federal and provincial personal income tax systems.

1 Failures in the current tax system

The traditional evaluative criteria for tax policy are efficiency, fairness, and simplicity. Comparing today's tax system with a flat tax according to these three criteria results in a strong case for the introduction of reforms based on a flat tax. The following section summarizes the failures of the current system and shows how a flat-tax system based on the work of Hall and Rabushka overcomes such problems.

Efficiency

Efficiency requires that economic distortions be minimized when taxes are imposed. The current Canadian tax system distorts economic decisions and, therefore, the allocation of resources in many ways. These distortions show up as tax incentives that effectively make some activities less expensive than others.

For example, there are a number of tax-based distortions in the field of investments. Such tax incentive programs, for instance, target resource exploration and venture capital investment. They effectively reduce the cost of making investments in these areas and, therefore, implicitly increase the relative marginal cost of making investments in other areas.

Another example of a tax-based distortion exists in the area of education. The tax system makes formal post-secondary education at an accredited university or college less expensive through the provision of tax credits. This, therefore, makes those programs that are not eligible for tax credits, such as professional and job-specific training programs relatively more expensive. This type of tax-based distortion leads to the allocation of too many resources to formal post-secondary education and not enough resources allocated to professional and job-specific training.

A flat tax removes all or nearly all of these tax-based biases. It minimizes the economic distortions attributable to the tax system and allows a more efficient allocation of resources.

Equity

Equity, also often called fairness, has two components, horizontal and vertical.

Horizontal equity

Horizontal equity requires that individuals or households with similar incomes face similar tax burdens, something not present in today's system. Certain types of income, such as some work-related benefits, face no taxation while other types of income, particularly business-related income, face multiple layers of taxation.

For instance, income earned from investments in corporations is taxed several times. First, the underlying investment is subject to corporate income tax and a variety of other taxes. The investor then pays income tax on any remittances from the corporation received in the form of dividends. The investor also pays capital gains taxes when the asset is sold, assuming that there is a nominal gain.

The government has responded to this particular issue by taxing different types of income at different rates. For example, the current top marginal federal tax rates are: 29.0% for interest and ordinary labour income, 14.5% for capital gains, and 19.6% for Canadian dividends (PricewaterhouseCoopers 2001). It is obvious that this tax structure adds considerably to the complexity of the system.

There are also biases towards two-income families and against one-income families. These biases are due to a difference between the value of the basic and spousal exemption and the fact that concentrated income by one earner reaches higher marginal tax rates than the same level of income earned by multiple earners. The analysis contained in *Flat Tax: Principles and Issues* shows how the personal income taxes of two sample families with similar incomes and similar deductions (credits) vary considerably. For example, a family with a combined income of $55,000, paid over $3,500 more in income taxes if the income came from one dominant earner than in a similar family with income earned more evenly between the spouses. Other studies have confirmed this bias in the tax system (Boessenkool 1999; Boessenkool and Davies 1998).

Interestingly, a similar phenomenon exists in the business tax system. The amount of taxation levied on corporations can vary considerably depending on the industry and the province in which the firm operates. For instance, prior to the 2000 federal budget, there were different corporate income tax rates applied to manufacturers and processors. Many provinces still maintain this preferential tax treatment. Similar differences among industries and provinces exist in the taxation of capital. Thus, two firms with similar incomes, profitability, and assets can bear significantly different tax burdens depending on their industry and province of operation.

Vertical equity

The second component of fairness is vertical equity. It is based on the notion that the higher the income people earn, the greater their ability to pay tax. This principle is used to justify the progressive income tax structure in Canada under which, as people earn more, they pay more tax. Table 1 summarizes the 2001 federal statutory personal income tax rates and the thresholds at which they apply.

It is important to note that this tax structure has two effects as incomes increase. First, the average tax rate payable on the total amount of income is raised. Second, there are higher tax rates on additional income beyond the various thresholds.

Recently, the federal and provincial income tax systems have been de-linked in most provinces. As a result, thresholds for marginal tax rates now differ from one jurisdiction to another. Tables 2 and 3 summarize the combined federal and provincial statutory tax rates and the applicable thresholds for the provinces of British Columbia and Alberta. The effect of de-linking can readily be observed in tables 2 and 3. British Columbia now maintains nine statutory tax rates once the federal personal income tax rates are combined

Table 1: Federal Statutory PIT Rates and Thresholds (2001)

Bracket	Interest & Ordinary Income	Capital Gains	Canadian Dividends
$100,000 & over	29.00%	14.50%	19.58%
$61,509–$99,999	26.00%	13.00%	15.83%
$30,754–$61,508	22.00%	11.00%	10.83%
$7,412–$30,753	16.00%	8.00%	3.33%
$0–$7,411	0.00%	0.00%	0.00%

Sources: Federal Department of Finance, Budget 2000 and October Mini-Budget; CIBC / PricewaterhouseCoopers, Statutory Rate Update.

Table 2: Combined Federal-Provincial Statutory PIT Rates and Thresholds (BC)

Bracket	Interest & Ordinary Income	Capital Gains	Canadian Dividends
$100,000 & over	45.70%	22.85%	33.08%
$85,000–$99,999	42.70%	21.35%	29.33%
$70,000–$84,999	41.70%	20.85%	28.08%
$61,509–$69,999	39.70%	19.85%	25.58%
$60,969–$61,508	35.70%	17.85%	20.58%
$30,754–$60,968	32.50%	16.25%	16.58%
$30,484–$30,753	26.50%	13.25%	9.08%
$8,000–$30,483	23.30%	11.65%	5.08%
$7,412–$7,999	16.00%	8.00%	3.33%
$0–$7,411	0.00%	0.00%	0.00%

Sources: Federal Department of Finance, Budget 2000 and October Mini-Budget; CIBC / PricewaterhouseCoopers, Statutory Rate Update.

Table 3: Combined Federal–Provincial Statutory PIT Rates and Thresholds (AB)

Bracket	Interest & Ordinary Income	Capital Gains	Canadian Dividends
$100,000 & over	39.00%	19.50%	24.08%
$61,509–$99,999	36.00%	18.00%	20.33%
$30,754–$61,508	32.00%	16.00%	15.33%
$12,900–$30,753	26.00%	13.00%	7.83%
$7,412–$12,899	16.00%	8.00%	3.33%
$0–7,411	0.00%	0.00%	0.00%

Sources: Federal Department of Finance, Budget 2000 and October Mini-Budget; CIBC / PricewaterhouseCoopers, Statutory Rate Update.

with the provincial personal income tax rates. These nine rates are in addition to the exemption value, which is technically an additional statutory tax bracket carrying a rate of 0.0%. Had the previous "tax-on-tax" system been maintained, British Columbia would have only four statutory tax brackets, plus the personal exemption.

A better example of the effect of de-linking on tax brackets is Alberta (table 3). Although the Province of Alberta maintains a single-rate tax, once the federal and provincial personal income tax rates and thresholds are combined, citizens of the province face five statutory tax brackets plus the exemption.

The move towards a "tax-on-income" at the provincial level (de-linking) has given the provinces greater power over tax policy. However, this increased decentralization has come at a price: increased complexity. The current system clearly has more statutory tax brackets, each with increasing marginal rate of taxation.

Economic effects of high and increasing marginal tax rates

The Canadian federal and provincial tax structure just discussed causes economic distortions and inefficiencies due to the disincentive effects of high and increasing marginal tax rates. When people decide to work an additional hour, to increase their human capital through education, or to invest their savings, they consider the marginal tax rate since it directly affects the proportion of increased income that accrues to them after they paid their taxes. The higher the marginal tax rate, the lower the return to productive activity and, thus, the lower the incentive for the individual, family, or business to engage in the additional productive activity.

The folly of demanding higher marginal tax rates for those in the upper income brackets is that higher rates will create disincentives for the most productive members of society to increase their productivity. In so much as this reduces the economic growth that benefits all members of society, increases in marginal tax rates in the long run result cause all of us to be worse off than we might otherwise have been.

The negative economic effects of high and increasing marginal tax rates have been studied widely. Following are brief summaries of some important studies.

Sillamaa and Veall (2001)

This paper used panel data to investigate the effects of the 1988 flattening of marginal tax rates in Canada. The study concluded that the responsiveness of income to changes in marginal taxes is positive, as expected, but smaller in Canada than in the United States. The authors also found evidence of a much higher response in self-employment income and in the labour income of seniors and from those with high incomes.

M. Feldstein (1995)

Using data from the 1986 tax reform in the United States, Feldstein concludes that "a decrease in marginal tax rates causes not only an increase in labour supply (broadly defined), but also a shift in the form of compensation and a reduction in deductible expenses ... Taxable income therefore rises substantially more than aggregate hours." He also concluded that capital gains realizations are far more sensitive to tax rates than had been assumed by government agencies.

M. Feldstein and D. Feenberg (1995)

This paper assesses the economic effects of increasing the former top statutory tax rate from 31% to 36% and the introduction of a new top rate of 39.6% at $250,000 in 1993 in the United States. The study concludes that high-income taxpayers would have reported 7.8% more taxable income had the tax rates not been increased. The decline in taxable income for these groups caused the Treasury to lose more than half the extra revenue that would have been collected if taxpayers had not changed their behaviour. In fact, the overall losses in efficiency associated with the higher marginal tax rates (including the effect upon labour supply) was estimated at roughly twice the $8 billion in revenue raised by the tax increase.

Carroll, Holtz-Eakin, Rider, and Rosen (1998)

Carroll et al. investigated the effects of high marginal tax rates on capital formation. The study found that "a 5 percentage point rise in marginal tax rates would reduce the proportion of entrepreneurs who make new capital investment by 10.4%. Further, such a tax increase would lower mean capital outlays by 9.9%." In other words, an increase in marginal tax rates results in less investment by entrepreneurs and subsequently less aggregate capital formation.

Gustavo Ventura (1999)

Ventura concluded that the elimination of taxes on capital, based on a tax reform of the type suggested by Hall and Rabushka, would have a positive effect on capital accumulation and that aggregate labour supply, measured in efficiency units would increase.

Koester and Kormendi (1989)

This study isolated marginal tax effects from average tax effects. They found that, after controlling for average tax rates, increases in marginal tax rates had negative effects on the level of economic activity. In other words, reducing the "progressivity" of the tax system while allowing the government the same tax revenue (measured as a percent of GDP) led to higher levels of national income.

Mullen and Williams (1994)

Mullen and Williams, using methods similar to those employed by Koester and Kormendi (1989), used state-based data in the United States to assess the relationship between marginal tax rates and growth in the capital stock and labour force. They concluded that "lowering marginal tax rates can have a considerable positive impact on growth ... creating a less confiscatory tax structure, while maintaining the same average level of taxation, enabling sub-national governments to spur economic growth."

F. Padovano and E. Galli (2001)

This study adjusts the underlying data used in previous studies to specify marginal tax rates properly across income groups and different countries. After doing so, the authors conclude that high marginal tax rates and tax progressivity are negatively correlated with long-run economic growth.

Becsi (1996)

Becsi, again using a method similar to that of Koester and Kormendi (1989), derived marginal tax rates for the American states to assess the relationship between marginal tax rates and economic growth.

He found that differences in marginal tax rates across states have a statistically significant effect on relative economic growth rates.

J. Long (1999)

This study assesses the relationship between marginal tax rates and taxable income across American states. It concludes that an increase in the marginal tax rate reduces taxable income. It also concluded that high-income taxpayers were much more responsive than lower-income individuals to changes in tax rates.

Engen and Skinner (1996)

This study reviewed previously completed research investigating marginal tax rates and economic growth. Engen and Skinner concluded "a major tax reform reducing all marginal rates by 5 percentage points, and average tax rates by 2.5 percentage points, is predicted to increase long term growth rates by between 0.2 and 0.3 percentage points." While this may appear small, the cumulative effect can be enormous. The authors speculated that, if a less efficient tax structure had been in place in the United States from 1960 to 1996, the amount of output currently lost would have totalled more than $500 billion annually or 6.4% of 1996 GDP.

Gruber and Saez (2000)

The finding of this study is that for each of the tax-spending cases investigated, the optimal structure of marginal tax rates should be declining as you move up from lower to higher income brackets. In other words, the marginal rates of taxation should be relatively higher for low-income earners and relatively lower for high-income earners. Given the behavioural responses of individuals, the authors conclude that in order to maximize social welfare "the optimal tax system should feature declining (or at least not increasing) marginal rates."

There can be little doubt that these studies confirm that high and increasing marginal tax rates impede the formation of capital, retard economic growth, hinder per-capita income growth, and constrain aggregate labour supply. This seems a high price to pay for vertical equity and progressivity, which could be achieved with a flat tax.

An advantage of a flat tax is that it can be designed to meet the criteria of horizontal and vertical equity. Horizontal equity is achieved by the inclusion of all sources of income into the base upon which a single or flat rate of taxation is levied. Vertical equity is achieved through the use of a basic personal and spousal exemption of income. Since the flat rate is imposed only on income beyond this exemption threshold, the average tax rate increases with income and approaches the flat rate for the highest income earners. Most important, by eliminating increasing marginal tax rates, a flat tax avoids many, if not all, of the costs outlined in the literature reviewed above, namely, lower economic growth, reduced savings and investment, and lower aggregate labour supply.

Simplicity

The flat tax also brings the benefit of simplicity, which makes it easier and less costly for citizens and business to comply with tax laws. The increased simplicity would bring large savings since the complexity of the tax code and the many tax forms and regulations in Canada have spurred an entire industry of tax accountants, lawyers, and planners who do nothing but attempt to reduce their clients' tax bills legally. Much of this industry would disappear if a flat tax were adopted and the resources in the industry would find employment in other industries meeting the genuine needs of Canadians.

The administrative and compliance costs associated with business taxes have been estimated by Robert E. Plamondon and David Zussman (1998). They found the cost to be between $2.3 billion and $4.5 billion in 1996. The midpoint of this range is $3.4 billion, which represented ⅖ of 1% of GDP or 1.5% of total tax revenue in 1996.

Two studies completed by Professor Brian Erard of Carleton University for the Technical Committee on Business Taxation (otherwise referred to as the "Mintz Commission") provide estimates of business compliance costs that buttress the estimates of Plamondon and Zussman. One of Erard's studies showed that the burden for the 500 largest non-financial corporations in Canada in 1995 was $250 million, or about 5% of total taxes paid (Erard 1997a).

Professor Erard's second study for the Mintz Commission confirmed that many small and medium-sized businesses feel overwhelmed by the compliance requirements associated with Canadian taxation. In fact, the central finding of the study was that the vast majority of small and medium-sized enterprises relied on outside professional assistance to comply with the tax system and that the principal compliance cost identified by these businesses were fees paid to these professionals (Erard 1997b).

There also exist estimates of the administrative and compliance costs of taxation for individuals. In a major study for the Canadian Tax Foundation, Francois Vaillancourt (1989) estimated that for the 1985 tax year, the average taxpayer spent 5.5 hours completing tax returns or spent roughly $69 (1985 dollars) to have a professional do the job. He then included other related costs to arrive at a total cost per taxpayer of $117.20 (1985 dollars) in administrative and compliance costs. This translates into roughly $1.8 billion in administrative and compliance costs for 1985 for individual taxpayers. Although somewhat dated, the study provides an important foundation for understanding the extent of costs associated with the personal income tax system.

Finally, there is cost of collection by government. The Fraser Institute recently estimated that the federal government alone spent some $2.6 billion in 1997/1998 to collect taxes and other revenues (Jones and Graf 2001).

The simplification of the tax system is a central part of flat tax reform. The simplification is achieved by the removal of most exemptions and nearly all deductions and tax credits and through the elimination of different treatment of income by type. As a result of the latter provision, there is no benefit in declaring income as one type or another since all income is taxed once and at the same rate.

2 The Hall-Rabushka Model

The tax reform proposed by Professors Robert E. Hall and Alvin Rabushka of the Hoover Institution is based on the use of a single rate of taxation for all sources of income. This proposal represents a fundamental change from the way governments currently collect tax revenue. The proposal achieves simplicity, economic efficiency, and fairness, the traditional measures of effective taxation, while collecting the necessary revenues required to finance government operations. Those wishing to study the proposals of Hall and Rabushka in greater detail will find their works on the Internet at the Hoover

Institution (www.hoover.org) and the American Enterprise Institute (www.aei.org) as well as in their book (Hall and Rabushka 1995), which will be found in most major bookstores and libraries.

The flat tax differs from the single-rate tax

The reforms to the personal income tax announced in the Province of Alberta in 1999 replaced the multiple tax rates applied to personal income with a single tax rate, thus eliminating the progressivity in the personal income tax structure that existed previously. The tax reform proposed by the Canadian Alliance during the federal election campaign in 2000 would initially replace the multiple federal statutory personal income tax rates with two rates, retaining some of the higher marginal tax rates as a function of income. The Alliance's proposal envisaged that, near the end of the party's first mandate, the two rates would be replaced by one, along the lines of Alberta's single-rate tax system. However, the replacement of multiple tax rates with a single rate is but one step in the process of broad-based tax reform based on a flat tax model.

Hall-Rabushka flat tax

Under the current tax system in both the United States and in Canada, certain types of income, such as some fringe benefits, are not taxed at all while other sources of income, such as dividends and capital gains, are taxed more than once. Under the reform proposed by Hall and Rabushka, all sources of income would be taxed only once and at one uniform rate.

Under the present system in the two countries, there exists an additional problem. Different sources of income are often taxed at different rates. This is the case for income from dividends, wages and benefits. Under the Hall-Rabushka proposal, all sources of income would be taxed at the same rate.

Hall and Rabushka argue that the imposition in the United States of a federal rate of flat tax of 19% on all sources of income would raise the same amount of revenue as the current system, which has 5 personal federal rates (15%, 28%, 31%, 36%, and 39.6%) and a number of business tax rates. They proposed that the 19% rate of taxation be payable only after generous personal exemptions, which for a family of four in 1995 would have been US$25,500 (CDN$32,986). These exemptions mean that a family with income below $25,000 pays no tax whatsoever. Those with incomes above $25,000 pay 19% on the income in excess of the exemption.

It is important to note that under the Hall-Rabushka proposal only wages, salaries and pension benefits are subject to personal income tax. Dividends, capital gains, interest, and fringe benefits are not included in the personal income tax base because they are subject to taxation under the corporate income tax.

One frequently overlooked aspect of Hall-Rabushka is its rejection of alternative taxes such as a national sales tax or a value-added tax to replace revenue lost from the elimination of multiple taxation and the adoption of uniform rates on all incomes. They reject the alternative taxes because they make it impossible or extremely costly to exempt lower-income individuals and families from taxation, as is done under their proposal through the use of the generous basic exemptions.

The Hall-Rabushka flat tax would also allow "postcard-size tax returns": individuals and families would simply sum their income from wages, salaries, and retirement benefits and subtract the personal exemption to calculate their taxable income. This amount is then multiplied by one rate (19%) to determine the individual or family tax bill for the year. The amount withheld is then compared to the amount owed to calculate whether a refund is due from, or a payment is owing to, the federal government. All of this information could easily fit on a post card. One of the main reasons that the tax return under the Hall-Rabushka system is so short and simple is that there are no opportunities to adjust the income base of the tax payable for tax credits, deductions, or additional exemptions and the type of income, which makes the present tax returns so complicated and time-consuming to prepare.

Another important aspect of the Hall-Rabushka proposal and, indeed, most flat-tax proposals, is the reform of the corporate or business income tax. According to their proposal, the tax base for business equals all business income minus the cost of inputs, salaries, wages, pensions, and investment in plant and equipment. The tax base is broadened through the elimination of tax-based incentives for business, the taxation of certain benefits that currently escape taxation, and by removing interest deductibility. As a result, they are able to maintain revenue neutrality in spite of the lower uniform tax rate of 19%.

Under the proposed system, businesses cannot deduct the cost of interest, dividends, fringe benefits, or any other payments to owners as expenses, as they do under the present system. This aspect of the Hall-Rebushka reform of business taxes is seen as quite radical by many. But, it is necessary to assure that these payments to individuals are taxed at the source and, under the principle of taxing income only once, do not have to be reported as taxable income by individuals receiving them. The proposed reform of business taxation, under which interest costs and depreciation expenses are no longer considered to be deductible expenses, brings another important benefit. It eliminates the present preferential treatment accorded debt relative to equity financing.

Perhaps the single most important and controversial proposal for the reform of business taxation made by Hall and Rabushka is the elimination of depreciation expenses. Businesses are currently able to write-off or deduct from pre-tax income the cost of investing in new plants and equipment on an incremental basis. The amount deductible every year is a percentage of the cost, which is a function of the economic life of the investment and is specified by the tax authorities. Hall and Rabushka propose that the entire cost of the investment is deductible as an expense in the year of purchase. There would then be no conflicts over whether the purchase of a certain piece of equipment is an investment and therefore subject to depreciation or if it is an expense and eligible to be written off in the year it is incurred. Depreciation schedules and the bureaucracy required to interpret them (accountants and lawyers) and to enforce them (government revenue officials) are eliminated or, at least, drastically reduced in number.

Focus on consumption

One of the main, though often overlooked, benefits of the Hall-Rabushka proposal is that it effectively moves personal and business taxation from an income base towards a consumption base. Economists generally agree that the taxation of consumption is the most efficient manner in which to raise tax revenue (Jorgensen and Yun 1991; Kesselman 1997; Grubel 2000; OECD 1997; and Kneller, Bleaney, and Gemmell 1999). Hall and Rabushka achieve this goal by excluding all investment activities from the tax base[2] and, thus, taxing only income that is consumed, that is, spent rather than saved. In addition, the Hall-Rabushka reform would also eliminate the present heavy taxation of returns to savings, which would create highly desirable incentives for increased savings and the formation of capital.

Economic considerations

From an economic perspective, the most important benefits of the Hall-Rabushka tax reform proposals are their creation of improved incentives for work, increased entrepreneurial activity, and greater formation of capital, which will lead to higher levels of national output and a higher standard of living. These economic benefits, in the longer run, are almost certain to be more important than the immediate and more obvious savings from the simplification of the system of taxation that will accrue to taxpayers directly and, through reduced government costs, indirectly.

In addition, some of the specific tax reforms proposed by Hall and Rabushka will lead to increases in the efficiency of capital formation through the elimination of the present tax-based incentives in the form of tax credits and subsidies that tend to redirect capital to less efficient uses. For example, the current system promotes debt-financed investment by permitting interest deductibility while penalizing equity-financed investment through double taxation of dividends and capital gains. The net result is less entrepreneurial activity and greater debt-financed (lower risk) investment. Auerbach and Kotlikoff (1987; cited in Hall-Rabushka) estimate that a flat tax would increase capital formation as a percent of GDP from 5.0% to 6.2% and, as a consequence, increase GDP by between 2.0% and 4.0% within seven years.

The Hall-Rabushka reform proposal also creates strong incentives for individuals to increase their work effort by reducing the disincentive effects associated with high and increasing marginal tax rates. Hall and Rabushka estimate that GDP will increase by approximately 3% simply due to the proposed elimination of disincentives for work.

The preceding summary hardly does justice to the wide ranging and comprehensive tax reforms proposed by Hall and Rabushka. However, our brief summary is sufficient to show that the proposals offer far-reaching economic benefits through significant increases in the simplicity, efficiency, and fairness in the tax system.

3 What would a flat tax look like in Canada?

We used Statistics Canada's Social Policy Simulation Database and Model (SPSD/M) to quantify the changes in tax rates that would arise from the application in Canada of the principles of the personal income tax reform proposed by Hall and Rabushka. We calculated what would happen to the income tax obligations of Canadians after the introduction of a flat tax under nine different scenarios. Unfortunately, we were not able to calculate integrated personal and business income estimates because of limitations in the data found in the SPSD/M. For this reason, it is important to remember that our results are not strictly comparable to those of Hall and Rabushka, since their model reforms both personal and business income taxes.

Table 4 shows the results of our calculations. The first seven analyses are for flat tax rates that preserve the present revenues under different assumptions about the level of exemptions, the retention of RRSP/RPP contributions, and deductions for charitable contributions. The remaining two calculations provide less tax revenue than is currently collected; in other words, there is a reduction in taxes.[3]

There are several important observations to be gleamed from table 4. First, assuming a simplified system with only personal and spousal exemptions, and child deductions, the federal flat tax rate required to raise the same amount of revenues as the current system is 18.3% with a provincial average rate of 10.3% (Scenario 5). This implies an average personal income tax rate of 28.6%. The result is that all income groups earning above $50,000 receive a tax reduction while those earning between $10,000 and $50,000 experience a marginal increase. (Clemens and Emes 2001 contains tables outlining the distributional effects of such a change.)

Scenario 6 considers the effect of including (retaining) RRSP and RPP deductibility, which effectively creates a consumption-based tax system. The flat rate rates required to raise the same amount of revenue as is currently collected are 19.9% at the federal level and 11.1% at the provincial level (average rate). This results in a combined federal-provincial flat tax rate of 31.0%, an increase of 2.4 percentage-points or roughly 8.4% over the flat tax rate in scenario 5. Distributional analyses in Clemens and Emes 2001 show that those earning in excess of $50,000 a year experience a net reduction in their taxes while those earning between $10,000 and $50,000 experience a marginal increase in their taxes. It is important to note that the inclusion of an RRSP/RPP deduction represents a tax deferral rather than a current tax expenditure, implying that the long-term tax revenue collection of the government would not be affected (see ACPM 2000).

Increasing the basic and spousal exemptions, as presented in Scenarios 8 and 9, results in a decrease across the board in personal income taxes paid for all income groups. Both cases represent a fairly simple system—basic and spousal exemption of $11,834, child exemption of $2,000, and current RRSP/RPP deductibility—but are coupled with tax and expenditure reductions at the federal level. In other words, the increase in the basic and spousal exemptions are financed through a moderate (scenario 8) and a substantial (scenario 9) tax and expenditure reduction.

As suggested by Hall and Rabushka, the system should remain as "clean" as possible, avoiding the introduction of additional exemptions, deductions, and tax credits. In particular, they caution against making exceptions for specific programs or requirements since such initiatives are seen as the beginning of a slippery slope to a complex, inefficient, and unfair tax system (See the discussion of scenario 7 in Clemens and Emes 2001 for more details and a discussion of this topic).

Competitive advantages of a flat tax

Canada is currently searching for ways to make its economy more competitive with that of the United States. The federal tax reductions enacted in 2000 were officially justified on these grounds by the Minister of Finance in the 2000 Budget speech. Unfortunately, the Canadian government has ignored the possibility of creating a competitive tax advantage over the United States through the overhaul of the tax system. The simplification of the tax system made possible by the introduction of a flat tax would give Canada an immediate and substantial competitive advantage. Currently, there are some 740 different tax forms in the United States with 250 or so publications explaining the forms. The US Tax Foundation estimates that Americans spend about 4.3 billion hours a year filling tax forms at a cost to the economy of $125 billion. Some tax

Table 4: Flat Tax Rates for Canada and the Provinces

Scenario	Personal Exemption	Child Exemption	Change in Revenue Collected[1]	Deduction for RRSPs and RPPs[2]
1	$0	$0	$0	
2	$7,231	$0	$0	
3	$8,766	$0	$0	
4	$17,532	$0	$0	
5	$8,766	$2,000	$0	
6	$8,766	$2,000	$0	√
7	$8,766	$2,000	$0	√
8	$11,834	$2,000	–$13.4	√
9	$11,834	$2,000	–$22.4	√

(1) Refers to the Federal Government only. Any change in the amount of revenue collected implies an expenditure and tax reduction at the federal level only. Stated in billions of dollars.
(2) RRSP/RPP contributions and charitable donations, if present, are treated as they currently exist in the federal tax system.

reform proposals introduced in Congress envision the creation of new income tax brackets with different marginal tax rates, which would make the American system even more complex. The present and possibly increasing complexity of the American tax system provide Canada with a unique opportunity to establish a real economic advantage over our neighbour. The adoption of a flat tax based on the Hall-Rabushka model would make Canada's system much simpler and at the same time more efficient while retaining most of its horizontal and vertical equity. The economic advantage gained by Canada through such a tax reform in the longer run would allow the country to narrow the gap in real per-capita income that has developed during the last 25 years.

Deduction for Charitable Donations[2]	Federal Flat-Tax Rate	Average Provincial Flat-Tax Rate	Ontario Provincial Flat-Tax Rate[3]
	12.7	7.0	5.8
	16.7	9.4	7.5
	17.8	10.0	7.9
	26.1	14.8	11.2
	18.3	10.3	8.1
	19.9	11.1	8.8
√	20.1	11.2	8.9
	19.0	12.9	10.0
	16.5	12.9	10.0

(3) Presented for illustrative purposes only.
Note: Distributional analysis of the scenarios are available in the main paper, available on the Internet at www.fraserinstitute.ca.
Source: Emes and Clemens, 2001.

Conclusion

The flat tax offers Canada the opportunity to adopt a fair, efficient, and simple tax system. Such a system would provide large positive incentives for work, savings, investment, and risk-taking. Empirical evidence suggests that the direct savings and economic benefits over the longer run of implementing a flat tax system would raise Canada's rate of economic growth, which in turn would lead to higher per-capita incomes and make affordable higher levels of government spending on social programs.

Notes

1 Rodger Scott was a Fiscal Studies Intern in 2001 and aided in the updating of the study. Both authors wish to express their thanks to Rodger for his efforts and contributions to the Fiscal Studies Department.

2 Poddar and English (1999) estimate that, in the current Canadian tax system, 75% of domestic savings are tax exempt (1999). This is due to the fact that the overwhelming majority of Canadians save exclusively within the confines of Registered Retirement Savings Plans (RRSPs) and Registered Pension Plans (RPPs). Thus, the inclusion of an RRSP/RPP deduction within a flat tax system would essentially mirror a national consumption tax or move considerably towards one.

3 Readers interested in more detail about the different assumptions and results can find them in our paper (Clemens and Emes 2001), which is available on the Internet at www.fraserinstitute.ca.

References

Aaron, H., and J. Pechman (eds) (1981). *How Taxes Affect Economic Behaviour.* Washington, DC: Brookings Institution.

Altig, David, and Charles T. Carlstrom (1994). The Efficiency and Welfare Effects of Tax Reform: Are Fewer Brackets Better Than More? *Economic Review* 30, 4: 30–42. Federal Reserve Bank of Cleveland.

Association of Canadian Pension Management (2000). *Dependence or Self-Reliance: Which Way for Canada's Retirement Income System?* Digital document available at www.acpm.com.

Besci, Zsolt (1996). Do State and Local Taxes Affect Relative State Growth? *Economic Review* 81, 2: 18–36. Federal Reserve Bank of Atlanta.

Boessenkool, Kenneth J. (1999). Putting Tax Policy in Its Place: How Social Policy Took over the Tax Treatment of the Family. In Douglas W. Allen and John Richards (eds.), *It Takes Two: The Family in Law and Finance* (Policy Study 33; Toronto: CD Howe Institute).

Boessenkool, Kenneth J., and James B. Davies (1998). *Giving Mom and Dad a Break: Returning Fairness to Families in Canada's Tax and Transfer System.* CD Howe Institute Commentary 117 (November). Toronto: CD Howe Institute.

Browning, Edgar K. (1987). On the Marginal Welfare Cost of Taxation. *American Economic Review* 77, 1 (March): 199–219.

Carroll, Robert, Dougals Holtz-Eakin, Mark Rider, and Harvey S. Rosen (1998). *Entrepreneurs, Income Taxes and Investment.* Working Paper 6374. Cambridge, MA: National Bureau of Economic Research.

Davies, James (1998). *Marginal Tax Rates in Canada: High and Getting Higher.* CD Howe Institute Commentary 103 (March). Toronto: CD Howe Institute.

Du Pont, Pete (2001). A Complicated Cut. *Wall Street Journal* (May 30). Digital document available at http://interactive.wsj.com/.

Emes, Joel, and Jason Clemens (2001). *Flat Tax: Principles and Issues.* Critical Issues Bulletin. Vancouver, BC: The Fraser Institute. Available at www.fraserinstitute.ca/.

Engen, Eric, and Jonathan Skinner (1996). *Taxation and Economic Growth.* Working Paper 5826. Cambridge, MA: National Bureau of Economic Research.

Erard, Brian (1997a). *The Income Tax Compliance Burden on Canadian Big Business.* Working paper 97-2. Prepared for the Technical Committee on Business Taxation. Dep't of Finance, Gov't of Canada.

Erard, Brian (1997b). *The Income Tax Compliance Burden on Small and Medium-sized Canadian Businesses.* Working paper 97-12. Prepared for the Technical Committee on Business Taxation. Dep't of Finance, Gov't of Canada.

Feldstein, Martin (1995). Behavioral Responses to Tax Rates: Evidence from Tax Reform Act of 1986. *American Economic Review* 85, 2 (Papers and Proceedings).

Feldstein, Martin, and Daniel Feenberg (1995). *The Effect of Increased Tax Rates on Taxable Income and Economic Efficiency: A Preliminary Analysis of the 1993 Tax Rate Increases.* NBER Working Paper 5370. Cambridge, MA: National Bureau of Economic Research.

Garay, Mark (2001). *Seeds of Change.* Deloitte & Touche. Digital document available at http://www.dttus.com/.

Grubel, Herbert (2000). *Unlocking Canadian Capital: The Case for Capital Gains Tax Reform.* Vancouver, BC: The Fraser Institute.

Gruber, Jon, and Emmanuel Saez (2000). *The Elasticity of Taxable Income: Evidence and Implications.* Working Paper 7512. Cambridge, MA: National Bureau of Economic Research.

Hall, Robert E., and Alvin Rabushka (1995). *The Flat Tax*. Third Edition. Stanford, CA: Hoover Institution Press.

Jones, Laura, and Stephen Graf (2001). *Canada's Regulatory Burden: How Many Regulations? At What Cost?* Special Issue, *Fraser Forum*. Vancouver, BC: The Fraser Institute.

Jorgenson, Dale W., and Yun Kun-Young (1991). The Excess Burden of Taxation in the United States. *Journal of Accounting, Auditing, and Finance* 6, 4 (Fall): 487–508.

Kesselman, Jonathan R. (1990). *Rate Structure and Personal Taxation: Flat Rate or Dual Rate?* Victoria, BC: Victoria University Press/Institute of Policy Studies.

Kesselman, Jonathan R. (1997). *General Payroll Taxes: Economics, Politics, and Design*. Toronto: Canadian Tax Foundation.

Kesselman, Jonathan R. (1998). Tax Cuts for Growth and Fairness. *Policy Options* (December): 13–16.

Kesselman, Jonathan R. (1999). Rate Cuts and Base Reforms: The Best Mix for Personal Taxes. Prepared for the Canadian Tax Foundation's Tax Policy Conference, Personal Income Tax Reform: Building a Better Mousetrap, Ottawa, Ontario (April 9/10).

Kesselman, Jonathan R. (2000). *Flat Taxes, Dual Taxes, Smart Taxes: Making the Best Choices*. IRPP Study. Montreal, QC: Institute for Research on Public Policy.

Kneller, Richard, Michael F. Bleaney, and Norman Gemmell (1999). Fiscal Policy and Growth: Evidence from OECD Countries. *Journal of Public Economics* 74, 2 (November): 171–90.

Koester, Reinhard, and Roger Kormendi (1989). Taxation, Aggregate Activity and Economic Growth: Cross-Country Evidence on Some Supply-Side Hypotheses. *Economic Inquiry* 27: 367–86.

Long, John E. (1999). The Impact of Marginal Tax Rates on Taxable Income: Evidence from State Income Tax Differentials. *Southern Economic Journal* 65, 4.

Mullen, John, and Martin Williams (1994). Marginal Tax Rates and State Economic Growth. *Regional Science and Urban Economics* 24, 6: 687–705.

Organisation for Economic Cooperation and Development [OECD] (1997). *OECD Economic Surveys 1997, Canada*. Paris: OECD.

Padovano, Fabio, and Emma Galli (2001). Tax Rates and Economic Growth in the OECD Countries (1950–1990). *Economic Inquiry* 39, 1 (January).

Plamondon, Robert E., and David Zussman (1998). The Compliance Costs of Canada's Major Tax Systems and the Impact of Single Administration. *Canadian Tax Journal* 46, 4.

Poddar, Satyar, and Morley English (1999). Canadian Taxation of Personal Investment Income. *Canadian Tax Journal* 47, 5: 1270–304.

PricewaterhouseCoopers (2001). *Federal and Provincial Statutory PIT Rates.*

Sillamaa, Mary-Anne, and Michael R. Veall (2001). The Effect of Marginal Tax Rates on Taxable Income: A Panel Study of the 1988 Tax Flattening in Canada. *Journal of Public Economics* 80, 3: 341–56.

Vaillancourt, Francois (1989). *The Administrative and Compliance Costs of the Personal Income Tax and Payroll Tax System in Canada, 1986*. Canadian Tax Paper No. 86. Toronto, ON: Canadian Tax Foundation.

Ventura, Gustavo (1999). Flat Tax Reform: A Quantitative Exploration. *Journal of Economic Dynamics & Control* 23: 1425–58.

Restructuring the Canadian tax system by changing the mix of direct and indirect taxes

Bev Dahlby

John Stuart Mill defined a direct tax as one that is levied on the individual or firm that is "intended" to pay it. By default, indirect taxes are those taxes where the individual or firm from whom the taxes are collected is not intended to bear the burden of the tax. This distinction between direct and indirect taxes is often highly imprecise because it is frequently difficult, if not impossible, to discern the legislators' intentions with regard to who should bear the burden of a tax. It is similarly difficult or impossible to know whether legislators know how the tax burden is likely to be shifted through the adjustment of market prices.

Over time, indirect taxes have come to mean sales and excise taxes on goods and services, while direct taxes usually refer to personal and corporate income taxes. Canada, like most countries in the OECD, relies on a mix of direct and indirect taxes. As figure 1 indicates, Canada, the United States, Australia, New Zealand and Japan rely more on taxes on income and profits and less on taxes

Figure 1: International comparison of tax mixes in 1997

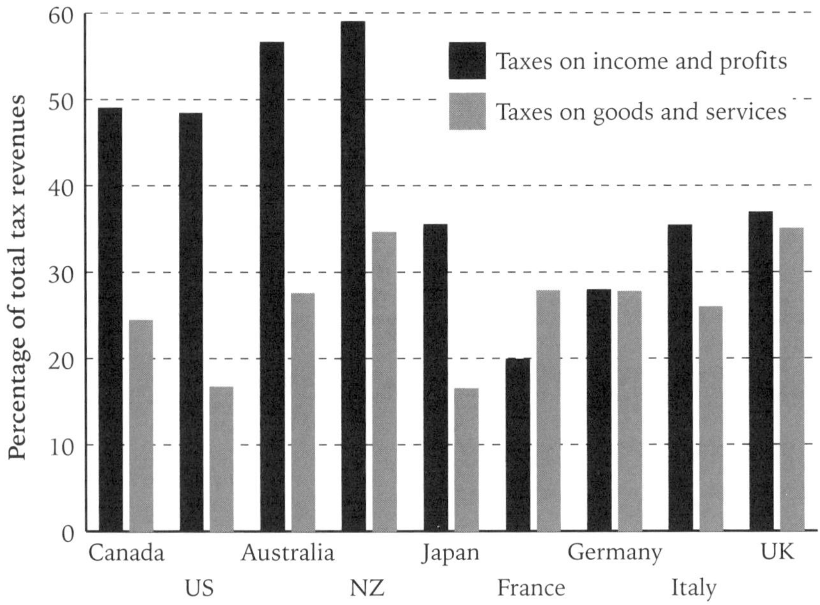

Source: OECD 1999.

on goods and services than the European countries of France, Germany, Italy and the United Kingdom.[1]

Determining the mix of direct and indirect taxes is a fundamental tax-policy choice.[2] On what basis should this choice be made? I will approach this issue by first noting that the taxation of goods and services is a form of consumption taxation. Therefore, the decision to rely to a greater or lesser degree on indirect taxes is ultimately a decision concerning the level of consumption taxation.

In section 1, I review the theoretical models and some of the empirical evidence regarding the consequences of consumption taxes for efficiency. My reading of the evidence suggests that while the level effects (static efficiency gains) from adopting a consumption tax are ambiguous, there is mounting evidence from simulation models and econometric studies that switching to consumption taxation has very significant growth effects (dynamic efficiency gains). In Section 2, I argue that consumption taxation is a fair or equitable form of taxation if we adopt the intuitively appealing notion that those with a higher standard of living should pay higher taxes.

Increasing reliance upon consumption taxation does not necessarily imply an increased reliance on indirect taxes because consumption taxes can be imposed through an expenditure tax, which is a form of direct taxation. In section 3 of the paper, I briefly compare direct and indirect tax mixes under a consumption-tax system. I argue that one would want to impose both direct and indirect taxes under a consumption tax system because both types of taxes are subject to different forms of tax evasion and avoidance. Therefore, a combination of direct and indirect consumption taxes would produce a more efficient and equitable tax system than simple reliance on one form of consumption taxation. The final section of the paper summarizes my conclusions and the policy implications.

1 Efficiency arguments for consumption taxation

The output of the economic system can be thought of as an "economic pie," where the size of the pie is the total value of the goods and services produced in the economy, including non-market activities such as leisure and the quality of the environment. The tax system can affect the size and distribution of the economic pie because taxes affect the decisions of households about labour supply and savings and the decisions of firms about output, employment, and investment. Taxes alter economic incentives by changing the net returns that households and firms receive from the inputs that they provide or from the products that they sell. If, in the absence of taxation, markets allocate resources to maximize the size of the economic pie, then the tax system, by changing the allocation of resources, will shrink the size of the economic pie. The shrinkage of the economic pie is what economists mean by the efficiency cost of the tax system.[3]

In discussing how the tax system affects economic performance, it is important to distinguish between level effects and growth effects.[4] In its purest form, a level effect has a once-and-for-all-impact on the size of the economic pie but it does not affect the long-term growth rate of the economy. However, the economic adjustments to a tax reform usually do not occur instantaneously. It takes time for households and firms to adjust their behaviour to a change in the tax regime and for changes in their decisions to have an impact on the economy.[5] If there is a gradual adjustment to a change in tax policy, then the growth rate of the economy will be temporarily higher along the transition path to the new equilibrium but, once all of the economic adjustments have occurred, the growth rate of the economy will return to its previous rate. Thus, the defining characteristic of a level effect is that it has, at most, a temporary impact on the growth rate of the economy. By contrast, the growth effect from a tax reform alters the long-term growth rate of the economy.

It is useful to distinguish between level effects and growth effects because some tax reforms will only have level effects, while other tax reforms may have a growth effect or both a level and a growth effect. An important point to bear in mind is that even seemingly small growth effects can have a major impact on living standards over a period of 20 to 30 years.

The level effects of switching to consumption taxation

A tax on investment income distorts an individual's savings decisions because it is equivalent to imposing a tax on future consumption. In contrast, a consumption tax, imposed at a constant rate over time, does not affect the rate of return on savings and does not distort savings decisions.

The gain from replacing a tax on the return on savings with a consumption tax is illustrated in figure 2 using the standard two-period model of consumption and savings decisions.[6] C_1 is consumption in the first period, which we will consider the individual's working life. C_2 is the individual's consumption in the second period, which we can think of as his retirement years. In this model, it will be assumed that the individual's earnings, *E*, are fixed and equal to *E* and that there is no precautionary or bequest motive for savings. It is also assumed that savings are completely unresponsive to the rate of return on savings in order to show that there is a gain from switching to a consumption tax even if savings elasticity is zero, a point that was first emphasized by Feldstein (1978).

In the absence of taxation, the individual's intertemporal budget constraint would be *EE′*. With a tax on the return to savings, the individual's intertemporal budget constraint is *BE*. The slope of the budget constraint reflects the reduced rate of return on savings or, equivalently, the increase in the price of future consumption. The

Figure 2: The gain from substituting a consumption tax for an interest income tax when earnings are fixed

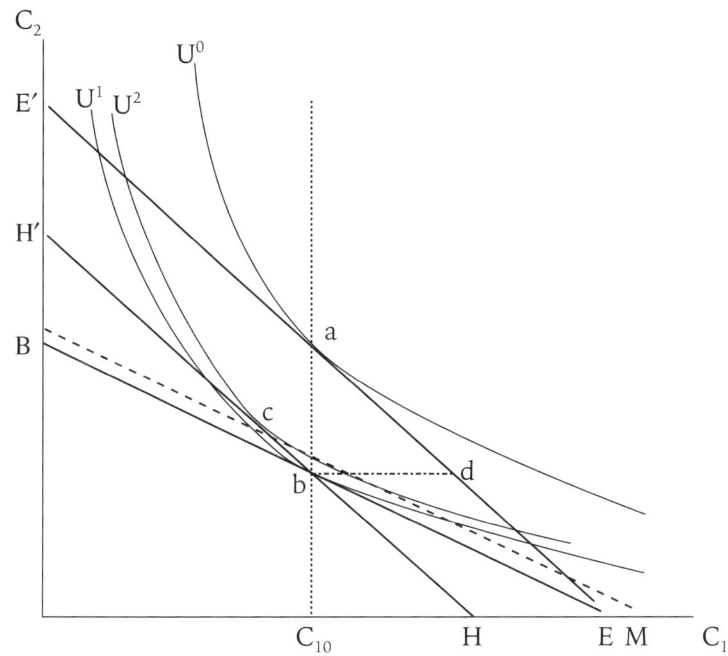

individual's optimal consumption bundle is at *b* on the indifference curve U^1 where the individual consumes C_{10} in the first period and saves $E - C_{10}$. The present value of the tax revenues collected from the individual is equal to the distance *bd*.

A consumption tax that collected the same tax revenues would have the same slope as EE′ and would pass through point *b*. The budget line *HH′* is the individual's intertemporal budget constraint with revenue-neutral switch to a consumption tax. Given this budget constraint, the individual maximizes the utility by consuming at *c* on the indifference curve U^2. The gain, *G*, from switching to the consumption tax is the "distance" between the indifference curves U^1 and U^2. This gain is given by the distance *EM*.

As figure 2 illustrates, there is a gain from switching to a consumption tax even though the savings rate is completely unresponsive to the rate of return on savings. What is crucial for determining the magnitude of the gain is the elasticity of substitution between consumption in the two periods, σ, not the savings elasticity. Only if the indifference curves are "elbow shaped", indicating no substitution effect from a change in the price of future consumption, would there be no gain from eliminating the intertemporal price distortion by substituting a consumption tax.

Intuitively, the efficiency gain is achieved by replacing a highly distortive, or high "cost", tax with a less distortive, less costly, source of tax revenues. Consequently, the gain from switching to a consumption tax per dollar of tax revenue, *G/R*, can be approximated by the following:

$$G/R \approx 1/2\,[MCF_{\tau_r} - MCF_{\tau_c}] \qquad (1)$$

where MCF_{τ_r} is the marginal cost of public funds obtained from taxing the return on savings and MCF_{τ_c} is the marginal cost of public funds from a consumption tax. (See Dahlby 2001b for a survey of the concept and applications of the marginal cost of public funds.) Within the context of this model, the *MCF*s for the two taxes can be shown to equal the following:[7]

$$MCF_{\tau_r} = \frac{q_2}{p_2 \cdot [1 + \tau_r\, r\, q_2\, (1 + \varepsilon_{22})]} = \frac{q_2}{p_2 \cdot [1 - \tau_r\, \varepsilon_S]} \qquad (2)$$

$$\mathrm{MCF}_{\tau_c} = \frac{1}{1 - p_2\, \tau_r\, r b_2\, \theta_2} \qquad (3)$$

where:

q_2 is the distorted price of second period consumption, $(1 + (1 - \tau_r)\, r)^{-1}$;

r is the pre-tax rate of return on savings;

τ_r is the tax rate on the return to savings;

ε_{22} is the elasticity of demand for second period consumption with respect to the price of second price consumption;

p_2 is the undistorted price of second period consumption, $(1 + r)^{-1}$;

ε_S is the elasticity of savings with respect to the net rate of return on savings;

b_2 is the share of the individual's earnings that are devoted to second period consumption;

θ_2 is the elasticity of second period consumption with respect to the individual's earnings.

The two equivalent expressions for MCF_{τ_r} arise because savings, S, are related to second period consumption by $S = q_2C_2$. Consequently, $\varepsilon_S = -rq_2(1 + \varepsilon_2)$. Note that if the savings elasticity is zero, the $MCF_{\tau_r} = q_2/p_2 = (1 + r)/(1 + (1 - \tau)r) > 1$. Note also that since the income elasticity of C_2 is positive, $MCF_{\tau_c} > 1$ for $\tau_r > 0$ because, although the consumption tax is equivalent to a lump-sum tax in this model (given the fixed earnings assumption), a consumption tax increase causes a reduction in second-period consumption and therefore a decline in revenue from the interest tax. This revenue slippage implies that the MCF_{τ_c} to be greater than one.

Equation (1) is used to calculate the G/R for the parameter values shown in table 1. These parameter values have been chosen so that the first period can be interpreted as a working life of 40 years and the second period is a retirement period of 15 years. It is assumed that the marginal tax rate on savings is 0.4, p_2 is 0.286, and q_2 is 0.40. In other words, the individual has to save \$400 during his working life to have \$1000 of consumption in retirement, which is what would be implied if savings accumulated over a 25-year period at a real after-tax rate of return of 3.0%. Table 1 shows how the gain per dollar of tax revenue varies with the assumed value of the elasticity of substitution between first-period and second-period consumption, σ, and the elasticity of future consumption with respect to earnings, θ_2.

One would expect the latter parameter to be positive and close to one, given that most people probably want to increase their retirement consumption in proportion to any increase in earnings. The table also shows the implied values of the savings elasticity given the values of σ and θ_2. Most studies of savings behaviour indicate that savings elasticity is close to zero.[8] In our base case calculation, with $\sigma = 1$ and $\theta_2 = 1$, the individual has a Cobb-Douglas utility function with a zero savings elasticity and the gain from replacing a tax on interest income with a consumption tax is 18.3 cents per dollar of tax revenue. In other words, the gain is almost one fifth of

Table 1: Measuring the gain from replacing an interest income tax with a consumption tax when earnings are fixed

The Income Elasticity of Future Consumption (θ_2)		The Elasticity of Substitution between Current and Future Consumption (σ)		
		0.25	**0.50**	**1.00**
0.50	G/R	0.035	0.075	0.175
	ε_s	–0.721	–0.500	–0.059
1.00	G/R	0.036	0.078	0.183
	ε_s	–0.662	–0.441	0.00
1.50	G/R	0.037	0.081	0.190
	ε_s	–0.603	–0.382	0.059

Notes: Computations based on p_2 = 0.286, q_2 = 0.40, r = 2.5, b_2 = 0.118, τ_r = 0.40.

the revenue of collected from the tax on the return to savings. Most would consider this a relatively large social gain from restructuring the tax system. If the earnings elasticity of future consumption is 1.5, then the gain increases to 19 cents per dollar of tax revenue and implied savings elasticity is 0.059. If the earnings elasticity is 0.5, then the gain is only slightly lower, at 17.5 cents per dollar of tax revenue.

As noted above, the elasticity of substitution is a critical parameter in determining the gain from replacing the distortionary tax on future consumption and some empirical studies suggest that σ is substantially less than one (see Bernheim 1999). Table 1 shows that the gain from restructuring the tax system is substantially reduced (to about 3.5 cents per dollar of tax revenue) but the implied savings elasticities are negative and relatively large in absolute value.

While these values are not implausible, they imply that individuals significantly reduce their lifetime savings in response to higher real after-tax rates of return. Such responses do not seem consistent with our casual observations about how individuals respond to rates of return on savings and at least some of the econometric evidence on savings behaviour. However, as Bernheim has admitted, our empirical knowledge about savings behaviour is very limited. That said, the conventional wisdom that savings elasticities are low or close to zero, and the intuitively appealing idea that the earnings elasticities of retirement consumption is close to one suggest that the relatively large *G/R* values in the last column of table 1 may be the empirically relevant ones.

There are two serious deficiencies with this analysis of the gain from substituting a consumption tax for a tax on interest income. First, it treats the consumption tax as a lump-sum tax. In reality, a consumption tax distorts an individual's work-leisure decision because it reduces the individual's real wage rate.[9] A consumption tax is in many respects similar to a wage tax because the lifetime consumption tax base for an individual is equal to the present value of the individual's labour income plus the value of any inheritances less bequests. Therefore, the disincentives to work need to be taken into account when computing the cost of raising revenue through a consumption tax.

A second neglected issue is the interaction of the two tax bases. Taxpayers generally change their behaviour in ways that reduce the base on which a tax is levied. However, in changing their behaviour, taxpayers may also affect the sizes of the other tax bases. If the change in their behaviour causes other tax bases to expand, some of the other tax-induced distortions in the economy are reduced and the total distortions caused by the tax system might be relatively small. Indeed, there might even be an improvement in resource allocation. Alternatively, an increase in a tax on one tax base might lead to adjustments in behaviour that reduce other tax bases, thereby exacerbating the tax distortions caused by other taxes. In such cases, the total efficiency losses induced by a particular tax may be much greater than the losses it induces with respect to its own tax base. Consequently, we need to assess the interactions between the interest-income base and the consumption base in assessing the costs of raising tax revenues from either of these two tax sources.

$$MCF_{\tau_r} = \frac{q_2}{[p_2 (1 - \tau_r \varepsilon_S)] + \tau_c \left[\frac{-b_0}{b_2} \varepsilon^c_{02} + b_0\theta_0 - (1 + \tau_r r \varepsilon_{22}) \right]} \tag{4}$$

$$MCF_{\tau_c} = \frac{1}{\left[\left(\frac{C_1 + p_2 C_2}{C_1 + q_2 C_2} \right) (1 + \tau_c) - \tau_c (1 + \varepsilon_H) \right] + \tau_r [p_2 r (1 - \tau_c)(-b_0 \varepsilon^c_{02} - b_2 \theta_2)]} \tag{5}$$

If one introduces leisure time as a third "good" in the two-period intertemporal choice model, then the following expressions can be derived for the marginal cost of raising revenue from either a consumption tax or a tax on interest income.[10]

Even in this simple framework, the expressions for the *MCF*s for the two taxes are relatively complex. In both expressions, the denominators indicate how total tax revenues respond changes in τ_r and τ_c respectively. The first set of terms in square brackets indicates how revenues from the own-tax base respond to changes in the tax rate. (The more tax-sensitive the tax base, the lower the "own" revenue response, and the higher the *MCF*.) The second set of terms in square brackets shows how the revenues from the other tax base respond to changes in the given tax rate. Each tax's *MCF* is higher the greater the reduction in revenues from the other tax base.

The three key parameters determining the costs of raising revenues from these two tax sources are:[11]

ε_S the elasticity of demand for savings, which determines the cost of the savings distortion caused by taxing interest income;

ε_H the elasticity of labour supply which determines the cost of the labour supply distortion caused by taxing consumption; and

ε^c_{02} the compensated elasticity of demand for leisure with respect to the price of second-period consumption that determines the interactions between the tax bases.

The ε_S and ε_H parameters determine the "own" revenue effects of the interest and consumption taxes. In theory, these parameters can be either positive or negative, because of offsetting substitution and income effects. Most empirical studies indicate that the savings elasticities and labour-supply elasticities are relatively small. The third parameter, ε^c_{02}, is positive, if an individual views leisure and future consumption as "net" substitutes, or negative, if they are viewed as "net" complements. To my knowledge, no empirical studies have yielded estimates of this parameter, that is, how labour supply is affected by the net real rate of return on savings. My economic intuition suggests that if the price of future consumption increases but I am compensated through a lump-sum transfer so that I am no worse off than before, then working to save for the future is less attractive, making leisure and future consumption net substitutes. But, this is not a deeply held belief and other people may have different tastes. In other words, we do not have econometric estimates or strong intuition that help us place numerical values on this key parameter.

Table 2 shows how the calculated values of the MCFs for these two taxes vary with different values for the three key parameters.[12] The first line of the table, which I will refer to as the base case, shows the *MCF*s when all three key parameters are zero. The difference between the *MCF*s for the two taxes is much smaller than in the corresponding case in table 1 with $\varepsilon_S = 0$. However, the MCF_{τ_r} continues to be greater than the MCF_{τ_c}, so there would still be a gain from a revenue-neutral switch from a tax on interest income to consumption taxation.

The second row of the table shows the impact of increasing the elasticity of savings. Contrary to expectations, a higher savings elasticity *reduces* the marginal cost of public funds from taxing interest incomes because, while own-revenues are less responsive to an increase in τ_r, thereby increasing the MCF_{τ_r}, there is an increase in consumption-tax revenues that more than offsets this effect. (When ε_S increases, ε_{22} is larger in absolute value, which makes the reduction in future consumption larger for a given increase in τ_r. The shift in consumption from the future to the present increases the present value of the government's consumption tax revenues.) With these parameter values, the *MCF*s for the two taxes are virtually identical, indicating that there would be no gain from small

Table 2: The marginal cost of public funds from taxing interest and consumption

Key Parameters			Marginal Cost of Public Funds	
Savings Elasticity (ε_s)	Labour Supply Elasticity (ε_H)	Compensated Elasticity of Demand for Leisure with respect to the Price of Second Period Consumption (ε^c_{02}.)	Tax on Interest Income ($MCF_{\tau r}$)	Tax on Consumption ($MCF_{\tau c}$)
0.00	0.00	0.00	1.135	1.067
0.10	0.00	0.00	1.069	1.067
0.00	0.10	0.00	1.135	1.106
0.00	0.00	0.10	1.898	1.078
0.00	0.00	–0.10	0.810	1.056

Note: Calculations based on $\tau_c = 0.333$, $\tau_r = 0.40$, $b_2 = 0.11765$. The marginal propensity to "spend" on leisure is 0.20. Taxes represent 36.8% of lifetime consumption.

changes in the tax mix. The third row shows that, if the labour supply elasticity is 0.10 while the other two key parameters are zero, then the MCF_{τ_c} increases somewhat, but it is still below the MCF_{τ_r}.

The last two rows show the sensitivity of the MCFs to the assumed value of the ε^c_{02}. If leisure and second-period consumption are net substitutes (as my intuition weakly suggests), an increase in τ_r reduces hours of work, thereby reducing consumption tax revenues. The MCF_{τ_r} is much higher than in the base case while the MCF_{τ_c} is only slightly higher and there would be a large gain in substituting a consumption tax for a tax on interest income.

If leisure and retirement consumption are net complements, however (as the last row in the table indicates), taxing interest income will induce people to work harder, which lowers the distortionary cost of taxing interest income. These calculations would justify higher taxes on interest incomes.

To summarize, this analysis has indicated that the efficiency gain from replacing an income tax with a consumption tax depends critically upon the substitutability or complementarity of future consumption and leisure. Since we do not have direct estimates of this parameter and economic intuition does not provide much guidance, we have to conclude that the static efficiency gains from replacing an income tax with a consumption tax are ambiguous or at least highly uncertain.

Two further points regarding the substitution of a consumption tax for an income tax should be mentioned. First, our current system is a hybrid income-consumption tax that does not tax the returns on certain types of investment income, such as the return on consumer durables like owner-occupied housing or the return on investment income held in registered retirement savings and investment plans. Indeed, it has been estimated that our current income tax system only taxes about one-quarter of the total return to savings (see Poddar and English 1999). For many individuals, the current personal tax system is effectively an expenditure tax. Moving completely to a consumption tax system would have little or no impact on them.

However, there could still be gains in moving completely to an expenditure tax. First, some savers are taxed under the current system. Removing the limits on contributions to RRSPs and RPPs would eliminate the marginal taxation of their savings. Since the average rate of tax is less than the marginal rate of tax on savings because of the features of the tax system referred to above, eliminating the residual taxation of savings would tend to have a relatively strong pro-savings effect. This is so because the "income" effect of the change (which tends to reduce the incentive to save) would be relatively weak compared to the substitution effect, which is determined by the marginal tax rate on the return on the last dollar saved. Thus, the stimulative effect of eliminating the taxation of savings under the current system for those who are currently taxed on their savings is likely to be much larger than the conventional low savings elasticity would suggest. Furthermore, the distortion in the choice of investments, particularly the bias in favour of investment in owner-occupied housing under the current tax regime, would be eliminated if a comprehensive consumption-tax regime were adopted, leading to a further improvement in resource allocation.

Finally, the calculated *MCF* for the consumption tax did not include the efficiency gain that arises from the fact that a consumption tax serves as a lump-sum tax on the initial stock of wealth. The lump-sum aspect of consumption taxation is one of the ways in which it differs from a proportional wage tax and would lower its *MCF*. It also has implications for the distributional impact of the tax. The consumption tax can be viewed as enhancing equity, because the lump-sum aspect falls disproportionately on the wealthy, or as inequitable because it falls disproportionately on accumulated wealth of the elderly. These equity aspects of switching to a consumption tax are addressed in Section 2 of the paper.

The growth effects of switching to consumption taxation

In analyzing the growth effects of restructuring the personal tax system, I will use as a framework a class of endogenous growth models that have been developed by economists over the last 15 years. These models stress the importance of investment in human capital—the skill and knowledge embodied in the workforce—in explaining an economy's rate of economic growth. Thus, they focus on a central feature of the knowledge-based economy: success depends on having a highly skilled and educated workforce that can take advantage of the technological innovations, the scientific breakthroughs, and the communication revolution that are occurring throughout the world.

The basic endogenous growth model will only be described here in broad brush strokes.[13] A key feature of this model is that it describes the growth effects of tax reforms for a small open economy where the prices of exported and imported goods and the after-tax rate of return on investment are determined in world markets. In particular, it is assumed that investment funds will flow into the economy from the rest of the world if the expected rate of return on investments in Canada is above the rate of return that investors can get elsewhere in the world. Similarly, capital can readily flow out of Canada if the expected after-tax rate of return is below the rate that investors can earn in other parts of the world. This high degree of capital mobility means that the rate of return on capital invested in the Canadian economy will adjust in the long-run so that investors can earn the same net rate of return that can be earned on investments elsewhere in the world.

At the heart of any model of economic growth is the aggregate relationship between the growth rate of per-capita output, the growth rates of inputs, the population growth rate, and the rate of the technological change. This basic *growth-accounting* relationship is presented below:

$$\dot{y} = (1 - \alpha)\,\dot{A} + \alpha\dot{K} + (1 - \alpha)\,\dot{H} - \dot{N} \qquad (6)$$

where

$\dot{y}$ is the growth rate of per-capita output;

$\dot{A}$ is the productivity growth rate;

α is a parameter equal to physical capital's share of the cost of production, which in most economies is around one third;

$\dot{K}$ is the growth rate of the physical capital stock;

$\dot{H}$ is the growth rate of the stock of human-capital population;

$\dot{N}$ is the growth rate of the population.

Per-capita output will grow at a faster rate the higher the productivity growth rate and the more rapid the growth rate of physical and human capital. It will grow more slowly when the population growth rate is higher, assuming that the other variables that affect the rate of economic growth are unchanged, because a given level of output is spread over a larger population when the population growth rate is higher.

This growth-accounting relationship is useful for *describing* the sources of economic growth but not for *explaining* the economic growth rate because it does not explain why each component of the accounting relationship grows at any particular rate. In order to explain how changes in public policy affect the growth rate of the economy, we need a model of the behavioural relationships between the variables in the growth-accounting model.

The human-capital variant of the endogenous growth model focuses on the behavioural relationships that determine the growth rates of human and physical capital. Investment in human capital is determined by the savings decisions of the residents of the economy. They will invest in human capital (by, for example, undertaking education and training course) up to the point where the after-tax return that they can earn from acquiring more human capital is equal to the after-tax return that they can earn from investing in financial assets. Investment in physical capital is determined by "foreign" investors who require a net rate of return, adjusted for risk, that is equal to what they can earn on investments in other countries. The physical capital stock will grow faster when the productivity growth rate is higher, when the growth rate of human capital is higher, or when output prices are growing at a faster rate. It will grow more slowly when the required gross rate of return on investment is increasing.

From the relationships determining $\dot{H}$ and $\dot{K}$ the growth-accounting relationship can be transformed into the following predictive model of the growth rate of per-capita output:

$$\dot{y} = \dot{A} + s(1 - \tau_r)r + \frac{\alpha}{1 - \alpha}\dot{P} - \frac{\alpha}{1 - \alpha}\dot{r}_g \qquad (7)$$

where

s is the savings rate;

$\dot{P}$ is the rate of increase in the price of the economy's output; and

$\dot{r}_g$ is the rate of increase in the required gross rate of return that on investment.

The model predicts that the growth rate of per-capita output will be higher in an economy with a higher savings rate because individuals will invest in human capital at a faster rate. A more rapid growth rate for human capital means that investment in physical capital will be more profitable, and the stock of physical capital will also grow at this more rapid rate. With constant returns to scale in production, per-capita output will also grow at this faster rate. Thus, the key mechanism linking a higher savings rate with faster economic growth is individuals investing in human capital at a faster rate.

That a higher savings rate is predicted to lead to a higher growth rate may seem obvious to the "man in the street." However, this is one of the features that distinguishes endogenous growth models from the neo-classical growth model, which was developed in the mid-1950s by Robert Solow (1956), a Nobel prize-winning economist. The neo-classical model predicts that an increase in the savings rate can temporarily boost the growth rate as the ratio of capital to labour in the economy increases but once the new equilibrium between capital and labour is achieved, the growth rate will return to its previous rate.[14] In other words, the neo-classical model predicts that an increase in the savings rate would have a level effect but not a growth effect.[15]

The model predicts that a reduction in the tax rate on the return to savings will increase the growth rate as follows:

$$\frac{\partial \dot{y}}{\partial \tau_r} = -s(1 + \varepsilon_S)r < 0 \tag{8}$$

Even if the savings elasticity is zero, a reduction in the tax rate on return to savings would still increase the long-term growth rate.

This simple model can be used to calculate the growth effect from eliminating the tax on the return to savings. Assuming that the real pre-tax rate of return on savings is 5% and that the savings rate is 10%, eliminating a 40% marginal tax rate on savings would increase the long-run economic growth rate by two tenths of a percentage point if elasticity of the savings rate is zero. If the savings rate elasticity were 0.15, the growth rate would increase 0.23 percentage points. If the savings elasticity were minus 0.15, the increase in the growth rate would still be 0.17 percentage points. Thus the size of the growth effect is not greatly affected by the assumed elasticity of savings.

While the endogenous growth model outlined above is very simple and our back-of-the-envelope calculations of the growth effects of restructuring the tax system are admittedly crude, they are consistent with the predictions of much more sophisticated endogenous growth models.[16] One of the interesting results from these simulations models is the growth effects of tax reforms are much larger (on the order of 10 times larger) in models of small open economies than in models of closed economies. The reason for the difference is that, in a small open economy, the gross rate of return on savings is determined on international markets. Therefore, eliminating the tax on the return to savings increases the return to savings by the full amount of the tax. In a closed economy, an increase in savings causes a one-for-one increase in investment, which leads to a lower rate of return on capital, thereby partially offsetting the initial increase in the return on savings. Since the Canadian economy represents less than 3% of the world economy and Canadian capital markets are highly integrated with world capital markets, it is unlikely that the return to capital would decline if the tax on the return on savings were eliminated. Therefore, one would expect that switching to consumption tax would have a powerful growth effect in Canada.

As Myles has noted, simulation models "introduce a range of issues that must be considered, but ... they do not provide any convincing or definitive answers" (2000:164). We therefore turn to the statistical studies of the growth effects of taxes, which try to determine whether the level or the composition of countries' taxes can explain international variations in growth rates.[17]

Some early econometric studies found taxation to have a significant negative effect upon growth. But, subsequent studies have concluded that these results are not robust because the sample of countries, the time periods, or the conditioning variables (such as initial per-capita income level or level of education) affect them. These variables are included in the regression equation to reflect the other variables that affect the rate of economic growth.[18] Three recent studies—Mendoza et al. 1997, Kneller et al. 1999, and Widmalm 2001—have overcome many of the problems that plagued the earlier studies and their results are now discussed in some detail.

Mendoza et al. (1997) studied the growth effects of taxes using data based on 5-year averages for 18 OECD countries (including Canada) for the period from 1965 to 1991. They found strong negative relationships between the investment rate and the rate of wage and capital taxation and a positive relationship between the investment rate and the rate of consumption taxation. The authors concluded that shifting the tax burden from capital and wages to consumption would increase a country's investment rate. They interpreted this effect as a level effect—which alters the transition growth rate of the economy—not a growth effect.

Kneller et al. (1999) argued that Mendoza et al. (1997) and other studies have produced biased and unstable estimates of the growth effects of taxes because they failed to incorporate the government's budget constraint in their estimate equations. They noted that if one fiscal variable, such as the consumption tax rate, changes, then there must be a change in another fiscal variable, such as the level of expenditures, or in the government's budget surplus. They argued that Mendoza et al. (1997) found insignificant growth effects from taxes because their model implicitly assumed that an increase in taxes is offset by an increase in productive government expenditures, such as expenditures on infrastructure. Therefore, the coefficient estimates in Mendoza et al.'s growth-rate regressions actually reflect the difference between the effect of a tax increase and the effect of a productive expenditure increase, which may be small and not statistically significant.

Kneller et al. estimated a model that incorporated the governments' budget constraints using 5-year average data for 22 OECD countries for the period from 1970 to 1995. The authors classified taxes on income, profit, payrolls, and property as "distortionary" taxes and taxes on domestic goods and services as "non-distortionary" taxes. They classified expenditures on defence, education, health, housing, and transportation and communication as "productive" expenditures and expenditures on social security, welfare, recreation, and economic services as "non-productive." They maintained the hypothesis that non-distortionary taxes (i.e. consumption taxes) and non-productive expenditures would have negligible growth effects and, therefore, these fiscal variables were excluded from their main regression equations. Their results indicated that the distortionary taxes have significant negative growth effects, reducing the rate of growth rate by 0.41 percentage points for an increase in the distortionary taxes of 1.0% of GDP. Overall, Kneller et al. concluded that even their lowest coefficient estimates indicate that "increasing productive expenditure or reducing distortionary taxes by 1% of GDP can modestly increase the growth rate (by between 0.1% and 0.2% per year)" (1999: 188).

Finally, a recent study by Widmalm (2001) has examined the effects of the tax structures on economic growth based on data for 23 OECD countries between 1965 and 1990. She found a robust negative correlation between economic growth rates and the share of tax revenue from personal income taxes and a measure of the progressivity of the tax system. She also found that reliance on consumption taxes tends to be growth-enhancing. Widmalm concluded that "personal income taxes affect growth, not so much via physical capital accumulation, as through resource allocation efficiency or the accumulation of human capital" (2001: 211), a result that is consistent with the endogenous growth model outlined above.

To conclude, endogenous growth models and recent econometric studies indicate that switching the tax mix toward consumption taxes can significantly increase the growth rate of the economy. An increase in the annual economic growth rate on the order of two-tenths of a percentage point—as predicted by the simple open-economy endogenous growth model—would have a dramatic impact on Canadian living standards over time. The present value of the additional per-capita output from increasing the annual growth rate by two-tenths of a percentage point is 238% of current output, which represents an enormous gain.

The endogenous growth model is admittedly highly simplistic and might exaggerate the increase in the growth rate that would occur from switching to a consumption tax. However, the cumulative impact of very small increases in the growth rate are so large that even if we have overstated the growth effect of switching to a consumption tax by a factor of 10, and the growth rate were only to increase by two one-hundredths of a percentage point, the present value of the increase in per-capita output would still be 22.3% of current output—a very significant gain.

The preceding analysis suggests that, in setting our tax policies, we need to pay particular attention to their growth effects. Theoretical models and empirical evidence predict a significant boost to the growth rate from switching to consumption taxation. Although, in setting economic policies, there is never enough evidence to be 100% sure that the predicted outcome will occur, the potential payoffs for our society from switching to a consumption tax base are so significant that switching to consumption taxation has to be high on our policy agenda.

2 Equity arguments for consumption taxation

Consumption taxes, such as the GST, are probably the most unpopular taxes in Canada because they are said to be "regressive." If we are going to reap the efficiency gains from switching to consumption taxation, we are going to have to overcome this fundamental misconception.

To some degree, economists have been responsible for the mislabeling of consumption taxes as regressive taxes because, in discussing what constitutes a fair tax system, we inevitably trot out the "ability-to-pay" principle. The very use of the words "ability to pay" makes it almost inevitable that annual income will be adopted as the standard for measuring ability to pay. Instead, we should adopt more neutral terminology: that the tax burden should be distributed according to an individual's standard of living. As a result, the concept of fairness in taxation could be approached more even-handedly.

This change is not just a matter of semantics. I believe that in discussing equity issues, the public is essentially concerned about the standard of living not the ability to pay. Indeed, ability to pay is not so much an equity concept as an efficiency concept. When a bank robber was asked why he robbed banks, he replied "because that's where the money is." In much the same way, governments have come to rely on the income tax base because "that's where the money is."

Most people—and almost all economists—are closet utilitarians. It is time to come out of the closet and declare openly that a person's standard of living is best measured by his consumption of goods and services. Ideally, a broad measure of consumption should be adopted that would include private goods and services obtained through market transactions, publicly provided goods and services, environmental quality, and "leisure" activity, which also includes home production of goods and services. However, it is very difficult to include the last three categories in any index of consumption used for tax purposes, and the consumption of marketed goods and services is, for practical purposes, the index of consumption that we have to adopt. Still, consumption of marketed goods and services is the primary determinant of standards of living in our society.

Consumption is a flow since it is measured per unit of time. Therefore, it is essential that we address the question: Over what time period do we measure consumption? Any short period of time, such as an hour, a day, or a month, leads to an unreliable index given the normal temporal fluctuations in measured consumption activity. Generally speaking, the longer the time period, the more reliable measured consumption becomes as an index of well-being. What timeframe should we adopt—a year, a decade, a generation, a lifetime? As a practical matter, taxes probably have to assessed at least once a year but a basic principle of horizontal equity dictates that two people with the same lifetime consumption (in present-value terms) should pay the same amount in taxes (again in present-value terms). This implies that, at least in principle, the progressivity of the tax system should be measured by the individual's tax burden paid as a percentage of lifetime consumption.

If we continue to use taxes paid as a percentage of annual income as the standard by which to measure the progressivity of the tax system, it is inevitable that other taxes will look regressive, or at least less progressive, than a personal income-tax system. It is a mug's game to compare the progressivity of a consumption tax with the progressivity of an income tax if progressivity is measured by taxes as a percentage of annual income. A consumption tax is bound to lose by comparison. Using annual income, which is a flawed index of one's standard of living, only perpetuates misconceptions about the fairness of the tax system and horizontal inequities that a personal income tax system inevitably produces.

Using lifetime consumption as measure of an individual's standard of living, a broad sales tax, such as the GST or a single rate expenditure tax, is proportional or slightly progressive. How progressive should the tax system be? Inevitably, there is an trade-off between efficiency and equity. A progressive expenditure tax would distort an individual's labour supply and as well as savings decisions just as a tax on interest income does. Whether the gain in fairness is worth the shrinkage of the pie depends on the strength of one's preferences for egalitarian outcomes.

However, it should be remembered that the current personal tax system is not highly progressive, even when progressivity is measured using taxes as a percentage of annual income. Most economists who have studied the redistributive role of government have concluded that the bulk of the net redistribution through the public fisc occurs through the expenditure side of the budget, not the tax side. This condition may well be due to the fact that basically, it is much more costly to achieve significant increases in redistribution through taxation than it is through government expenditures. Those who favour a greater degree of redistribution by Canadian governments should focus their efforts and policy proposals on the expenditure side of the budget rather than the tax side. This is not to say that redistribution through the expenditure side is costless, because it does involve some administrative costs and disincentive effects. The conclusion is based on the fact that expenditures have a higher benefit-cost ratio than taxes. Furthermore, as the saying goes, "a rising tide floats all ships" so that a higher rate of economic growth brought about by the proposed shift to expenditure taxes will, over time, improve the standard of living of the rich as well as poor.

There are distributional implications of switching to consumption taxation that have to be addressed. These arise from the fact that, on average, the elderly have accumulated more wealth than younger generations. As a result, an increase in consumption taxation imposes a higher burden on older age groups. Many simulation models, such as Akerloff and Kotlikoff 1987 and Altig et al. 1997, support this proposition. In addition, the elderly suffer relative to the young from the switch to an expenditure tax because they do not benefit from the greater economic growth, which the switch is expected to produce.

How to resolve this problem? Given the substantial efficiency gains to be derived from switching to a consumption tax, our society could afford to be more generous to those who will not benefit from the faster rate of economic growth, such as the elderly who are no longer part of the workforce. Growing a bigger economic pie means that we can provide higher transfer payments, such as social assistance payments and seniors' benefits, so that virtually everyone benefits from the tax reform.

A second possibility is to expand the tax-reform package to include at least a temporary increase in payroll or wage taxes, which would shift the burden to the younger generations who will benefit from the higher future rate of economic growth. Finally, a tax reform that is not revenue neutral would also help to assuage the intergenerational consequences of switching to a consumption tax. This goal could be reached by substituting a low rate of consumption taxation for investment income taxes and running a deficit during a transition period. This strategy would transfer the tax burden to future generations who will be the main the beneficiaries of the higher rates of economic growth. However, because Canada's ratio of public-sector debt to GDP is still relatively high, a tax reform that is not revenue neutral is a risky policy measure given the volatility of the world economy. Therefore, the other two options—higher transfer payments to the elderly and the disabled and higher payroll taxes during a transition period—are better ways of redistributing the tax burden to the younger generations who are likely to be the primary beneficiaries of the tax reforms.

3 Direct and indirect consumption taxes

The strong equity and efficiency arguments for consumption taxation give rise to the question whether we should impose a direct consumption tax in the form of an expenditure tax or an indirect consumption tax in the form of a sales tax such as the GST. In my view, the answer is simple. We need both. Both forms of consumption taxation are needed because both types of taxes are subject to somewhat different forms of tax avoidance and tax evasion behaviour. Therefore, it is preferable to have two systems of consumption taxation, each levied at a moderate rate, rather than have one consumption tax system levied at the full rate.

As noted above, under an expenditure tax, consumption is directly taxed by exempting from taxation all income not spent, which is equal to the taxpayer's savings. Presently, this objective is achieved partly by allowing individuals to deduct savings invested in a *designated asset* account, which are taxed when the assets are withdrawn, or by exempting the return on assets purchased out of after-tax dollars. RRSPs are an example of a designated asset. Our current tax treatment of housing, where savings in the form of increases of the homeowner's equity are not deductible but the return on owner-occupied housing—implicit rental income plus capital gains—is not taxed, is an example of the so-called *tax-prepaid* approach.

Our current personal tax system is a hybrid system, which combines income taxation with consumption taxes on consumer durables, the return to human capital, and retirement savings. The system could be fully converted to an expenditure tax by removing the limits on RRSP and RPP contributions.

Kesselman and Poshmann (2001) have proposed a savings plan where taxes are prepaid as an attractive alternative to the existing RRSP system. This alternative is attractive because it avoids the distortions that occur under the designated-asset plans when the marginal tax rate on contributions is different from the marginal tax rate imposed when assets are withdrawn. Kesselman and Poshmann (2001: table 3) show numerically that when the marginal tax rate at the time of contribution is higher than the marginal tax rate on withdrawal, a designated asset system effectively subsidizes the return to savings. Conversely, it imposes a tax on the return to savings if the marginal tax rate on withdrawals exceeds the marginal tax rate at the time of contribution. Thus, designated-asset treatment can either tax or subsidize the return to savings even though it is nominally a component of the expenditure tax.

Since no one can confidently predict tax rates 20 to 30 years in the future, the designated-asset approach also introduces a great deal of uncertainty concerning the net rate of return on savings. Furthermore, as Kesselman and Poshmann (2001) point out, consumption out of a savings plan where taxes are prepaid could be exempt from the present GIS tax-back, thereby eliminating this potential disincentive to save for retirement. For these reasons, the use of savings plan where taxes are prepaid might be the preferred way of converting our current hybrid personal tax system to a full expenditure tax system.

If we had a personal expenditure tax system, would we need to levy a broad sales tax such as the GST or the provincial sales tax? In my view, we should levy both direct and indirect consumption taxes because they are subject to different forms of tax evasion and avoidance.[19] Direct taxes, levied on a residence basis lead to evasion or under-reporting of income from, for example, off-shore sources. Sales taxes levied on a destination basis lead to incentives to consume outside Canada and to engage in cross-border shopping. The optimal tax mix under a consumption-tax regime would involve levying both direct and indirect taxes.

Another reason for the levy of both direct and indirect consumption taxes is that it would improve the transparency of the tax system. There would be greater transparency if the federal government imposed the direct consumption tax and the provincial governments levied the indirect consumption taxes. Under such a scheme, the federal government would levy the GST, since the imposition of a uniform, national rate would be most efficient. The provinces would levy an expenditure tax on a common, harmonized base.

4 Conclusions and policy implications

Endogenous growth models and recent econometric studies indicate that increasing reliance on consumption taxes can boost the long-run growth rate of the economy. Therefore, an increased reliance of consumption taxes would raise Canadian living standards significantly over time.

The chief obstacle to the adoption of consumption taxation is the perception that consumption taxes are regressive while most Canadians favour a progressive tax burden under which those with a higher income bear a higher share of the tax burden than those with lower incomes. However, income is not a proper base for measuring the progressivity of a tax system. As argued above, the proper base is individuals' consumption of goods and services over a number of years since it reflects their real standard of living. It follows that the progressivity of the tax system should be measured by individuals' tax burdens as a percentage of consumption over a long period of time. Measuring tax progressivity in this way means that consumption taxes are proportional or slightly progressive, not regressive.

Redistributive policy objectives should be pursued through government expenditures rather than taxes because redistributive expenditures are more cost effective than highly progressive taxes. Finally, and most importantly, in discussing the redistributive effects of switching to consumption taxes, we must not overlook "the rising tide that floats all ships." A higher rate of economic growth due to the switch to growth-enhancing consumption taxes will, over time, improve everyone's standard of living, rich as well as poor.

The policy implications that flow from this analysis are relatively straightforward and "do-able." Canada's personal income-tax system, which is already three-quarters of the way to a consumption tax system, should be fully converted to a consumption tax system. This goal could be reached easily by removing existing limits on RRSP and RPP contributions and by introducing a savings plan where taxes are prepaid, along the lines of the Kesselman and Poshmann proposal. Any reductions in tax revenues from these reforms should be offset through increases in the GST rate.

The provincial governments that have not already done so should adopt the GST as the base for their sales taxes. Some realignment of tax powers between federal and provincial governments would be desirable to improve transparency and accountability, with the federal government having the dominant role in the sales tax field, and the provincial governments having a larger role, if not the dominant role, in the expenditure tax area.

The potential payoffs for Canadian society from switching to a consumption tax system are so significant that these tax policy changes must receive serious consideration.

Acknowledgments

I would like to thank the Donner Canadian Foundation for their on-going support for my research on restructuring of the Canadian tax system and Jonathan Kesselman and Herbert Grubel for their comments on a draft of this paper.

Notes

1 This pattern is not significantly altered if employee payroll taxes are classified as direct taxes and employer payroll taxes are classified as indirect taxes.

2 See Kesselman 1986a and 1986b for comprehensive discussions of the tax-mix issues.

3 The administration of the tax system and the compliance activities of taxpayers also use up resources and this contributes to the shrinkage of the economic pie. In this paper, we focus on the efficiency cost of the tax system caused by the reallocation of resources rather than on the administration and compliance costs.

4 See Myles 2000: 146–47 on the distinction between level and growth effects.

5 For example, Loayza, Schmidt-Hebbel, and Servén in a study of the determinants of savings across countries, found that changes in savings behaviour in response to changes in economic conditions "are fully realized only after a number of years, with long-run responses estimated to be more than two times larger than short-run (within a year) ones" (2000: 180).

6 The gain from replacing source-based capital taxes, such as the corporate income tax, with a consumption tax is not considered in this paper. The efficiency effects of taxing capital in a small open economy are analyzed in Dahlby 2001a.

7 Detailed derivations of these expressions are available from the author upon request.

8 See Bernheim 1999 for a survey of the research on the determinants of savings.

9 Sales taxes may also induce cross-border shopping, thereby distorting the location of an individual's consumption decision.

10 Detailed derivations are available from the author upon request.

11 The only other new parameters are b_0, the share of the individual's resources that are "spent" on leisure and θ_0, the income elasticity of demand for leisure.

12 The values of the other parameters are given at the bottom of the table.

13 See Dahby 2000 for a more detailed description of the model.

14 This is the neo-classical model's prediction for a closed economy. For a small open economy, the neo-classical model predicts that a higher savings rate will not affect per-capita output or the long-term growth rate. It would only affect the degree to which the residents of the economy are net debtors (or net creditors) vis-à-vis the rest of the world.

15 The domestic savings rates are highly correlated with domestic investment rates. This empirical regularity has been interpreted as indicating that capital is not highly mobile across countries. However, the observed positive correlation would arise, even with perfect capital mobility, if the governments run zero deficits and exports equal imports. Furthermore, the open-economy endogenous growth model described above also predicts that domestic savings rates will be highly correlated with investment rates in physical capital. Consequently, the observed correlation of savings rates and investment rates is not a powerful test of capital mobility.

16 See Milesi-Ferretti and Roubini 1998 on the growth effects of income and consumption taxes in endogenous growth models. King and Rebelo 1990, Rebelo and Stokey 1995, Pecorino 1994, and Coleman 2000 have simulated the endogenous growth models that replicate the basic characteristics of the American economy. Endogenous growth models that mimic the characteristics of Canadian economy have been developed by Mérette 1997 and Xu 1997 and 1999. All of these models have indicated that there are positive growth-rate effects from replacing a tax on investment income with a consumption tax.

17 For a review of these studies, see Ahn and Hemmings 2000.

18 See, for example, Garrison and Lee 1992.

19 See Kesselman 1993, Boadway, Marchand, and Pestieau 1994, and Richter and Boadway 2001 on the mix of direct and indirect taxes when the two tax bases are subject to evasion.

References

Ahn, S., and P. Hemmings (2000). Policy Influences on Economic Growth in OECD Countries: An Evaluation of the Evidence. OECD Economics Department Working Papers (June).

Altig, David, Alan J. Auerbach, Laurence Kotlikoff, Kent A. Smetters, and Jan Walliser (1997). Simulating US Tax Reform. NBER Working Paper 6248. Cambridge, MA: National Bureau of Economic Research.

Auerbach, Alan J. and Laurence Kotlikoff (1987). *Dynamic Fiscal Policy*, Cambridge: Cambridge University Press.

Bernheim, Douglas (1999). Taxation and Saving. Department of Economics, Stanford University, Stanford, CA.

Boadway, Robin W., Maurice Marchand, and Pierre Pestieau (1994). Towards a Theory of Tax Structure: Direct versus Indirect Taxation. *Journal of Public Economics* 55: 71–88.

Coleman II, W.J. (2000). Welfare and Optimum Dynamic Taxation of Consumption and Income. *Journal of Public Economics* 76, 1 (April): 1–39.

Dahlby, Bev (2000). *Tax Reform and Economic Growth in Alberta*. Calgary, AB: Canada West Foundation.

——— (2001a). Economic Integration: Implications for Business Taxation. Paper presented at Industry Canada's Conference, North American Linkages: Opportunities and Challenges for Canada, Calgary, AB (June 20–22).

——— (2001b). Using the Marginal Cost of Public Funds to Evaluate Public Expenditure Programs. Unpublished paper. Department of Economics, University of Alberta, Edmonton, AB.

Feldstein, Martin (1978). The Welfare Cost of Capital Income Taxation. *Journal of Political Economy* 86, 2, pt. 2: S29–S51.

Garrison, C.B., and F.Y. Lee (1992). Taxation, Aggregate Activity and Economic Growth: Further Cross-Country Evidence on Some Supply-Side Hypotheses. *Economic Inquiry* 30, 1 (January): 172–76.

Kesselman, Jonathan (1986a). The BTT, the Tax Mix, and Tax Reform. *Report of the Proceedings of the Thirty-eighth Tax Conference,* Canadian Tax Foundation, Toronto.

——— (1986b). Role of the Tax Mix in Tax Reform. In John G. Head (ed), *Changing the Tax Mix* (Sydney, AUS: Australian Tax Research Foundation).

——— (1993). Evasion Effects of Changing the Tax Mix. *Economic Record* 69, 205: 131–48.

Kesselman, Jonathan, and Finn Poshmann (2001). *A New Option for Retirement Savings: Tax-Prepaid Savings Plans.* Commentary No. 149. Toronto, ON: CD Howe Institute.

King, R.G., and S. Rebelo (1990). Public Policy and Economic Growth: Developing Neoclassical Implications. *Journal of Political Economy* 98, 5: 126–50.

Kneller, R., M.F. Bleaney, and N. Gemmell (1999). Fiscal Policy and Growth: Evidence from OECD Countries. *Journal of Public Economics* 74: 171–90.

Loayza, N., K. Schmidt-Hebbel, and L. Servén (2000). What Drives Private Saving across the World? *The Review of Economics and Statistics* 82, 2 (May): 165–81.

Mendoza, E.G., G.M. Milesi-Ferretti, and P. Asea (1997). On the Ineffectiveness of Tax Policy in Altering Long-Run Growth: Harberger's Superneutrality Conjecture. *Journal of Public Economics* 66: 99–126.

Mérette, M. (1997). *Income Taxes, Life-Cycles and Growth.* Working Paper 97-06. Ottawa, ON: Department of Finance.

Milesi-Ferretti, G.M., and N. Roubini (1998). Growth Effects of Income and Consumption Taxes. *Journal of Money, Credit, and Banking* 30, 4 (November): 721–44.

Myles, G. (2000). "Taxation and Economic Growth," *Fiscal Studies* 21(1): 141-168.

Organization for Economic Co-operation and Development (1999). *Revenue Statistics,* Paris: OECD.

Pecorino, P. (1994). The Growth Rate Effects of Tax Reform. *Oxford Economic Papers* 46, 3 (July): 492–501.

Poddar, Satya, and Morley English (1999). Canadian Taxation of Personal Investment Income. *Canadian Tax Journal* 47, 5: 1270–304.

Rebelo, S, and N.L. Stokey (1995). Growth Effects of Flat-Rate Taxes. *Journal of Political Economy* 103, 3 (June): 519–50.

Richter, Wolfram, and Robin W. Boadway (2001). *Trading Off Tax Distortion and Tax Evasion.* CESifo Working Paper No. 505. Munich: Center for Economic Studies and Ifo Institute for Economic Research.

Solow, R.M. (1956). A Contribution to the Theory of Economic Growth. *Quarterly Journal of Economics* 52, 1 (Feb.): 65–94.

Widmalm, Frida (2001). Tax Structure and Growth: Are Some Taxes Better than Others. *Public Choice* 107, 3–4 (June): 199–219.

Xu, J. (1997). *The Dynamic Effects of Taxes and Government Spending in a Calibrated Canadian Endogenous Growth Model.* Working Paper 97-02. Ottawa: Department of Finance.

——— (1999). *Taxation and Economic Performance: A Cross-Country Comparison and Model Sensitivity Analysis.* Working Paper 99-01. Ottawa: Department of Finance.

An evaluation of business taxes in Canada

Thomas A. Wilson

Businesses in Canada are taxed in a variety of ways. The most important tax on business is the corporate income tax (CIT) but a variety of other taxes are also levied on businesses. There are the personal income tax (PIT) levied on unincorporated businesses, the taxation of corporate dividends and business capital gains under the PIT, federal and provincial taxes on corporate capital and municipal and provincial property taxes on commercial and industrial property.

The employer component of federal and provincial payroll taxes is the second most important set of taxes paid by businesses. In 1995, payroll taxes paid by business actually exceeded corporate income taxes paid. In 2000, total corporate taxes paid were almost $46 billion, whereas total payroll taxes paid by business were $28.6 billion. Table 1 presents details on corporate income, capital and payroll taxes.

In this chapter, I evaluate the costs and benefits of the corporate income tax and the issues surrounding the possible integration of the personal and corporate income taxes.[1] In my evaluation of the corporate income tax and the integration of the personal and corporate taxes, I assume that the basic structure of the income tax

Table 1: Corporate income, capital and payroll taxes (CDN$ millions), 1971–2000

	Corporate Income Tax		Capital Tax	Payroll Taxes[c]		
	Federal[a]	Provincial[b]	Provincial	Federal	Provincial	CPP/QPP
1971	2,477	869	104	232	350	414
1972	2,901	1,019	128	305	404	446
1973	3,643	1,436	138	395	503	488
1974	5,012	2,039	166	675	641	603
1975	5,380	2,114	185	854	803	714
1976	5,061	2,067	211	1,083	1,182	827
1977	5,135	2,103	241	1,116	1,319	915
1978	5,737	2,451	349	1,231	1,503	1,022
1979	6,860	3,178	423	1,225	1,638	1,158
1980	8,406	3,672	451	1,367	1,761	1,327
1981	9,323	3,473	651	2,064	2,425	1,489
1982	9,212	2,543	831	2,097	2,891	1,779
1983	9,536	2,784	921	3,070	3053	1,709
1984	11,319	3,665	976	3,337	3,361	1,929
1985	11,586	3,977	1,172	3,829	3,653	2,139
1986	10,302	4,271	1,280	4,207	4,190	2,342
1987	11,864	5,126	1,387	4,484	4,877	2,674
1988	11,857	5,729	1,490	5,091	5,663	2,976
1989	12,132	6,434	1,885	4,513	6,223	3,300
1990	10,442	6,392	1,917	5,699	8,270	3,794
1991	9,892	5,123	1,863	6,591	8,127	4,068
1992	9,981	4,536	2,089	7,841	8,269	4,359
1993	10,695	5,568	2,387	8,146	8,561	4,578
1994	12,200	7,142	2,611	8,724	9,000	4,849
1995	13,372	8,766	2,810	8,530	9,686	5,421
1996	16,225	10,014	3,162	8,236	9,788	5,535
1997	20,229	12,021	3,430	8,843	9,689	5,850
1998	19,331	11,131	3,743	8,315	9,913	6,855
1999	24,173	12,494	3,860	8,163	10,343	7,875
2000	30,353	15,682	3,987	8,200	10,958	9,480

Source: National Income Accounts and author's calculations. **Note a**: Federal corporate income tax includes the large corporation tax and capital taxes on financial institutions. **Note b**: Provincial corporate income tax includes taxes on mining and logging profits. **Note c**: 58% of EI contributions, 100% of provincial payroll taxes and 50% of CPP/QPP contributions are paid by employers. Following the Mintz Committee (Table 2.1) we assume that ¾ of employer payroll taxes are paid by businesses.

system remains unchanged. In other words, I assume that no radical reforms such as a switch from an income base to a consumption base are undertaken at the same time. This means that I evaluate the corporate income tax within an income-based tax system.

Reasons for a separate corporate income tax

Why tax corporate profits at all? Since these profits are ultimately either distributed as dividends or generate capital gains, both of which are taxed under the personal income tax system, it has been argued that a corporate income tax is redundant and involves an element of double taxation of corporate source income.

In Canada, the issue of double taxation has been dealt with by the partial integration of the PIT and CIT, under which taxpayers are allowed to deduct from taxes due on corporate dividends part of the CIT paid by the corporation. In practice, this integration requires the application of a tax credit to dividend income that has been the "grossed-up", i.e. taxable dividends are 125% pof dividends received. The full integration of the PIT and CIT eliminates all elements of double taxation, though in Canada full integration in this sense has not been achieved (except for small corporations).

I believe that a separate but integrated corporate income tax is required in an income tax system for several reasons. First, taxing corporate income at the corporate level protects the personal income tax base. If there were no corporate income tax, profits could be reinvested rather than distributed. Since the resultant increase in the value of the corporation is taxed only upon realization of capital gains, the reinvestment of corporate earnings would permit the owners of corporations significant opportunities to defer the payment of income taxes. Taxes at the corporate level mitigate or eliminate this problem. Second, taxing corporate income enables Canada to tax profits of foreign-owned enterprises, which otherwise would be taxed only in the home country of the investors. Third, a separate corporate income tax effectively taxes on an accrual basis excess profits or "rents" of corporations, which can be taxed without inducing economic distortions and therefore are highly efficient.[2]

Existing corporate income taxes in Canada

In Canada, corporate profits are taxed by both the federal and provincial governments. Seven of the provinces levy their tax on the federal base and have the federal government collect the tax on their behalf. Three important provinces, Alberta, Ontario, and Quebec, have separate corporate taxes, which allow them to use definitions of taxable income different from that used by the federal government.

Statutory and effective rates of tax vary by industry, by size, by type of asset and by province. Following are some major features of the existing CIT system.

1 A preferential rate for manufacturing.

2 Special allowances and deductions for certain resource industries.

3 A favourable rate for small Canadian controlled private companies (CCPCs). For dividend income, the corporate taxation of these companies is approximately fully integrated with personal taxes.

4 Dividends receive a credit under the "gross-up" and credit mechanism, and capital gains are taxed at one half the rate of ordinary income. It is important to note that these measures amount to the partial integration of the CIT and PIT for large companies.

Current Canadian statutory rates for corporate taxes are higher than the American rate for non-manufacturing companies and lower than the American rate for manufacturing companies. Other features of the corporate tax like deductions and credits cause the marginal effective tax rate for manufacturing to be about the same in Canada as in the United States. However, Canadian marginal effective tax rates for services are higher than American marginal rates. Sweden, the United Kingdom, and Ireland have lower marginal effective tax rates. Canada has a lower statutory corporate tax rate from small business than the United States.

At the start of the new millennium, Canada began a process of lowering corporate tax rates. Thus, the federal government reduced the general statutory rate by one percentage point on January 1, 2001 and is committed to reducing this rate by six more percentage points over the following three years. Ontario reduced its general corporate tax rate by 1.5 percentage points in 2001 and is committed to a further reduction of six percentage points over the following five years. Alberta reduced its rate to 13.9% in 2001 and is committed to reducing the rate to 8.0% over the following five years. British Columbia has adopted a three precentage point reduction, effective on January 1, 2002. When these federal and provincial rate reductions are fully implemented in 2006, the average statutory corporate rate for large corporations in Canada will be reduced to 32%. Because of the existing different rates of taxation for different types of corporations in Canada noted above, the new average level represents a decline of 11.3% for large non-manufacturing firms and a decline of 3.0% for large manufacturing firms from levels in 2000.

These large reductions in statutory rates generate significant reductions in marginal effective tax rates (METRs) for most non-manufacturing firms. With the exception of the oil and gas, and mining sectors, large non-manufacturing firms will experience declines in METRs of 3.6 to 7.2 percentage points. The METR for large manufacturers is projected to decline by 2.5 percentage points. These planned rate reductions will put METRs in Canada 2.5 to 3 percentage points below present American rates. The statutory rate for large corporations will be about 7 percentage points below the American rate. Even with these rate reductions, however, corporate taxes for large firms will be higher in Canada than those in the United Kingdom, Sweden and Ireland.

Principles for efficient taxation of corporations

The existing corporate tax system was examined extensively by the Technical Committee on Business Taxation (The "Mintz Committee"). Following other reviews of the corporate income tax, the Mintz Committee argued that the most basic general principle of business taxation should be neutrality. Such neutrality assures that the tax system does not distort business decisions by favouring particular industries, investments, or activities. The Mintz Committee also emphasized that the level of business taxation should be internationally competitive by having tax rates no higher than those of Canada's major trading partners.

Neutral tax treatment also entails equal marginal effective rates of tax for all asset types and industries. The Committee found, however, that such neutrality did not exist in Canada and that there is substantial room for improvement of Canada's corporate tax structure.

Non-neutral treatment is appropriate where market imperfections affect investment decisions. Such market imperfections exist in the case of investment in Research and Development (R&D), which can generate significant spillovers or externalities that are not captured by the investing firm. While such externalities justify R&D tax incentives under the corporate income tax, the Mintz Committee found that Canada's tax treatment of R&D is so generous that substantial tax credits and deductions presently generate large negative marginal effective tax rates.

Many small businesses have limited access to capital or face prohibitive capital costs because of imperfections in the capital market. Such capital rationing can be mitigated by a lower rate of tax on the retained earnings of small businesses. The existence of capital market imperfections for small businesses provides the most important justification for Canada's generous treatment of small CCPCs. The other justification is the integration of the personal and corporate taxes, which is considered in the next section.

Integration of the corporate and personal taxes

Ultimately all income and general taxes paid by corporations and businesses are borne by individuals in their capacity as shareholders, investors, consumers, or employees. Some business taxes, like payroll taxes, are primarily shifted back to employees in the form of lower wages. Others, like sales taxes, are shifted forward to consumers through higher product prices. In the case of the corporate income tax, the incidence of the tax is ambiguous. The Technical Committee took an eclectic view, arguing that some portion of the CIT is borne by investors in Canada and some by foreign treasuries.

To the extent that the corporate tax is borne by investors, savings and investment and, therefore, the future rate of growth of potential output are reduced. As a result, the average level and growth of real income of Canadians are diminished. It is, therefore, most important to design a corporate income tax that minimizes these negative effects.

Another issue concerning the efficiency of the corporate tax involves the presently unequal taxation of debt and equity. This inequality is due to the absence of a deduction for the cost of equity and the deductibility of interest costs in the calculation of corporate income-tax obligations. This distortion can be eliminated by the full integration of the CIT and PIT discussed above or, alternatively, by allowing interest deductions only at the PIT level.

The full integration of the CIT and PIT has the further benefit of eliminating another non-neutrality of the existing corporate income tax in Canada, the distortion of incorporation decisions. Without full integration, the combined taxation of corporate source income exceeds the taxation of comparable unincorporated businesses.[3]

The Canadian Tax Reforms of 1971 created a mechanism for integrating the CIT and PIT taxes. Under this mechanism, personal income tax returns allow taxpayers to gross-up their dividend income and then apply a tax credit to adjust the amount of taxes payable. The rates of gross-up and credit were set to achieve the full integration for small businesses. But, since the large business corporate tax rate is higher, the present rates do not result in a full integration for dividend income of corporations.

Since its creation in 1972, the dividend credit as well as statutory corporate tax rates have changed. As a result, in some years there has been over-integration for small business in the sense that the dividend credit was generous enough to reduce the combined tax on dividend income below that on other income. With the provinces levying differential rates of corporate tax on small business, and with federal and provincial surtaxes, the situation has become more complex. At present there is over-integration in some provinces and under-integration in others, though it should be noted that the departures from full integration are not large.

Recommendations of the Technical Committee on Business Taxation

The recommendations of the Technical Committee were constrained by the requirement that the overall package of changes in tax rates and mix had to be "revenue-neutral." Unless rate reductions were "self-financing" through stimulative effects upon economic activity, rate reductions had to be financed by base-broadening measures. Furthermore, the requirement for revenue neutrality had to include the cost of any transitional relief provided to industries adversely affected by the proposed changes in tax rates and structure.

Since the committee was established in 1996, at a time when deficit reduction dominated the fiscal policy agenda, this revenue neutral requirement was an understandable constraint. Now that Canada is achieving fiscal surpluses and the debate is about allocating the future "fiscal dividend," this revenue-neutral constraint should no longer be binding. There should be room to provide transitional relief to industries that face increased tax burdens through proposed reforms that involve base-broadening measures.

The key base-broadening recommendations made by the Committee include:

- reduction of Capital Cost Allowance (CCA) rates for certain classes of investment;
- phasing out of the 100% write-off of R&D Capital Assets and reduction of R&D credits;
- restructuring of the resource allowance so that it applies to resource revenues net of all deductions—to be undertaken in consultation with the Provinces;
- reduction of the rate of write-off of development costs from 30% to 25%;
- replacement of the present immediate write-off of development expenses in mining by a 25% deduction on a declining balance basis—to be put into effect five years after its announcement;
- various limitations on the deductibility of interest expenses for investment in foreign affiliates and other measures to tighten the taxation of international investment income;
- phasing out of the Atlantic Investment Credit;
- harmonization of the capital tax bases of the federal and provincial governments, together with the elimination of the deductibility of provincial capital taxes.

The Committee's estimates of the revenues to be gained by these base-broadening measures are summarized in table 2, which shows that these recommended corporate tax measures would have generated about $2 billion in revenue in 1997.

The Mintz Committee also addressed the issue of integration and the taxation of capital gains. It supported the continuation of the gross-up and credit system for dividends. However, it was concerned that the credit was too generous in cases where corporate income tax paid was less than the amount credited. Such conditions arise when dividends are distributed from corporate income that has been sheltered by deductions or credits.

The Mintz Committee also proposed a dividend distribution tax of 25% payable by corporations. Federal and provincial taxes on corporate profits would be fully creditable against this dividend distribution tax. Therefore, the dividend distribution tax would mainly affect corporations not paying taxes and, to a lesser extent, CCPCs in provinces where there is over-integration of dividend income. The Committee estimated that this measure would generate a revenue increase of $525 million, of which $350 million would accrue to the federal government and $175 million to the provinces.

The taxation of capital gains represents another component of a system that integrates the CIT and PIT. Thus, when capital gains

Table 2: Revenue Impacts (CDN$millions) of Proposed Corporate Tax Measures

	Federal	Provincial	Total
Reduced CCA Allowances	105	60	165
Reduced R&D Deduction & Credits	200	10	210
Resource Allowances & Deductions	215	130	345
International Income Measures	400	250	650
Eliminating Atlantic Investment Credit	95	—	95
Non-deductibility of Capital Taxes	375	200	575
Total	1,390	650	2,040

Source: *Report of the Technical Committee*, Table 1.1.

are taxed at the same rate as dividends under the PIT, dividends and retained earnings are subject to the same degree of integration. The Committee reviewed the argument for taxing capital gains at rates below the rate on other income and concluded that the inclusion rate of 75% of the value of the capital gains in effect in 1996 was appropriate. I question this conclusion, since the effective rate of tax on capital gains was higher than the effective rate on tax on dividends for top-bracket taxpayers. Instead, the appropriate inclusion rate is two thirds to achieve the the desired equality in the rate of taxation of capital gains and other sources of income. By this reasoning, the 50% inclusion rate in effect since 2001 distorts this neutrality and favours capital gains

The Committee also recommended that the current $500,000 lifetime capital-gains exemption for farmers and owners of shares of CCPCs should be eliminated and that it should be replaced with enhanced RRSP contributions that would treat such capital gains as equivalent to earned income on a lifetime basis. The Committee estimated that this measure would generate an additional $450 million of revenue, of which $275 million would accrue to the federal government and $175 million to the provinces.

The Committee estimated that the increased revenue from the corporate tax changes, the implementation of the dividend distribution tax and the changed treatment of capital gains would generate about two billion dollars to the federal government and one billion dollars to the provincial governments. These higher revenues were estimated to be sufficient to finance the revenue losses resulting from the Committee's recommendation that the general federal corporate tax rate be reduced to 20% and the provincial rate to 13%.

The Committee also studied the contributions to the Employment Insurance (EI) system made by employers, which is the only federal payroll tax. This payroll tax represents 58% of the total EI premiums collected by the government. The rest is paid directly by employees. Employer payments by business represent 75% of all EI premiums paid, the rest is contributed by governments and nonprofit institutions. The Committee recognized that in the long run payroll taxes are largely, but not completely, shifted back to workers. However, the Committee also recognized that in the short run increases in the employer contribution rate raise labour costs with adverse effects on employment and economic growth.

The Committee was mainly concerned with the distribution of the costs and benefits of EI payments among different industries. A small number of industries have very high ratios of benefits received by their workers over contributions made by the employers and the workers. In effect, these industries are subsidized by payroll taxes paid by other industries. To deal with the inequity and inefficiencies implicit in the different ratios of benefits and costs of some industries, the Committee recommended that an experience rating system for employers by gradually phased in. Such a policy was to be financed out of the large surplus in the EI "Account" and implemented by granting greater reductions in contribution rates to industries for which the ratio of benefits to costs is below one and smaller reductions (or, zero reductions) to industries for which the ratio is greater than one. Because governments have a ratio smaller than one, the implementation of experience rating would have reduced government payroll tax costs by almost $300 million.

The Committee also expressed the view that the federal government should reduce average EI premiums over time in order to bring revenues down to the long-run cost of the program. However, no explicit rate targets were recommended and, therefore, no estimates of revenue impacts were provided.

What has happened since the report of the Technical Committee?

Key federal tax measures since 1997

The federal government did not act immediately to implement any of the Committee's recommendations. The federal budget of 1998 provided some reductions in personal income tax targeted to low- to middle-income taxpayers. The basic contribution rates for EI were reduced by $0.20 and $0.28 for employees and employers, respectively.[4] Otherwise, no significant changes to business taxes were introduced.

Prior to the 1999 budget, EI premia were again reduced by $0.15 for employees and BY $0.21 for employers. The 1999 budget expanded PIT relief to include middle- to higher-income taxpayers. In the field of business taxation, the 1999 budget introduced a measure that reduced effective tax rates for companies generating electricity by extending the Manufacturing and Processing credit to these firms. This measure was phased in over four years and will reduce the statutory federal corporate rate by 7 percentage points when fully implemented in 2002. While specific to the electrical generation industry, this measure can be viewed as a small initial step towards the more general corporate rate reductions recommended by the Technical Committee.

The federal budget of 2000 finally made a major commitment to reduce corporate income taxes by one percentage point in 2001 and by six additional percentage points within five years. Importantly, these rate reductions were targeted to those firms that were paying the highest statutory and effective rates. This means that there were no rate reductions for firms in the manufacturing and processing, mining, and oil and gas sectors. The budget did not reduce tax rates for small businesses with profits below $200 thousand but it reduced the statutory rate on profits between $200 and $300 thousand to 21% in 2001.[5] Two months before the budget, EI premiums were again reduced, by $0.15 for employees and $0.21 for employers. The 2000 budget also reduced the capital gains inclusion rate from 75% to 66.6%. This measure brought the top marginal rate applicable to these gains in line with the top marginal rate applicable to dividends.[6]

Although the corporate rate reductions announced in the 2000 budget represented an important step towards improved international competitiveness and inter-industry rebalancing, there was a great deal of uncertainty about the timing of the tax cuts. This uncertainty was substantially reduced by the *Economic Statement and Budget Update*, October 18, 2000 (hereafter "October 2000 Statement"). This statement lays out a timetable of successive cuts in the corporate rate of two percentage points, which will bring the general federal corporate tax rate down to 21% by 2004.[7] The October 2000 Statement also accelerated and enhanced the PIT reductions laid out in Budget 2000. The "high income" surtax was eliminated, the low-bracket rate was reduced to 16%, the middle-bracket rate was reduced to 22%, and a new upper-middle bracket was created with a rate of 26%. The threshold for the top marginal rate was raised and the brackets themselves were indexed to inflation.[8]

The October 2000 Statement also lowered the capital gains inclusion rate from ⅔ to ½. With the top federal marginal rate on capital gains reduced to 14.5% and reduced tax rates in many provinces, tax rates on capital gains in Canada are competitive with tax rates on long term capital gains in the United States. Without changes to the dividend credit, however, the tax rate on capital gains is now below the tax rate on dividends for top bracket taxpayers. This raises the prospect of "surplus stripping" and administrative countermeasures, which would increase tax complexity. I address this issue in the section on recommendations below.

Key provincial tax measures since 1997

In 1998 British Columbia, Alberta, Saskatchewan, and Manitoba introduced personal income tax reductions, while Ontario continued to implement its multi-year PIT tax reduction. The corporate tax rate for small businesses was reduced to 8.5% in British Columbia and Ontario. Several provinces introduced tax incentives for R&D and specified investments such as film production.[9]

In 1999, several provinces announced reductions in personal income tax rates. The corporate rate for small business was reduced to 5.5% in British Columbia. In Ontario, the phased reduction in corporate tax rates for small business continued, with the rate dropping to 8%.[10]

In the year 2000, nine of the 10 provinces switched from a system under which they imposed their tax on the basis of the federal tax obligation to a tax on income, where income is defined by the provincial code. The tax-on-income system will permit greater flexibility in the design of provincial personal income tax systems. In 2000, personal income taxes were also reduced in several provinces. Alberta adopted a single rate for its PIT, set originally at 11% and then lowered to 10.5%. At the same time, Alberta increased personal exemptions substantially. Corporate tax rates for small business were reduced by 4.75% in British Columbia and Manitoba and to 6.5% in Ontario and 4.5% in New Brunswick. In Ontario, the rate for large corporations was reduced to 12% for manufacturers and 14% for other firms. Ontario also announced a number of incentives for specific activities involving film, publishing, and other media.[11]

In 2001, all provinces and territories adopted the tax on income as the basis for personal income taxes. In British Columbia, the new government adopted a major reduction in personal income taxes. Small reductions in PIT were implemented in other provinces, partly through matching the changes to brackets and indexing adopted by the federal government in 2000. Corporate tax rates were reduced in British Columbia to 13.5%. Alberta announced a plan to reduce all corporate tax rates: by 2004, for large corporations the rate will be 8% and for small corporations, 3%. Saskatchewan reduced its corporate rate for small business to 6%. Manitoba reduced its rate for small business to 5%, and announced a phased reduction in general corporate rates of 0.5% per year over four years. Ontario announced a plan to reduce corporate taxes over four years so that, by 2005, for large corporations the rate will be 8% and for small corporations, 4%. New Brunswick reduced its general corporate rate to 16% and its small business rate to 4%.[12]

Overview of statutory corporate tax rates

Tables 3 and 4 summarize recent changes in general corporate income tax rates for large corporations and small businesses as well as those planned in the future. Table 3 shows that one of the major recommendations of the Mintz Committee is being implemented. By the year 2006, combined federal and provincial statutory tax rates for large firms in Alberta and Ontario will be lowered to 30% and in Quebec to 31%. Given the importance of these three provinces, the weighted average combined statutory rate for Canada as a whole will be reduced to 32%. This level represents a decline of 11 percentage points relative to 1997. The weighted average level of the combined rate of tax for all provinces will in fact be one percentage point lower than the 33% recommended by the Technical Committee although the Federal statutory rate would be about two percentage points higher.

Table 4 shows that the small business federal statutory tax rate will not change by 2006 but that many provincial rates had been reduced by 2001 and, in Alberta, Ontario and Saskatchewan, further rate cuts are planned. When fully implemented, the combined statutory rates for small corporations will be only 16.1% in Alberta, and 17.1% in Ontario.

It is important to note that these low rates of corporate income tax for small businesses mean over-integration of the corporate and personal taxes in all provinces and territories except for Prince Edward Island and Quebec.[13]

Table 3: General[a] Corporate Income Tax Rates

	1988	1995	2001	2006
Newfoundland	16.0	14.0	14.0	14.0
Prince Edward Island	15.0	15.0	16.0	16.0
Nova Scotia	15.0	16.0	16.0	16.0
New Brunswick	16.0	17.0	16.0	16.0
Quebec	13.9	16.3	9.0	8.9
Ontario	15.5	15.5	14.0	8.0
Manitoba	17.0	17.0	17.0	15.0
Saskatchewan	17.0	17.0	17.0	17.0
Alberta	15.0	15.5	13.9	8.0
British Columbia[b]	14.0	16.5	16.5	13.5
Northwest Territories	10.0	14.0	14.0	14.0
Nunavut	10.0	14.0	14.0	14.0
Yukon	10.0	15.0	15.0	15.0
Federal (inc. surtax)	32.5	29.1	28.1	22.1

Note a: These are rates applicable to large firms outside the manufacturing, mining, and oil and gas sectors. *Note* b: The rate for BC for 2006 is from a BC Ministry of Finance News Release, *Tax Relief, Sound Fiscal Management to Boost the Economy* (July 30, 2001).

Table 4: Corporate Income Tax Rates for Small Business

	1988	1995	2001	2006
Newfoundland	10.0	5.0	5.0	5.0
Prince Edward Island	10.0	7.5	7.5	7.5
Nova Scotia	10.0	5.0	5.0	5.0
New Brunswick	5.0	7.0	4.0	4.0
Quebec	3.2	5.8	9.0	8.9
Ontario	10.0	9.5	6.5	4.0
Manitoba	10.0	9.0	6.0	5.0
Saskatchewan	10.0	8.0	7.0	6.0
Alberta	5.0	6.0	5.3	3.0
British Columbia	10.0	10.0	4.5	4.5
Northwest Territories	10.0	5.0	5.0	5.0
Nunavut	10.0	5.0	5.0	5.0
Yukon	5.0	6.0	6.0	6.0
Federal (inc. surtax)	13.4	13.1	13.1	13.1

Source for Tables 3 & 4: Canadian Tax Foundation, *Canadian Tax Highlights* 9, 5 (May 2001).

Broadening the tax base and other recommended measures

With the exception of certain measures designed to tighten the taxation of international investment income and business profits of foreign-owned corporations, the corporate base-broadening recommendations of the Technical Committee have so far been ignored. This means that the federal corporate rate reductions have largely been financed from the "fiscal dividend." The upside of this situation is that potential revenues from broadening the tax base remain to finance other desirable tax changes.

The recommendations of the Committee to implement a dividend distribution tax and to replace the $500,000 capital gains tax exemption have also so far been ignored. Finally, the Committee's recommendation for the gradual implementation of experience rating for the EI contributions of businesses has not been acted upon. However, as noted above, EI contribution rates have been reduced each year.

At the provincial level, we have witnessed the implementation of a variety of corporate tax measures that provide favourable tax treatment to designated activities. By and large, these represent deviations from the principle of tax neutrality endorsed by the Technical Committee.

An evaluation of the effects of reductions in the corporate rate and other measures[14]

Most economic studies have suggested that the most distortionary revenue sources in Canada are related to business taxes, particularly the corporate income tax. Effective tax rates on capital vary by industry, type of asset, size of firm, and business organization. The business tax system is not only distortionary but also quite complicated. Some studies have suggested that each additional dollar of corporate income tax levied causes the Canadian economy to lose nearly one dollar in economic output.[15] Therefore, the total cost of raising one dollar of corporate income tax revenue can be about two dollars, once these distortionary effects of the tax are taken into account.

An ideal business tax system would be neutral with respect to different industries, asset types, and different degrees of risk. Any non-neutralities in the system should be used to mitigate the effects of market imperfections. Examples of corrective non-neutralities in the tax system include favourable treatment of small business to offset capital-market rationing and incentives for research and development in recognition of the positive spillovers generated by an increase in knowledge or know-how.

In today's world, not only should business taxes be neutral but they should also be levied at rates that are competitive internationally. This is especially important for the corporate income tax. Given the relative ease with which corporations can shift income from countries with high taxes to those with low taxes without changing real economic activity, a country with a high corporate income tax rate could find its tax base eroded significantly. Recent studies have shown that as corporate income tax rates are increased, the gain in revenues is anywhere from 8% to 20% less than what would be expected if the tax base did not change.[16]

High effective marginal corporate rates deter investment and variations in the effective rates for different industries and different assets distort the allocation of capital. Consequently, a reduction in the level of marginal effective tax rates and a reduction in their variance are high priorities from the standpoints of growth and efficiency.

Effects of Budget 2000

With the 2000 Budget and the October 2000 Statement, the federal government committed itself to a reduction of one percentage point in corporate income tax rates for the broad service sector[17] in 2001, followed by four cuts of two percentage points each. the government indicated that it would reduce the corporate income tax rate from 28 points to 21 points by the year 2004/2005 for active business income in sectors other than the resource and manufacturing sectors. It also increased capital-cost write-offs for railway assets, utility equipment, and manufacturing equipment subject to obsolescence. The government also introduced a few tightening provisions: tighter thin-capitalization rules for debt owed to related non-residents, the abolition of the election to be treated as non-resident owned investment corporations and adjustments for research and development expense deductions for provincial deductions in lieu of investment tax credit programs.

The changes in business taxes in the 2000 Budget took many observers by surprise. The cut in corporate income tax rates, although small in the first year, are significant when fully implemented. The rate cuts, moreover, would be focussed on the broad service sector, thereby reducing inter-industry distortions. Tax rates on manufacturing and processing income as well as on resource profits would remain unchanged.

The impact of the 2000 budget changes and of planned provincial corporate rate reductions can be seen in table 5. The small changes introduced for the year 2001 have little impact on effective tax rates on capital. Significant variation in effective tax rates would remain across all sectors. When the proposed corporate rate reduc-

Table 5: Marginal Effective Tax Rates: Large-sized Tax-paying Firms Only

	2000	2001	2006
Forestry	32.5%	31.3%	26.0%
Mining	12.5%	12.1%	11.1%
Oil & Gas	4.7%	4.3%	3.2%
Manufacturing	24.2%	23.5%	21.0%
Construction	37.3%	35.9%	28.7%
Transportation[a]	28.2%	27.1%	21.7%
Communications	28.5%	27.8%	21.9%
Public Utilities[b]	26.1%	25.0%	21.4%
Wholesale Trade	34.8%	33.2%	27.0%
Retail Trade	34.0%	32.5%	26.5%
Services	28.9%	28.4%	21.9%

Note a: Estimate for the transportation sector reflects the higher CCA rate for railway equipment (i.e., 15% instead of 10%). *Note* b: The estimate is made by assuming that 50% of the public utility sector are in the power generating business, which started phasing in the M&P tax credit from year 2000 and may benefit from the higher tax allowance for CCA class 1 (i.e., 8% instead of 4%).
Source: Mintz and Wilson (2001): 102, table 1.

tions are fully in effect in 2004/2005, however, they have a much more dramatic impact. Most industries, except for mining, oil and gas, and manufacturing, would experience a sharp decline in the effective tax rate—over 4 percentage points. Although this tax reform takes us in the right direction, it still leaves considerable variation in effective tax rates on capital across industries and, in some cases, rates remain too high, thereby discouraging investment.

International comparisons and international competitiveness

In an open economy, the business tax structure must be designed with an eye to the likely response of multi-national corporations (MNCs) as well as to its longer term effects on international competitiveness. Attention should be paid to both statutory and effective marginal rates. Statutory rate differentials may provide incentives for MNCs to shift expenses to, and income away from, high tax jurisdictions through transfer pricing and debt management practices. Statutory rates differences may also influence location decisions.

Current and projected corporate statutory rates for OECD countries are presented in table 6. The corporate statutory rate for large manufacturers in Canada lies in the middle of this group of countries but the statutory rate for large non-manufacturing firms is currently above all the other countries (except for Germany and Japan). Projected rates for 2006 indicate that the Canadian corporate tax rate will be below the level of that in the United States, Japan, Germany, and France but will remain higher than many other countries.

In order to prevent substantial erosion of revenue, statutory rates should not be higher than rates typically found in other industrialized countries where investments by MNCs take place. In order to stimulate investment and provide economic growth, effective tax rates on capital should be lower than in other competing jurisdictions.

The implementation of reductions in the statutory corporate rates would establish Canada's rates at the OECD average and well below American statutory rates, thereby eliminating the principal sources of revenue erosion via debt shifting and transfer pricing.

Table 6: Statutory Corporate Income Tax Rates (%) in Selected OECD Countries[a]

	July 31, 1996	January 1, 1999	Change	Intentions (year)
Australia	36	36.0	—	30.0 (2000)
Canada[b]	34.9/43.2	35.0/43.3	—	32.0 (2006)[c]
Denmark	34	32.0	↓	
France	41.7	36.7/40.0[d]	↓	37.8 (2000)
Germany	56.1	51.9[e]	↓	35.0–38.0 (2001)[f]
Ireland	10.0/38.0	10.0/28.0	↓	12.5 (2003)
Italy	53.2	31.3–41.3[g]	↓	
Japan	52.2	48.0	↓	41.0 (2000)
Netherlands	37.0/35.0	35.0	↓	
Norway	28.0	28.0	—	
Poland	40.0	34.0	↓	22 (2004)
Sweden	28.0	28.0	—	
Switzerland	35.5	25.1	↓	
Turkey	44.0	33	↓	
United Kingdom	33.0	30.0[h]	↓	
United States[i]	39.2	39.2	—	

A reduction in the combined general corporate income tax rate to 30% instead of 32% accompanied by broadening of the base would reduce typical marginal effective tax rates for non-resource firms by about 1 to 1½ points. The lower statutory rate would also make Canada more attractive relative to other countries, providing added deterrence to debt shifting and transfer pricing by MNEs.

Because a reduction in corporate statutory rates would stimulate an increase in the tax base, the revenue costs are attenuated to some extent. The Technical Committee estimates that the elasticity of the corporate tax base with respect to a reduction in tax rates is about 0.15. Based on this elasticity, in 1998 for example, a 2% point reduction in all corporate tax rates would involve a revenue

Note a: The 1996 rates are based on the former Coopers & Lybrand, *1997 International Tax Summaries* and the 1999 rates are adopted from the KPMG *Corporate Tax Rates Survey,* January 1999, unless otherwise specified. **Note b:** The rate is a combination of the federal CIT rate (22.1% and 29.1% respectively for manufacturing and others) and the average of provincial CIT rates that is weighted by the provincial GDP by industry. The minor difference between the two years reflects some changes in provincial CIT rates. **Note c:** This is a weighted average of all industries. Note that the current general CIT rate of 43% will still be applicable to the resources sector, which also enjoys various preferential tax treatments unavailable to any non-resource sectors. **Note d:** The rate is a combination of the corporate income tax rate of 33 ⅓% and the surtax of 10% and 20% respectively. The lower surtax is applied to smaller-scaled firms that are mainly owned by individuals. For year 2000 and later, the lower rate will apply to all firms (see Ernst & Young, *1999 Worldwide Corporate Tax Guide,* for details). **Note e:** Our estimate based on to Ernst & Young, *2000 Worldwide Corporate Tax Guide.* It includes a corporate income tax rate of 40%, an average trade tax of 16.75% (ranging from 13% to 20.5%), which is deductible for CIT purposes, and a surcharge of 5.5% on CIT payable. **Note f:** Refer to *Tax Notes International* 20, 4 (January 24, 2000). **Note g:** The higher rate (41.3%) includes a general corporate income tax rate of 37% and a regional tax of 4.25%. The latter is levied on the Italian-source income from productive activities, which includes interest payments and cost of labour. The general CIT rate may be reduced to 19% for qualifying taxable income corresponding to the ordinary remuneration (currently 7%) of the net equity increase. However, the average corporate income tax rate for a company may not fall below 27%, which, combined with the regional tax rate of 4.25%, resulted in the lower aggregated income tax rate of 31.3%. **Note h:** Effective as of April 1, 1999. **Note i:** Our estimate based on an average state corporate income tax rate of 6.5% (ranging from 1% to 12%).

loss of about $1.3 billion of federal corporate tax revenue (representing about 7% of federal corporate tax revenues).[18] In future years, moreover, this relative revenue loss would be further attenuated, as the lower corporate tax rates lead to higher investment, a higher capital stock, and hence increased labour productivity and real output.

Differences in marginal effective tax rates provide incentives for MNCs to adjust their real capital stocks, increasing investment in countries with relatively low effective marginal rates relative to other countries. Table 7 presents current and prospective marginal effective tax rates (METRs) for Canada and eight other countries.

Table 7: Marginal Effective Tax Rates (METRs) for Domestic

	Canada	United States	United Kingdom	Germany
Manufacturing				
1996	23.5%	23.8%	19.4%	38.0%
2000	23.5%	23.6%	17.2%	34.4%
2001	23.4%	23.6%	17.2%	21.1%
Intention in 2006	21.0%			
Services				
1996	29.0%	25.0%	19.2%	37.5%
2000	29.0%	24.8%	17.2%	34.0%
2001	28.3%	24.8%	17.2%	20.8%
Intention in 2006	21.9%			

Source: Mintz and Wilson 2001: 102–3, table 2.
Note 1: To single out the tax impact, we as:sumed that the interest rate was 6.8% and the inflation rate, 1.4% across countries and periods. **Note 2:** The Canadian METR for the service sector in 2001 corresponds to the federal CIT rate of 28.12% (including the 4% sur-tax) combined with the weighted average provincial CIT rate of 14.15%. **Note 3:** The German METR for 2001 reflects the federal CIT reduction from the current 40% to 25%, starting in January 2001. The municipal trade tax (16.66% on average) and the solidarity surcharge (5.5%) will still apply.

In 1996, Canada's effective tax rate on capital invested in manufacturing was comparable to the United States, lower than that found in Germany, France, Italy, and Japan and higher than rates in the United Kingdom, Sweden and Ireland. The broad service sector was more highly taxed in Canada compared especially to the United States and to most countries, except Germany, Italy and Japan.

Since the Technical Committee's Report was released, developments abroad have made further lowering of effective corporate tax rates in Canada more important (Mintz 2001). Within the G7, Japan, Germany and Italy have all reduced effective marginal rates substantially. The United Kingdom, which previously had the lowest effective marginal rate, also reduced its rate by two percentage

Firms in G-7 Countries, 1996, 2000 and 2001

France	Italy	Japan	Sweden	Ireland		
				(1)	(2)	(3)
25.3%	31.6%	31.6%	14.4%	4.2%		
23.2%	18.1%	22.6%	14.4%	4.2%		
23.2%	18.1%	22.6%	14.4%	4.2%		
27.9%	35.5%	33.1%	14.2%	4.2%	8.7%	16.2%
25.8%	21.4%	24.0%	14.2%	4.2%	5.6%	11.3%
25.8%	21.4%	24.0%	14.2%	4.2%	4.3%	9.1%

Note 4: The general CIT rate in Ireland was 32% in 1996, 24% in 2000 and 20% in 2001. A lower rate of 10% is applicable for manufacturing and the international tradable service sector (i.e., financial service sector), to which a corresponding METR of 4.2% is shown in Case (1). Case (2) is for hotel services that are subject to the general CIT rate but enjoy a higher tax depreciation rate of 15% for hotel buildings. Case (3) is for other services subject to the general CIT rate and tax depreciation allowance. In 2004, Ireland's statuatory corporate rate will be 12.5% for all three sectors and the corresponding METR, 5.3%.

points. As a result, Canada has become an outlier, with the highest effective marginal rates of any of the G7 countries (except Japan).

Recent reforms in Scandinavia have resulted in companies being taxed at corporate income tax rates below 30% in Finland, Sweden and Norway, and 32% in Denmark. However, the aggressive business tax policies of Ireland are the most important case in point, since Ireland is the fastest growing OECD country of the past decade, virtually doubling its per-capita GDP in 10 years. While Ireland has reduced tax rates on manufacturing and financial service income to 10%,[19] it also eliminated a number of special ineffective preferences for investments. After pressure from the European Union, Ireland is implementing a corporate income tax rate of

12.5% by the year 2004 that will apply to all businesses. As shown later, Ireland and Sweden have a far more favourable tax treatment of investments compared to Canada.

Over the past five years, Canada's competitive position has eroded as a result of reforms in many countries. In 2000, Canada's effective tax rate in manufacturing, while still comparable to that of the United States, was only lower than that of Germany. However, in 2001, Germany's substantial reform of its system put its effective tax rate well below Canada's. For services, in the year 2001 Canada's effective tax rate was well above that of most countries.

With prospective reductions in federal and provincial statutory corporate tax rates, by 2006 Canada's effective tax rate on capital will be competitive with that of the United States but still above those of the United Kingdom, Sweden, and Ireland. However, it is likely that many of these countries will undertake further changes to their corporate income tax systems and it can be expected that in five years many countries will have reduced corporate income tax rates while broadening their tax bases.

Recommendations for corporate taxes

1 Implement the seven-percentage-point reduction in the general corporate rate in Budget 2000 on a timely basis, as laid out in the October 2000 Statement. The one-percentage-point rate reduction of January 1, 2001 and two-percentage-point rate reduction of January 1, 2002 should be followed by two annual reductions of two percentage points over the next two years.

2 Implement the base broadening and other recommendations of the Report of the Technical Committee (including the elimination of the 4% corporate surtax). This will permit additional reductions of federal and provincial statutory rates, bringing the combined rate close to 30%.

3 Provide selective investment credits that provide transitional relief for industries adversely affected by these reforms.

Recommendations for integrating corporate and personal income taxes

As noted above, amid growing concern that high tax rates affect Canada's international competitive position, the federal government has recently moved to lower taxes on capital gains substantially, and plans to reduce corporate tax rates significantly over the next 4 years. Some provinces have recently reduced these taxes, and others plan future reductions.

While these reductions in effective marginal rates on capital income are welcome, the reduction in capital gains taxes has created a differential between taxes on these gains and taxes on dividends, thereby providing an incentive for conversion of dividends into capital gains. Resolving this issue is now more difficult, because all provinces have moved to a tax on income basis. In this section I consider alternative ways of dealing with this problem.

There are several features of the existing income tax system that prevent the establishment of equal effective marginal tax rates on capital gains, dividends and other income. There is no full integration of the corporate and personal income tax system. While the system has been designed to approximately integrate corporate and personal taxes for small CCPCs, for all other corporations, integration is only partial. Since the rate of corporate tax for small CCPCs differs from that of other corporations, a common dividend credit rate alone cannot achieve perfect integration for both types of firms. Finally, the existence of the $500K capital gains exemption for shares of qualifying CCPCs prevents equalization of taxes on the three categories of income derived from such companies.

Since a major tax reform to equalize corporate rates, provide full integration and abolish the special capital gains exemption is not in the cards, what is the "second best" solution? As the differential treatment of small CCPCs lies at the heart of the problem, we first consider the appropriate tax rates on dividends for these firms, and then consider the tax treatment of other companies. For many small CCPCs the special capital gains exemption reduces the effective rate of tax on capital gains to zero. The existence of this exemption has necessitated the implementation of many rules to determine how firms may qualify for the exemption. These rules effectively prevent the generation of capital gains through either dividend strips or the accumulation of financial assets.

For small CCPCs, the most important issue is, therefore, the equalization of taxes on dividends and on other income paid by these firms (wages and salaries, bonuses, etc.) This can be accomplished by setting federal and provincial net dividend credit rates so as to achieve perfect integration of taxes on dividend income for these firms. One way of doing this is to implement dividend distribution taxes on dividends paid from income eligible for the small business deduction.

For other companies (public corporations, large CCPCs and other private corporations) the most important issue is the equalization of taxes on dividends and capital gains for top bracket tax payers. If the rate of tax on dividends is higher than the rate of tax on capital gains, these firms would have an incentive to convert dividends into capital gains through share buybacks and other financial arrangements.

How do we implement these recommendations? For all corporations except small CCPCs, I propose that the dividend gross-up and credit system be changed to equalize marginal rates on dividends and capital gains for individuals in the highest marginal rate bracket. Specifically, I recommend that the dividend gross-up factor be increased to one third, and the federal dividend credit be increased to set the top marginal federal tax rate on dividends at 14.5%, equal to the top marginal federal tax rate on realized capital gains.

I assume that participating provinces will accept the federal definition of taxable income, so that the 50% capital gains inclusion rate and the one-third dividend gross-up enter the provincial income tax base. Each province should then set its dividend credit so as to equalize its top marginal rate on dividends with its top marginal rate on capital gains.

At current corporate tax rates, this system will not provide complete integration for large corporations. However, the degree of integration will increase as planned future corporate rate reductions are put into effect.

Notes

1 For a discussion of the allocational and incentive effects of business payroll taxes, see Mintz and Wilson 2001 and Dungan 1998.

2 Boadway and Kitchen 1999: 220–21.

3 It is for this reason that the United States modifies its classical CIT through the use of sub chapter "S" corporations, which are taxable in the same way as partnerships.

4 As usual, these EI contribution rate changes were put into effect prior to the budget on January 1, 1998.

5 Other corporate changes included liberalization of capital cost allowance for certain assets, tightening of the thin capitalization rules for foreign owned corporations, repeal of non-resident investment corporation elections, and restrictions on "weak currency" borrowing.

6 Other measures permit deferral of tax on the exercise of employee stock options and the establishment of rollover provisions for certain small- and medium-sized business investments.

7 This would bring the general corporate rate down to the rate for manufacturers and processors. Note that the general federal rate for mining and oil and gas is to remain at 28%.

8 This income bracket is from \$60,000 (indexed after 2000) to \$100,000 (indexed after 2001).

9 See Perry 1998: 626–44.

10 Source is Ort and Perry 1999: 1194–213.

11 Source is Ort and Perry 2000: 710–33.

12 Source is Ort and Perry 2001: 674–707.

13 For perfect integration under the existing gross-up and credit for dividends, the combined corporate rate should be 20%. Rates above 20% indicate under-integration and rates below 20% indicate over-integration. The resolution of this problem will be discussed in the section on recommendations below.

14 This section draws upon Mintz and Wilson 2001: 95–133.

15 See Whalley 1997.

16 See Dungan, Murphy, and Wilson 1997 and Jog and Tang 1997.

17 The broad service sector includes all industries except manufacturing and processing and the resource sectors.

18 This revenue loss is less than the fiscal cost estimate derived from Finance, The Economic and Fiscal Update, Nov. 2, 1999 p. 113.

19 This rate is substantially below the 30% rate for other industries, resulting in less favourably taxed industries growing less quickly.

References

Boadway, Robin W., and Harry M. Kitchen (1999). *Canadian Tax Policy* (Third Edition). Canadian Tax Paper No. 103. Toronto: Canadian Tax Foundation.

Canada, Department of Finance (1999a). *The Economic and Fiscal Update* (November 2).

Canada, Department of Finance (1999b). *The Budget Plan 1999* (February 16).

Canada, Department of Finance (2000a). *The Budget Plan 2000* (February 28).

Canada, Department of Finance (2000b). *Economic Statement and Budget Update* (October 18).

Canadian Tax Foundation (2001) *Canadian Tax Highlights* 9, 5.

Coopers & Lybrand (1997). *1997 International Tax Summaries.*

Dungan, Peter (1998). *The CPP Payroll Tax Hike: Macroeconomic Transition Costs and Alternatives.* C.D. Howe Institute Commentary No. 116.

Dungan, Peter, Steve Murphy, and Thomas A. Wilson (1997). The Sensitivity of the Corporate Tax to the Statutory Rate. Working paper 97-1. Technical Committee on Business Taxation

Ernst & Young (1999). *1999 Worldwide Corporate Tax Guide.*

Ernst & Young (2000). *2000 Worldwide Corporate Tax Guide.*

Jog, Vijay, and Jianmin Tang (1997). Tax Reforms, Debt Shifting and Tax Revenues: Multinational Corporations in Canada. Working Paper 97-14. Technical Committee on Business Taxation.

KPMG 1999. *KPMG Corporate Tax Rates Survey* (January).

Mintz, Jack M. (2001). *Most Favoured Nations: Building a Framework for Smart Economic Policy.* Toronto, C.D. Howe Institute.

Mintz, Jack, and Thomas Wilson (2001). Taxes, Efficiency and Economic Growth. In Pat Grady and Andrew Sharpe (eds), *The State of Canadian Economics: A Festschift in Honor of David Slater* (Queen's University-McGill University Press): 95–133.

Ort, Deborah L., and David B. Perry (1999). Provincial Budget Roundup, 1999. *Canadian Tax Journal* 47, 5: 1194–213.

Ort, Deborah L., and David B. Perry (2000). Provincial Budget Roundup, 2000. *Canadian Tax Journal* 48, 3: 710–33.

Ort, Deborah L., and David B. Perry (2001). Provincial Budget Roundup, 2001. *Canadian Tax Journal* 49, 3: 674–707.

Perry, David B. (1998). Provincial Budget Roundup, 1998. *Canadian Tax Journal* 46, 3: 626–44.

Technical Committee on Business Taxation (1997). *Report of the Technical Committee on Business Taxation.* Ottawa, Department of Finance.

Whalley, John (1997). Efficiency Considerations of Business Tax Reform. Working Paper 97-8, Technical Committee on Business Taxation. Ottawa: Department of Finance.

Why there should be no capital gains tax

Herbert Grubel

"Harvest the fruit but do not cut the tree." "A buck is a buck." These two slogans define the battleground on which the fight over the existence of a capital gains tax in Canada is taking place. The first slogan has long dominated the thinking of economists. Just as cutting the tree necessarily lowers future harvests of fruit, so does taxing capital diminish its stock and future returns. Taxes on capital interfere with the efficient, intertemporal allocation of capital.

The second slogan was introduced into the public domain by the Carter Commission, whose report provided the rationale for the introduction of Canada's capital gains tax in 1972. The slogan's appeal is based on equity considerations. Someone with a capital gain can increase consumption just as if the money was earned as income. Since income is taxed, capital gains should be taxed also.

The equity slogan dominates the culture of Canada's Department of Finance also on the grounds that equal taxation of both sources of income eliminates incentives to shift financial resources between income and capital gains. As a result, the task of enforcing Canada's tax code is made much easier.

It is obvious from this brief description of the battleground that both positions have merit and that the fight cannot be decided on the grounds of principle alone. There is, in fact, a trade-off between efficiency and equity. Society as a whole needs to decide which point on this trade-off it chooses. In a free and democratic society like Canada's, this choice ultimately is made through the political process. However, voters' choices are influenced not only by value judgements—the kind of income distribution the people want—but also by empirical information about the trade-off.

The present paper provides available empirical information about the trade-off. In particular, it discusses the economic costs of the capital gains tax, the effects on the distribution of income and the implications for fiscal revenues.

Implications for efficiency

The implications of taxing the tree are best summarized by the following quotations.

> The tax on capital gains directly affects investment decisions, the mobility and flow of risk capital ... the ease or difficulty experienced by new ventures in obtaining capital, and thereby the strength and potential for growth in the economy. (President John F. Kennedy, 1963)

> The capital gains tax is so economically inefficient—because of its punitive effect on entrepreneurship, thrift, and investment—that the optimal economic policy for the United States would be to abolish the tax entirely. (S. Moore and J. Silvia, The ABCs of the Capital Gains Tax, *Policy Analysis*, Washington, DC: CATO Institute, 1995)

> The major impact (of the capital gains tax) is to impede entrepreneurial activity and capital formation. While all taxes impede economic growth to one extent or another, the capital gains tax is at the far end of the scale. I argued that the appropriate capital gains tax rate was zero. (Federal Reserve Chairman Alan Greenspan in testimony before the Senate Banking Committee, February 25, 1997)

The empirical judgements of these students of capital gains taxation are based on considerations discussed in the following three sections.

Lower capital stock

In today's integrated global capital market, investors equalize the risk-adjusted rates of return after taxes in all countries. Assume that the world is in equilibrium and that these returns are equal in all countries. If, under these conditions, a small country like Canada imposes a capital gains tax, investors reduce their investments in that country. The resultant lowering of the capital stock increases its marginal productivity in that country until the after-tax return is again equal to that in the rest of the world. Since productivity of labour is an increasing function of the capital stock, the smaller amount of capital in Canada is associated with lower output and living standards.

The impact of the imposition of the capital gains tax is slow since it takes time for the capital stock to fall. In fact, the effect may be swamped by the normal growth in the capital stock so that it is difficult to document that the stock would have been even higher if there had been no capital gains tax.

Knowledge capital and entrepreneurial innovation

Modern economic theory stresses that society's productive capital is made up not just of physical plant and equipment but also of human and knowledge capital. The latter is created by research and development and, most importantly, the efforts of entrepreneurs that turn the information into marketable products and services. The boom of the 1990s in the high-tech industries, as well as the increase in labour productivity in the rest of the economy, have been fuelled by entrepreneurship applying new knowledge. In many ways, entrepreneurs are the driving force behind all economic growth.

Entrepreneurs are people determined to make profits from an unproven innovation. They take risks by investing their own capital and time and borrowed capital in pursuing their dream. Unfortunately, a large proportion of entrepreneurial efforts fail. Only markets decide which innovative products, services and technologies are successful.

Entrepreneurs are like people buying lottery tickets. They hope to draw a winner but know that success comes only to a few. However, the expectation of drawing that lucky ticket or successful product is enough to keep people buying lottery tickets and becoming entrepreneurs.

The government of Canada does not tax lottery winnings because it knows that otherwise the net revenue from the lottery would be reduced because people would buy fewer tickets or the payoff ratio would have to be increased. However, the government imposes stiff capital gains taxes on entrepreneurs and the venture capitalists that finance them. Yet, there is little doubt that the reduced returns result in less innovative activity in Canada and it is curious that the same principles underlying the non-taxation of lottery gains are not applied to entrepreneurial gains. Because of this condition, economic growth and productivity gains in Canada are lower than they would be otherwise.

An argument can be made that the existence of venture capital firms deals with the problem that winners from innovation are taxed prohibitively. Such firms pool risks of investing in innovative activities and thus are able to offset wins against losses. Nevertheless, their total net profits are reduced by the capital gains tax and flows into venture capital activities are smaller than they would be in the absence of the tax. Moreover, many entrepreneurs are loners, perhaps because they necessarily fight established ways. These individuals cannot avail themselves of the risk-pooling benefits and the tax reduces their expected net returns. The lower the expected returns, the smaller will be the supply of entrepreneurs willing to take gambles on innovation.

Canada's record of innovative entrepreneurship is inferior to that of the United States. According to the preceding analysis, this result can be explained, at least in part, by the fact that Canada has a much higher capital gains tax than does the United States. To make up for lost ground and possibly pull ahead of the United States, Canada has to eliminate the capital gains tax.

The lock-in effect

The capital gains tax causes damage to the productivity of the existing capital stock by creating a so-called lock-in effect. This effect arises because the tax interferes with market incentives to move out of assets with low yields into assets with high yields. Consider an investor who owns an asset, the sale of which triggers a large capital gains tax obligation. As a result, the investor's cash available for a new investment is reduced by the amount of the tax. The yield on the new investment must be higher than that on the old by an amount sufficiently large to compensate for the smaller amount of money invested.[1] The lock-in effect prevents the prompt reallocation of capital from low into high yielding uses. It thus reduces the dynamic efficiency of the economy and results in lower income and living standards in Canada.

The government has recognized the damage done by the lock-in effect. For some types of investment, therefore, it instituted rollover provisions under which the capital gains tax is not payable if the reinvestment takes place under a strict set of rules. Assets held in tax-sheltered investments like RRSPs do not pay taxes on capital gains. However, these measures do not eliminate most of the lock-in effect, as many investors in stock markets have found out to their dismay during recent periods when stock markets boomed.

The marginal efficiency cost of taxes

The idea that taxes cause costly distortions and reduced supplies of the taxed factor of production have been formalized in the theory of the marginal efficiency cost of taxation. Essentially, the marginal efficiency cost of taxaton is higher, the easier it is for the taxpayer to avoid the specific tax.

Thus, a consumption tax tends to have the lowest efficiency cost since every person needs to buy goods and services to maintain desired living standards and, as a result, they cannot avoid payment of the tax. The highest efficiency costs in turn arise from the taxation of capital because it induces people to move their capital abroad, keep it locked up in less than optimal investments, or to consume it. Estimates made by the Department of Finance in Canada and published by the OECD (1997) suggest that the marginal efficiency cost of taxes on capital is $1.55. That is, if a private person has an investment yielding 10% and the government taxes it away, society will be poorer unless the government invests the money in a project yielding 25.5%.

The most important implication of the marginal efficiency cost models is that Canada's tax system could be improved greatly by the elimination of taxes on capital and their replacement by sales and personal taxes, which have efficiency costs of only $.17 and $.56, respectively.[2]

Quantitative estimates of the cost

Direct empirical estimates of the cost of capital gains taxes are very difficult because of the myriad of confounding changes in policies, technology, terms of trade, and demographics taking place at the same time changes in capital gains taxes are implemented. Moreover, there are few distinct, major changes in capital gains taxation levels and structure in Canada and other countries. And, as noted above, the effects of the tax on the capital stock and productivity take place over a prolonged period of time.

Nevertheless, there are two sets of empirical information that shed important light on the cost of the capital gains tax. The first set is based on the concept of the marginal efficiency cost of taxes and empirical studies made to estimate them in Canada and other countries. Dahlby (2002) in his contribution to this volume presents a careful review of such studies and concludes:

> [R]ecent econometric studies indicate that switching the tax mix toward consumption taxes can significantly increase the growth rate of the economy. An increase in the annual economic growth rate on the order of a two-tenths of a percentage point ... would have a dramatic impact on Canadian living standards over time. The present value of the additional per-capita output from increasing the annual growth rate by two-tenths of a percentage point is 238% of current output, which represents an enormous gain.
>
> ... [E]ven if we have overstated the growth effect of switching to a consumption tax by a factor of 10 ... the present value of the increase in per-capita output would still be 22.3% of current output—a very significant gain. (Dahlby 2002: 96)

Dahlby's conclusion draws on the findings of studies that considered the entire range of indirect taxes, mainly taxes on labour and capital. For this reason, the empirical estimate quoted is not entirely relevant to the capital gains tax alone, which produces only a small fraction of the entire revenue from indirect taxes.[3] On the other hand, the marginal efficiency of capital taxes generally is higher than that for other indirect taxes, which implies that its replacement with a direct tax would have a disproportionately large effect, albeit on a small base.

The second empirical study was produced by Kugler and Lenz (2001) for a Fraser Institute conference. This landmark study notes that the federal government of Switzerland does not have a capital gains tax but that, during the last 20 years, individual cantons have experimented with the tax. The authors show that the incomes of all cantons between 1978 and 1995 followed a very similar trend since the same external factors and federal policies affected the economies of all.

However, eight of the cantons during the period under study at some time eliminated the capital gains tax in their jurisdiction while the rest did not. Regression analysis showed that the cantons, which eliminated the tax, enjoyed a jump in cantonal income of 3.2% relative to the income of those that retained the tax. There also has been a beneficial effect on economic growth. The authors found that these gains were not achieved at the expense of cantons that did not eliminate their capital gains tax.

Finally, I made a very simple calculation of the rate of economic growth experienced in the period from 1990 to 1997 by OECD countries that do not have any capital gains tax imposed by their federal government. I found that Hong Kong, the Netherlands, New Zealand, Singapore and Switzerland, countries without the tax, had per-capita growth rates of 2.2% while the rest of the OECD countries grew at 1.2%.[4]

Summary and conclusions

Theoretical considerations suggest capital gains taxation imposes costs on society by lowering the stock of real and knowledge capital and by inducing its less efficient use through the lock-in effect and efforts to avoid the tax. All of these effects translate into lower productivity, per-capita incomes and living standards.

These theoretical considerations in turn have been used to make econometric estimates of the quantitative effect on income. The studies noted above are not specific enough to allow me to conclude that the elimination of the capital gains tax in Canada would result in a certain percentage increase in per-capita incomes. However, together, the empirical evidence implies strongly that the capital gains tax has reduced Canadian income by quantitatively significant amounts and that it will continue to do so in the future.

Effects upon equity

Many Canadians believe that a necessary part of a desirable, good society is a fair tax system and a fair distribution of income. The concept of fairness is value-laden and only the political process can decide on the merit of any given policy. In this spirit, the political establishment in the late 1960s decided to examine the effects of having no capital gains tax on the distribution of income. The examination and public mood resulted in the imposition of a capital gains tax in Canada in 1972.

Fairness of the system—"a buck is a buck"

The public mood at the time was influenced by the idea that people with the same level of income paid different amounts of taxes, depending on whether their income was derived through capital gains or from work. In economics jargon, the tax system did not meet the criterion of horizontal equity. The issue was popularized by the catchy slogan, "a buck is a buck," and strengthened by reference to the work of two serious scholars, Robert Haig (1921) and Henry Simons (1938). The so-called "Haig-Simons conditions"—that income from all sources should be taxed equally—continues to this day to dominate the discussion of academics and policy makers about the merit of capital gains taxation.

The basic case for the taxation of capital gains on the grounds of horizontal equity is logically valid as far as it goes. However, for a number of reasons, it rests on an incomplete understanding of the nature of capital gains.

First, as Bruce Bartlett argues in a scholarly paper (2001), capital gains are not like income at all. He supports his detailed arguments by reference to the important fact that capital gains are not counted as income in national accounts, which record the total value of goods and services produced in a country. He quotes Simon Kuznets, one of the creators of these national income accounts: "Capital gains and losses are not increments to, or drafts upon, the heap of goods produced by the economic system for consumption or for stock destined for future use, and hence they should be excluded" (Kuznets 1941: 12). In other words, GDP designed to measure the value of national income do not reflect capital gains or losses. Since Kuznets' principles for measuring national income are accepted almost universally by economists, the question is why capital gains are excluded from the aggregate measures but included in the individual levels of income. Bartlett's answer to this question is:

> In truth, their [Haig and Simons'] rationalization for taxation of capital gains rested more on ideological grounds than scientific analysis. As Haig once put it, "an income tax which would allow capital gains to escape unscathed would, in this country at least, be an ethical monstrosity." Simons too holds the same basic view. "The main and decisive case for inclusion of capital gains rests on the fact that equity among individuals is impossible under an income tax which disregards such items of gain and loss." (Bartlett 2001: 12-13; quoting Haig 1928: 120 and Simons 1938: 158).

Second, a large proportion of capital gains are illusory increases in spending power of their owners since they are caused by inflation. Thus, between 1972 and 1991 consumer prices rose 3.8 times while investments in the TSE increased only 2.9 times. Therefore, capital gains reported on such TSE investments were entirely nominal. Economic developments did not allow the owners of such capital gains to increase their spending as if the money had come from work. Their net worth was reduced.[5]

It is argued that the system of capital gains taxation in Canada takes account of inflation by requiring the inclusion in taxable income only one half of the realized capital gains. The preceding data on stock market investments over nearly 20 years show that this provision is not adequate. The exclusion from taxation of 50% of the nominal gains still meant that taxes were due on real losses. In addition, the inclusion rate introduces a bias in the rate at which investments are taxed depending on the length of time over which they have been held. Thus, when inflation is moderate, the 50% exemption is likely to more than compensate for capital gains held for a short period. On the other hand, for long-term investments, the exemption is not likely to equal the actual rate of inflation, as was the case in the stock-market example given in the preceding paragraph.[6]

The problem of assuring horizontal equity in a system without capital gains taxes is aggravated by the ability of people to engage in tax arbitrage, which means that they shift taxable personal and investment income into non-taxable capital gains. For this reason many tax experts, especially those in Canada's Department of Finance believe that a capital gains tax equal to the tax on income is needed to prevent this type of tax evasion. This important subject will be discussed below in more detail.

Vertical equity—"the rich get richer ..."

Politicians, reflecting public opinion in Canada are very much concerned about the fairness of the distribution of income and wealth or what economists call vertical equity. The public demands that tax and spending policies of government reduce the disposable income and wealth of the rich and enhance those of the poor. There are special concerns that the policies address the problem that "the rich get richer and poor get poorer," which is perceived to exist unless government intervenes.

Policies designed to create greater fairness in the distribution of income involve, among others, progressive income tax rates and the capital gains tax. In addition, there are expenditure programs like welfare, unemployment insurance, and pension benefits designed to help the poor.

Few people realize that the progressivity of the income tax has resulted in the fact that the top 10% of all income earners in Canada have traditionally paid around 45% of all income taxes[7] while the bottom 40% of all income earners pay no income taxes at all. This outcome is the result of the progressivity of marginal income tax rates and, important for the present analysis, also to the payment of capital gains taxes by those who earn high incomes. This presumption is based on the appealing notion that only high-income earners hold assets and incur capital gains tax obligations.

What is the empirical evidence on the payment of capital gains taxes by Canadians at different levels of income? One set of calculations supports the view that most capital gains accrue to the rich. Thus, Joel Emes, using a data-base supplied by Revenue Canada found that in 1992 families with incomes of $100,000 and more paid 78% of all capital gains taxes.[8] Families with income of $50,000 or less paid only 8% of the total. In looking at these numbers, it should be remembered that only 7.9% of all Canadian families in 1992 had incomes above $100,000.

However, these results are quite misleading because the income used to classify families includes capital gains and these gains often are a rare event. In other words, capital gains push some into high income brackets when normally they have much lower incomes. For example, the owners of small retail stores or restaurants often have low incomes and plow earnings back into their business to build up a nest egg for retirement. In the year that such people sell their business and retire, they appear as high-income earners in the statistics. In fact, of course, they are not the "rich" that the capital gains tax was designed to affect.

Emes examined this issue employing the same 1992 data he had used to produce the conventional statistics reported above. In the new calculation he excluded the capital gains reported from total income and made a new distribution. He found that those Canadian families with incomes other than capital gains over $100,000 in 1992 paid only 26.8% of all such taxes. Families with less than $50,000 of such non-capital gain incomes paid 52.1%.[9]

One explanation of the large amount of capital gains taxes paid by those with lower incomes is that many of them have investments in mutual funds. Capital gains made by such funds have to be reported as individual income in the year they are realized.[10]

Incidence of the tax

Economists are fond of pointing out that taxes often are not paid ultimately by people who send money to the tax collector. For example, excise taxes on cars are paid by the manufacturer, the GST is paid by every firm in the chain of production and distribution, tariffs are paid by importers. Yet, in the end all of these taxes raise the prices paid by consumers through higher prices of their purchases.

Economists are divided over the issue whether business income taxes are paid by their owners or whether they too are shifted to consumers like tariffs and sales and value-added taxes. Some believe that all business income taxes fall on workers and consumers on the grounds that the lower after-tax rates of return drive capital abroad or into consumption until the resultant lower stock of capital restores the original pre-tax rate of return on capital. Others believe that most business owners have insufficient alternative uses for their capital and so are forced to accept the lower rate of return forced upon them by the tax.

While the issue of the incidence of excise and business income taxes has been analyzed widely, the incidence of the capital gains tax has not.[11] Yet, the capital gains tax is a tax on business and capital, much like the corporation and small business income taxes. Therefore, it is quite uncertain who pays the capital gains tax. It may in the end be paid by workers and consumers, most of whom are not the "rich" at whom the tax was aimed.

Summary and conclusions

The capital gains tax is designed to create a fair system of income taxation. In particular, it is designed to assure that "a buck is a buck," that horizontal equity is achieved through the taxation of income whether it comes from ordinary income or capital gains.

The horizontal equity principle of taxation, however, is invalidated to the extent that capital gains in some important ways are not like other income. This fact is acknowledged in the official estimates of national income, which do not include capital gains. In addition, most capital gains are not real but due to inflation so that taxing them implies the confiscation of wealth.

The capital gains tax is also designed to equalize the distribution of after-tax income, to prevent "the rich from getting richer and the poor from getting poorer." The rationale for this policy is based on the conventional wisdom that only high income earners own capital and enjoy capital gains. However, this wisdom is incorrect in the light of the fact that capital gains taxes are paid by people who enjoy one or a few capital gains in their life-times but otherwise have only low or average incomes. Calculations show that, in fact, over half of capital gains taxes are paid by families earning less than $50,000 a year in other income.

The idea that capital gains taxes increase vertical equity suffers also from the neglect of hidden forces of market adjustment induced by the tax. Thus, it is likely that in a small country like Canada in a world of increasingly globalized capital markets, the incidence of capital gains taxes falls on workers and consumers, not the owners of capital.

In sum, we have found that the capital gains tax imposes significant cost on Canadians in terms of reduced living standards. We have also found that the benefits in terms of horizontal and vertical equity are much less than conventional wisdom suggests. This new information combined suggests that the old calculations of the ratio between the costs and benefits of the capital gains tax are no longer valid. Canadians would be better off if the tax were abolished.

Tax arbitrage

When a business has to pay a tax on profits but not on capital, incentives are created to use creative bookkeeping and legal manoeuvers to turn profits into capital gains. Small businesses, like those of lawyers and physicians, can reduce the pay of their employees and invest the savings in the firm. The value of the firm increases correspondingly and employees can realize the gains as non-taxable capital gains. These processes designed to take advantage of the absence of capital gains taxes are known as tax arbitrage or "surplus stripping," in the terminology used during the 1970s.[12]

A publication by the Canadian Department of Finance reviewed the history of tax arbitrage and reached the following conclusion: "The inability of the government to check surplus stripping abuses was, in fact, the primary impetus for the comprehensive review of the tax system in the early 1960s. It led to the establishment of the Royal Commission on Taxation" (Department of Finance 1980). The Carter Commission Report recommended the adoption of the capital gains tax to prevent surplus stripping. The government accepted this recommendation and adopted a capital gains tax in 1972.

How big is the problem of tax arbitrage in Canada? At the 1999 symposium on capital gains taxation at the Fraser Institute, a number of participants, who had been working in the financial sector during the 1960s, disputed the proposition that surplus stripping was a major problem at that time. They noted that such stripping is not possible for large, publicly held companies except through the reinvestment of profits and the repurchase of outstanding stocks. These latter practices are employed for many reasons other than tax arbitrage and have continued after the capital gains tax was introduced and raised above the tax rate applicable to other income.

On the other hand, small, privately held companies were able to engage in this kind of legal and financial maneuver. But, it was also true that the Department of Finance could quite easily have prohibited such manoeuvers, which so obviously had no other purpose than the avoidance of taxes. These observers suggested that surplus stripping was a red herring to divert public attention from an innovation in taxation that was motivated by a desire to equalize the distribution of income and expand the size of government.

The following view, attributed to one of the most respected American economists in public service in recent decades, supports the views of Canadian experts about the problem of tax arbitrage just discussed: "Alan Greenspan laboured in the Wall Street vineyards before he got his academic degrees in economics. He told me he had to spend decades trying to figure out how to convert ordinary income into capital gains and couldn't figure out how to do it" (Wanniski 1999). To shed further light on this issue, the Fraser Institute's 2000 symposium brought to Vancouver economists who were knowledgeable about the problems experienced in their countries as a result of having no capital gains taxation. The experience of Hong Kong is of special relevance to the present analysis. For evidence from other countries readers are directed to Grubel 2001.

Empirical evidence from Hong Kong

Berry Hsu and Chi-Wa Yuen (2000) discussed Hong Kong's experience. They provided a list of methods that can be used to turn profits into capital gains. Some are quite simple, like buying real estate with the intention of reselling it but claiming that the resulting profits were capital gains. Others are more sophisticated, like the sale of the right to a future stream of income, claiming it to be a capital gain. These and other schemes have been tried and have been challenged successfully by the Hong Kong revenue authorities. These authorities are guided in their actions by two, relatively simple, anti-avoidance principles:

> The first sets out to disregard any "artificial or fictitious" transactions that do not in fact take place and any that reduce or would reduce the amount of taxes payable. The second applies a "sole or dominant purpose" test to determine whether a transaction is conducted mainly for the purpose of obtaining tax benefits through the avoidance or postponement of the liability to pay tax or the reduction in the amount thereof. (Hsu and Yuen 2001: 43)

The decisions of the revenue authorities based on these principles are challenged regularly by the affected parties. A Board of Review adjudicates these appeals. Hsu and Yuen consider the rulings by the revenue authorities and of the review board to reflect the magnitude of the efforts of taxpayers to shift taxable income into non-taxable capital gains. They conclude: "On the basis of the indirect evidence available to us we conclude that the absence of a capital gains tax in Hong Kong has resulted in little, if any, inefficiencies and inequities" (Hsu and Yuen 2001: 50). Hong Kong is, in so many ways, like no other "country" in the world and its experiences may have only limited relevance to others. Most important, the low income and profits taxes, which keep low the returns to be gained by turning taxable income into non-taxable capital gains.

On the other hand, Hong Kong's practices for dealing with such tax avoidance efforts show that it should be possible for Canada's revenue agency to set out some simple anti-avoidance principles against which it, and an appeals court, can evaluate any practices that appear to be designed to avoid taxes. Such a task would not be new since the present more favourable rate of taxation of capital gains relative to other income already contains some incentives to avoid taxes by dividend stripping or the methods used in Hong Kong. Existing rules and regulations may be expected to apply fully in a regime completely without capital gains taxes though, of course, under these conditions the incentives to get around these rules and regulations would be stronger for the private sector.

Conclusion

There is no doubt that the absence of a capital gains tax in the presence of business and personal income taxes opens opportunities for tax arbitrage. Such tax arbitrage wastes resources, induces the inefficient allocation of resources and causes the tax system to be unfair.

These facts give rise to two questions. First, how large would such arbitrage be and, second, how difficult is it for the Government of Canada to prevent it. Evidence relevant to the first question is mixed. Before Canada introduced a capital gains tax, government experts considered it to be a major problem. On the other hand, practitioners from the private sector deny this. Evidence relevant to the second question suggests that the cost of avoiding arbitrage might be quite small, if the government armed itself with anti-avoidance principles as the base from which to evaluate and prevent the arbitrage.

Perhaps the views of capital market participants and the experience of Hong Kong are biased. But, it is also quite likely that the testimony of government experts is also biased. Their life has been made much easier by not having to prevent tax arbitrage.

On balance, the possibility of tax arbitrage and the cost of preventing it represent a cost of uncertain magnitude in eliminating the capital gains tax in Canada. It should, therefore, enter a rational calculation of the costs and benefits of such a policy discussed above. My own view is that the cost of arbitrage is unlikely to be greater than the benefits in terms of efficiency minus the net cost of reduced equity discussed above.

Implications for revenue

Any suggested changes in the tax system must be accompanied by consideration of their effect on overall fiscal revenues. In the context of the present discussion of the capital gains tax, the easiest way to handle this issue is to suggest that the government be required to raise other taxes to make up the lost revenue. Alternatively, at times when the government projects the development of fiscal surpluses, it may be assumed that the elimination of the capital gains tax is just one of the ways in which the surplus can be eliminated.

In either case, the size of the revenue losses from the elimination of the capital gains tax is important because it determines how significant are the required increases in other tax rates or how much of a surplus is required and, therefore, cannot be used for other purposes. Unfortunately, the Government of Canada does not publish how much revenue the capital gains tax generates. There are no relevant data in publications by the Department of Finance or Statistics Canada. In OECD publications, where estimates for other countries are presented, the entry for Canada is blank.

To make up for this lack of information, Joel Emes used a computerized model provided by Statistics Canada to examine a representative sample of personal income tax returns. He estimated that in 1992 total revenue from the capital gains taxation was $715.6 million, or less than .3% of the total tax revenue that year. This figure was disputed by the Department of Finance, which informed us that, according to their estimates, the revenue from the capital gains tax were about 3% of total revenue and that provincial governments collected additional amounts on their own accounts.[13]

Whatever the true size of the revenue from the capital gains tax, the available information suggests that it is relatively small. Therefore, it is almost certain that its elimination will have little impact on other taxes if revenue neutrality is desired or if it occurs at the cost of other uses of the fiscal surplus. As a practical matter, the increases in revenue generated by normal economic growth would quickly exceed the relatively small amount of revenue lost through the elimination of the tax and prevent it from causing, or adding to, any fiscal deficit.

Most important, however, is the fact that the elimination of the capital gains tax will almost certainly add to normal economic growth and, therefore, to revenues from all other tax sources. The prospect of such a favourable development follows directly from the analysis of the positive effects the policy would have on economic efficiency and incentives discussed above.

Unfortunately, the expected growth in income and other tax revenue is uncertain with respect to timing and magnitude. In addition, the link between increased growth and the elimination of the capital gains tax is not as transparent as one might wish. Therefore, the merit of the elimination of the capital gains tax is subject to much controversy among economists. If the government of Canada were to embrace the suggested elimination of the capital gains tax, politicians would encounter much opposition from organizations dedicated to the fostering of income equality, real and perceived. These politicians cannot expect support from the rest of Canadians since their gains in income will be relatively small and uncertain. They have only negligible incentives to lobby for their interests and threaten punishment at the ballot boxes. This asymmetry of pressures on politicians, formalized so ably by public-choice theory, haunts all efforts to create policies that improve overall economic performance but affect adversely small segments of society.

Summary and policy implications

At the risk of oversimplification, the battle over the retention or abolition of the capital gains tax is fought along lines characterized by two catchy slogans, "a buck is a buck" and "harvest the fruit but do not cut the tree." The first slogan is about the distribution of income and the fairness of the taxation system. The second is about the efficiency implications of the tax and how much it reduces economic growth and per-capita incomes. Most people agree that both fairness and efficiency should be considered in the design and operation of Canada's tax system. The crucial issue arises around the magnitudes of these two social objectives.

This paper discussed the growing evidence on the size of the efficiency losses due to the tax. The large number of studies using the concept of the marginal efficiency cost of taxes implies that the cost is substantial. The study of the Swiss experience is powerful and adds to the direct evidence on the effects of that tax on income.

A review of the issue of horizontal equity raises serious analytical questions about the relevance of the arguments suggesting the need to treat capital gains in the same way as other income. On the issue of vertical equity, recent calculations have shown that over half of the tax is paid by families with less than $50,000 annual income from other sources.

Available empirical evidence suggests that tax arbitrage would be much less of a problem for the economy than the Department of Finance believes. A strong case can be made that the practices used in Hong Kong could effectively limit tax arbitrage at a reasonable administrative costs in Canada.

In sum, new empirical and analytical knowledge implies that Canada would be better off without the capital gains tax. The resultant increases in output and prosperity would almost certainly outweigh the relatively minor effects on the fair distribution of income and the small cost associated with limiting tax arbitrage.

Notes

1 Consider an investor who holds an asset worth $100. The future rate of return is assessed to be 9% and thus brings $9 annually. In the absence of the capital gains tax, the asset would be sold and reinvested in a comparable company assumed to exist and with a return of 10%, bringing an annual income of $10. But, now consider that the sale of the asset gives rise to a $20 capital gains tax obligation, leaving only $80 for reinvestment in the higher yielding asset. If the investor holds on to the low yielding asset, the income is $9, more than the $8 earned by selling it, paying the capital gains tax and reinvesting in the higher yielding asset. The rational owner of the investment subject to the capital gains tax keeps his funds where they are and is privately better off than if the asset were sold. However, society is worse off because funds are prevented from flowing from the lower into the higher yielding investment—$1 per $100 in the preceding example.

2 In a study of the United States, Jorgensen and Yun (1989) estimated the capital income tax to have an efficiency cost of .924 while the sales and personal income tax costs were .256 and .598, respectively. The relatively small efficiency cost of capital taxation in the United States is not surprising since it is the one country in the world where the "small country assumption" does not hold. Capital inflows and outflows can be so large that they influence the "world" rate of return, in contrast with Canadian flows that are so small as to leave returns in the world unaffected.

3 According to one estimate, the capital gains tax revenue of the federal government in 1992 represented only .3% of all federal taxes collected (Grubel 2000: 14). Poddar and English estimated that federal capital gains taxes represented only 21.1% of the total federal tax on investment collected (Poddar and English 1999). For more on this subject, see the last section below.

4 The latter group excludes countries that index capital gains taxes to inflation (Australia, Ireland, Luxembourg, Mexico, and the United Kingdom). The per-capita growth rate of these countries from 1990 to 1997 was 2.3%.

5 See Grubel 2000: 40–42 for the sources of this information and a discussion of reasons why inflation indexing is used in only few countries. Eisner 1980: 343 shows that in the United States there were no real but only nominal capital gains during the period from 1946 to 1977.

6 These facts raise the question why capital gains taxes are not adjusted for inflation so that only real gains are taxed. I have not discovered any answers to this question. At the 2000 Fraser Institute symposium on capital gains taxation a number of economists reported on their countries' experiences with indexing. There are no theoretical objections and no practical pitfalls preventing the use of this system in Canada and other industrial countries. Unfortunately, its introduction in the presence of a 50% exemption rate, as prevails in Canada, would require the elimination of that exemption. Such a policy would be condemned widely as a tax increase, as it almost certainly would be during the relatively low rates of inflation that have prevailed in recent years and may be expected for some years to come.

7 A graph showing the share of all income taxes paid by the top 10% and 1% of all income earners between 1997 and 1995—regardless of the top marginal income tax rates—is found in Grubel 2000: 16.

8 See Grubel 2000 for more information about these calculations.

9 Jonathan Kesselman has indicated to me in private correspondence that the calculations made by Emes do not prove conclusively that lower-income and middle-income Canadians pay the bulk of the capital gains tax. He thinks that generally high-income earners can be expected to report their capital gains in years that their other incomes are below normal. I agree with him that this issue can be settled only by studies, which trace incomes and tax payments through time. Unfortunately, such panel data are not yet available in Canada.

10 As a result of this provision, many Canadians with low and modest incomes at income tax time face unanticipated tax obligations. Some are forced to sell part of their fund holdings to generate the cash needed to pay the tax collector, which contributes to economically inefficient turnover of investments.

11 I owe the point on the shifting of the capital gains tax to Professor John Chant, who made it in an unpublished note presented at the first Fraser Institute conference on capital gains taxation held in Vancouver in September 1999.

12 Essentially the process requires that the owners of a working company establish a dummy corporation. This dummy borrows money from a bank to buy all of the shares of a working company. The dummy company becomes the owner of all of the real assets of the working company plus the profits it earned in the preceding period. These profits are referred to as surplus and are to be turned into capital gains.

The next step in the process of stripping this surplus is for the working company to use the money it received from the dummy corporation to buy back all of its shares. It thus becomes once more the owner of its real assets but, by agreement, it leaves the surplus with the dummy corporation. The dummy then uses the money it received for the shares to repay the bank loan. However, it has left over the surplus, or profits, of the working corporation. The dummy corporation is dissolved and in the process declares a capital gain equal to the working company's profits. The owners of the dummy corporation in effect have turned the taxable profits of their working company into a non-taxable capital gain.

An analogous process can be used to convert the income of professionals like physicians and lawyers into a surplus of a business owned by them. See Grubel 2001 for the way in which such practices can be used to turn taxable personal income into non-taxable capital gains.

13 For more details, see Grubel 2000. I remain puzzled by the fact that the Department of Finance has data on the amount of revenue collected but does not publish it and makes it available, after delays, only to persons making persistent requests for the information.

References

Bartlett, Bruce (2001). *Why the Capital Gains Tax Rate Should Be Zero.* NCPA Policy Report No. 245 (August). Dallas, TX: National Center for Policy Analysis.

Dahlby, Bev (2002). Restructuring the Canadian tax system by changing the mix of direct and indirect taxes. This volume: 77–108.

Department of Finance (1980). *A Review of the Taxation of Capital Gains in Canada: An Examination of the Canadian Experience and of Issues Involved in Proposals for Change.* November.

Eisner, Robert (1980). Capital Gains and Income: Real Changes in the Value of Capital in the United States, 1946–77. In Dan Usher (ed.), *Measurement of Capital* (Chicago: University of Chicago Press).

Grubel, Herbert (2000). *Unlocking Canadian Capital: The Case for Capital Gains Tax Reform.* Vancouver, BC: The Fraser Institute.

——— (2001), *International Evidence on the Effects of Having No Capital Gains Taxes.* Vancouver, BC: The Fraser Institute.

Hsu, Berry F. C., and Chi-Wa Yuen (2001). Tax Avoidance Due to the Zero Capital Gains Tax: Some Indirect Evidence from Hong Kong. In Herbert Grubel (ed.), *Unlocking Canadian Capital: The Case for Capital Gains Tax Reform* (Vancouver, BC: The Fraser Institute, 2001): 39–54.

Haig, Robert M. (1921). The Concept of Income—Economic and Legal Aspects. In Robert M. Haig (ed.), *The Federal Income Tax* (New York: Columbia University Press).

Jorgensen, Dale, and Kun-Young Yun (1991). The Excess Burden of Taxation in the United States. *Journal of Accounting, Auditing and Finance* 6, 4: 487–509.

Kugler, Peter, and Carlos Lenz (2001). Capital Gains Taxation: Evidence from Switzerland. In Herbert Grubel (ed.), *Unlocking Canadian*

Capital: The Case for Capital Gains Tax Reform (Vancouver, BC: The Fraser Institute, 2001): 55–72.

Kuznets, Simon (1941). *National Income and Its Composition, 1919–38.* New York: National Bureau of Economic Research.

Organisation for Economic Co-operation and Development (1997). *Economic Surveys, Canada*. Paris, OECD.

Poddar, Satya, and M. English (1999). Canadian Taxation of Personal Investment Income. *Canadian Tax Journal,* 47, 5: 1270–304.

Simons, Henry C. (1938). *Personal Income Taxation*. Chicago: University of Chicago Press.

Wanniski, Jude (1999). *Supply-Side University Spring Semester Lesson #17.* Published on www.polyconomics.com on June 4.

The corporate capital tax—Canada's most damaging tax

Jason Clemens, Joel Emes, and Rodger Scott

Introduction

The corporate capital tax is a business tax little known outside the circles of academia, tax-planning, and corporate boardrooms. However, the corporate capital tax is one of, if not the most, damaging tax currently imposed by governments in Canada. Because of its cost and complexity and because Canada must compete with other industrialized countries, few of which use such a tax, it should be eliminated by all Canadian governments.

This chapter provides a brief overview of the detailed analysis contained in *The Corporate Capital Tax: Canada's Most Damaging Tax*[1] and gives two of the four sections in the main study: (1) a description and critical evaluation of corporate capital taxes (hereafter "capital taxes"); and (2) the measurement of capital tax usage in Canada. The two sections not presented examine trends over time and present a more developed analysis of the use of capital taxes in various Canadian jurisdictions.

1 Description and evaluation of capital taxes

What is a capital tax?

The capital tax generates revenue for governments by assessing a levy on corporations based on the amount of capital (essentially debt and equity) employed. There are two major categories of corporate capital taxes in Canada: those levied on financial institutions and those levied on non-financial companies.[2] The applicable rates vary from 0.0% in Alberta for both financial and non-financial corporations (i.e. there is no capital tax) to 0.64% in Quebec for non-financials and 4.0% in Newfoundland for financial institutions.

Like all business taxes, the burden of the capital tax, both the general and that specific to financial institutions, is borne by ordinary citizens through higher prices for goods and services, lower wages, and reduced rates of return on savings and investments.

Evaluating the capital tax

There are three traditional measures of tax effectiveness: efficiency, fairness (also referred to as equity), and simplicity.

1 Efficiency

Efficiency, as applied to taxation, requires that tax revenues be raised in the least distortionary manner, thus maximizing economic growth. The marginal efficiency cost (MEC) of taxation measures the cost of raising an additional dollar of tax revenue from an existing tax. Tables 1 and 2 give the results of two studies of MEC—*OECD Economic Surveys, 1996–1997* (Organisation for Economic Co-operation and Development 1997); The Excess Burden of Taxation in the United States (Jorgenson and Yun 1991)—that demonstrate the relatively high cost of raising tax revenues via capital-based taxes compared with the use of consumption and labour-based taxes.

The common finding in both studies of the MEC of different taxes is that business taxes are much less efficient than those with a labour income or consumption base. That is, payroll and sales (consumption) taxes are much more efficient than business taxes such as the corporate income tax.

Both studies found that using business taxes, specifically corporate income taxes, imposed a substantially higher cost to the economy than the use of either sales or payroll taxes. Thus, considerable

Table 1: Estimates of marginal efficiency cost (MEC) for selected Canadian taxes

Tax	MEC ($)
Corporate Income Tax	$1.55
Personal Income Tax	$0.56
Payroll Tax	$0.27
Sales Tax	$0.17

Source: Organisation for Economic Cooperation and Development 1997.

Table 2: Estimates of marginal efficiency cost (MEC) for various taxes

Tax	MEC ($)
Capital Income Taxes (Individual & Corporate)	$0.924
Corporate Income Tax	$0.838
Individual Income Tax	$0.598
Labour Income Tax	$0.482
Sales Tax	$0.256
Property Taxes	$0.174

Source: Jorgenson and Yun 1991.

efficiency gains can be achieved by simply reconfiguring the current tax mix to move away from corporate income and capital bases and toward labour income and consumption bases.

2 Fairness (equity)

The main concern for a capital tax in terms of fairness is whether or not it achieves horizontal fairness: firms with similar amounts of capital face similar corporate capital tax bills.

There are several reasons that capital taxes fail the test of horizontal fairness. First, because there are varying definitions of what constitutes an eligible large corporation and, thus, the exempted level of capital, firms with equivalent capital are not treated equally across jurisdictions. Second, financial institutions are taxed more heavily by the capital tax than non-financial institutions. Third, capital taxes fail the test of fairness because they place a higher burden on industries whose activities are more capital intensive than others. Growth-enhancing industries like software, biotechnology, and communications bear a heavier capital tax burden than other, less capital-dependent industries.

3 Simplicity

Simplicity refers to the cost to the government of collecting taxes as well as the costs incurred by businesses and individuals in complying with a tax system. The principle of simplicity requires that both sets of costs be minimized.

The Technical Committee on Business Taxation, one of the most important recent Canadian commissions to evaluate taxation concluded that "capital taxes are becoming increasing[ly] complex" (Technical Committee on Business Taxation 1997: 4.21). This is due to the inherent administrative complexity of taxing capital and to the lack of uniform interpretation of the capital tax legislation both in and across jurisdictions.

Corporations are required to calculate total capital tax payable by determining the taxable capital, investment allowance, and applicable exemptions, deductions, and credits. One study concluded that this requires accounting for 103 items simply to determine capital tax payable in a single jurisdiction.

Although the capital tax on its surface may appear to be relatively simple, in reality it is complex and becoming more so as additional credits and deductions are added.

Conclusion

The capital tax is a poor way to raise revenues for government because it violates the principles of fairness, simplicity, and efficiency, and ultimately impedes economic growth.

2 Measuring the use of capital taxes

International comparison

Canada is almost alone in its use of capital taxes, one of only three countries in the OECD that levies a direct tax on the capital of corporations at the federal level. The other two OECD countries, that impose capital taxes are Germany and Japan, but they do so to a much lesser extent. Several American states levy a minor tax equivalent to a capital tax but the amount and the effect are negligible. Canada's capital tax is levied at the highest rates, extracted from the broadest bases, and administered with the greatest degree of complexity compared with the few other jurisdictions using capital taxes.

Intra-Canadian comparisons

Four measures were used to rank the use of capital taxes by Canadian federal and provincial governments over the last 12 years: capital tax as a percent of (1) own-source revenue, (2) business profits, (3) gross domestic product (GDP), and (4) corporate income tax. The results are summarized in table 3.

Table 3: Use of capital taxes in Canada (2000/01)

	Capital tax as a percent of:				Average Rank
	(1) Own-source revenue	(2) Business profits	(3) GDP	(4) Corporate income tax revenues	
Canada	8	8	8	10	8.5
BC	5	4	4	3	4.0
AB	11	11	11	11	11.0
SK	1	2	1	1	1.3
MB	4	3	3	4	3.5
ON	3	5	5	7	5.0
QC	2	1	2	2	1.8
NB	7	7	7	6	6.8
NS	6	6	6	5	5.8
PEI	10	9	10	9	9.5
NF	9	10	9	8	9.0

Source: Clemens et al. 2002.
Note: updates using data for 2001/2002 are available in Clemens 2002.

The table shows that, in general, Saskatchewan and Quebec use the capital tax to the greatest extent. In fact, Saskatchewan's capital tax consistently generates more revenue than its corporate income tax. British Columbia is a relatively high user of capital taxes although it has announced it will eliminate its non-financial capital tax in 2002. Finally, Manitoba rounds out the group of Canadian jurisdictions that use capital taxes to a relatively high degree.

At the other end of the spectrum, Alberta no longer has a capital tax, having eliminated its captial tax on financial institutions on April 1, 2001. The federal government along with Newfoundland and Prince Edward Island are also relatively low users of capital taxes.

Below is a brief summary of the findings from four specific measures of the use of capital taxes by the federal and provincial grovernments in Canada.

1 Corporate capital tax as a percent of own-source revenue

This measures the proportion of revenues collected in a particular jurisdiction (i.e. own-source revenue) in the form of capital taxes (figure 1). Saskatchewan was the leader in capital tax revenue as a percentage of own-source revenues (5.40%). Quebec ranked second with 3.48%. Ontario, Manitoba, and British Columbia ranked third, fourth, and fifth, respectively. Alberta ranked last in the percentage of its own-source revenues provided by capital taxes: only 0.14 cents of every dollar collected in revenues were from capital taxes.

Saskatchewan and Quebec remained in first and second position throughout the period from 1989 to 2001. Alberta frequently ranked last, indicating the lowest reliance on capital taxes as a percent of own-source revenues over the twelve-year period. The federal government along with the Atlantic Provinces generally also ranked relatively low.

2 Corporate capital tax as a percent of business profits

This indicator measures the amount of capital tax collected compared to the profits generated by corporations (figure 2). Quebec's capital tax extracted the greatest amount of revenue as a percent of business profits (6.9%). Quebec was followed closely by Saskatchewan (6.1%). Manitoba (5.1%) and British Columbia (4.3%) followed in third and fourth positions. Alberta was again ranked last

Figure 1: Corporate capital tax as a percent of own-source revenue, 2000/2001

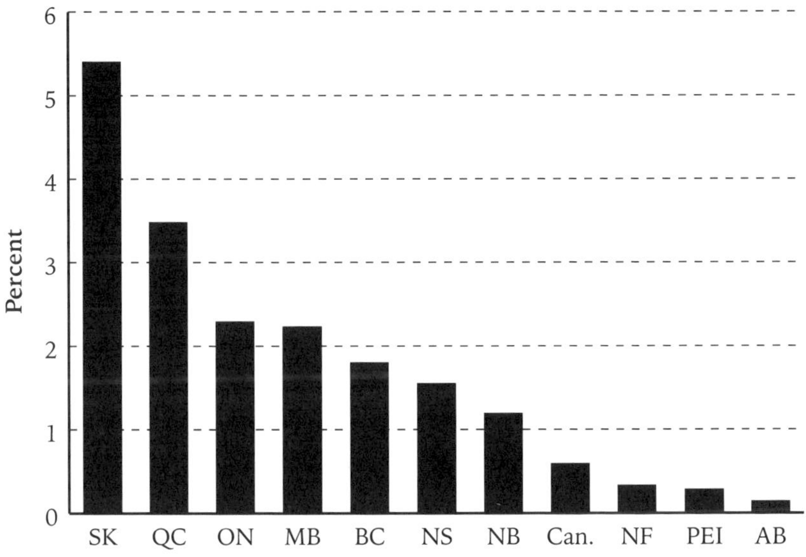

Figure 2: Corporate capital tax as a percent of business profits, 2000/2001

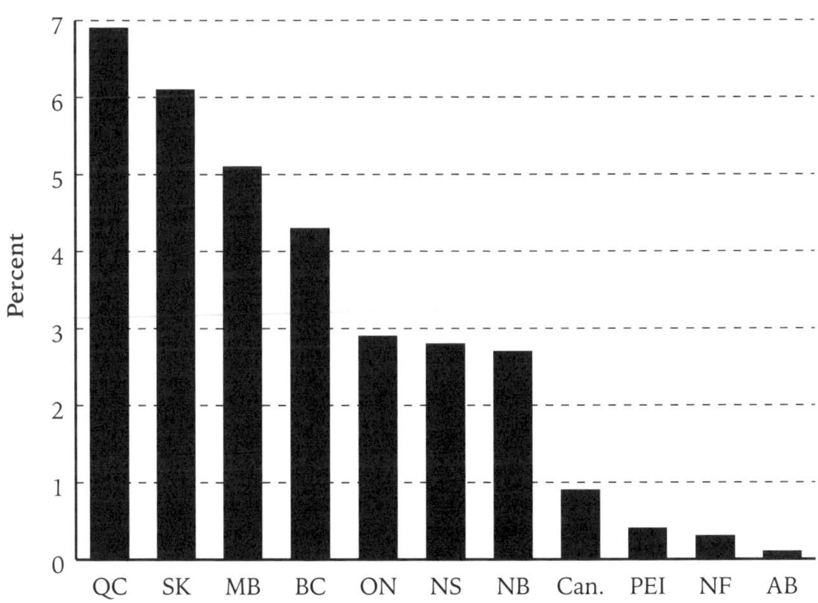

with capital taxes representing only 0.1% of business profits. Newfoundland and Prince Edward Island tied for tenth position.

Throughout the period from 1989 to 2001, Quebec ranked first in every year but one. Saskatchewan ranked second in every year but one, in which it was ranked first. Manitoba was consistently ranked third. Alberta, Prince Edward Island, Newfoundland, and New Brunswick generally extracted the least amount of capital tax revenues relative to business profits.

3 Corporate capital tax as a percent of GDP

This indicator measures the use of capital taxes relative to the size of the economy (figure 3). Saskatchewan ranked first in this indicator with capital taxes representing 0.98% of GDP. Quebec followed in second position with capital taxes representing 0.73% of GDP. Manitoba (0.40%) ranked third and British Columbia (0.34%), fourth. Alberta was ranked last with capital taxes representing a mere 0.03% of GDP in 2000/2001. Prince Edward Island and Newfoundland followed closely, tying for tenth position.

Saskatchewan and Quebec consistently ranked first and second throughout the period from 1989 to 2001. Manitoba and British Columbia (after 1992/1993) consistently held third or fourth. Alberta ranked last for 10 of the 12 years. Prince Edward Island and Newfoundland also regularly ranked low.

4 Corporate capital tax as a percent of corporate income tax

The fourth indicator compares the amount of capital tax revenue with the amount of revenue collected by the corporate income tax (figure 4). Saskatchewan ranked the highest of all jurisdictions. Saskatchewan was the only jurisdiction in which more revenues were raised from capital taxes than from corporate income taxes: $1.05 in capital taxes for every $1 in corporate income tax. Quebec ranked second in the amount of capital taxes raised relative to corporate income taxes, British Columbia, third, and Manitoba, fourth. Alberta, Prince Edward Island, and the federal government ranked low in their use of capital taxes relative to corporate income taxes.

Throughout the period from 1989 to 2001, Saskatchewan, on average, collected $1.21 in capital tax revenues for every $1.00 raised in corporate income tax. Saskatchewan is the only province to collect more, consistently, through capital taxes than through corporate

Figure 3: Corporate capital tax as a percent of GDP, 2000/2001

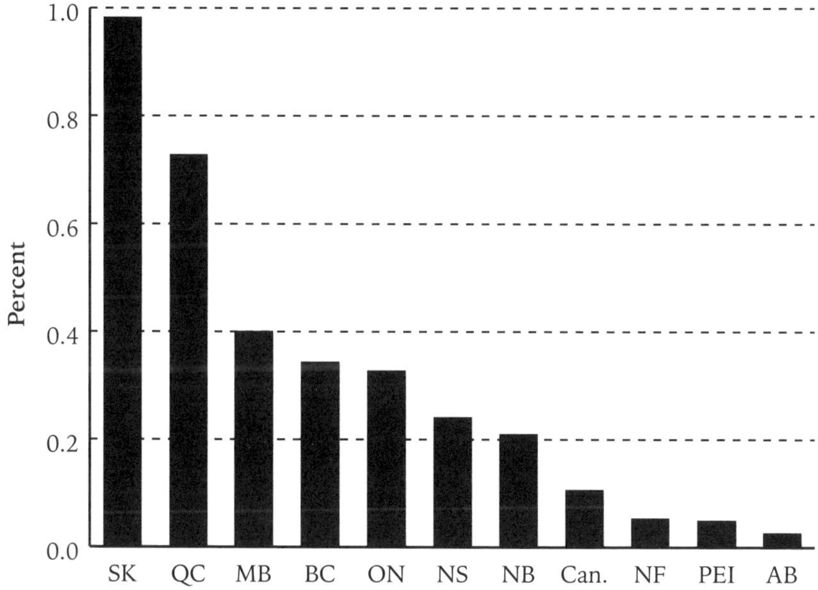

Figure 4: Corporate capital tax as a percent of corporate income tax, 2000/2001

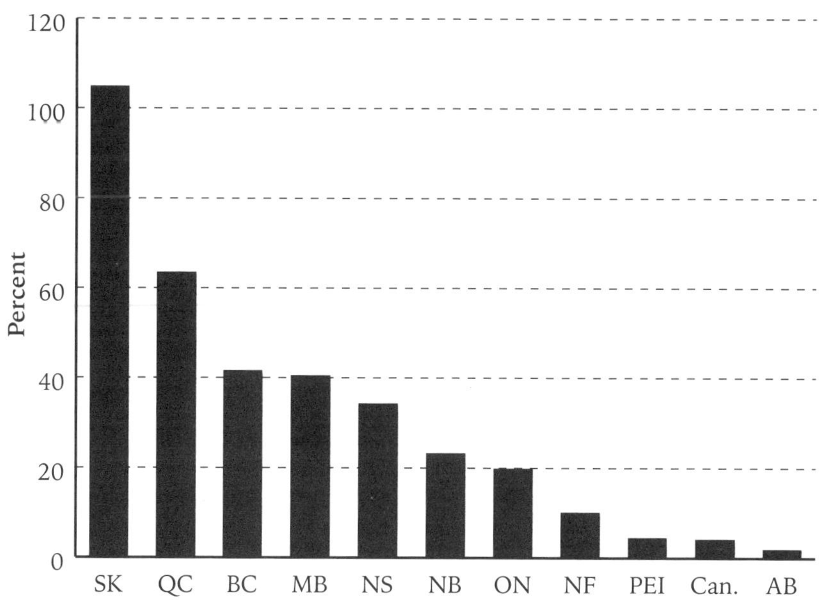

income taxes. Quebec consistently ranked second but was far behind Saskatchewan. Manitoba and British Columbia commonly alternated between third and fourth places. Alberta collected relatively low amounts of capital tax revenues compared with corporate income taxes consistently over the period. The federal government also received low rankings over the period.[3]

Conclusion

The combination of these four measures indicate quite strongly that Saskatchewan, Quebec, Manitoba, and British Columbia are the highest users of capital taxes in Canada. On the other end of the spectrum, Alberta, the federal government, and the maritime provinces tend to be relatively low users of capital taxes.

Recommendation

Given that there are high and unnecessary costs associated with using capital taxes and that Canada is one of only three OECD coutries to use them, it is imperative for all Canadian jurisdictions to follow the lead of Alberta and eliminate them. At the very least, capital taxes should be replaced with more efficient taxes such as payroll or sales taxes. However, the first and best option for every jurisdiction in Canada is the straightforward elimination of capital taxes—a tax reduction, like that in Alberta, rather than a tax replacement.

Notes

1 Clemens, Emes, and Scott 2002. Also available as a digital document (PDF) from www.fraserinstitute.ca.

2 Note that there is also a capital tax assessed on insurance companies that is not dealt with in this study.

3 Section 4 of Clemens, Emes and Scott 2002 provides detailed profiles of the use of capital taxes by each jurisdiction.

Reference

Clemens, Jason (2002). The Big News Is No News on the Corporate Capital Tax. *Fraser Forum* (November): 31–32.

Clemens, Jason, Joel Emes, and Rodger Scott 2002. *The Corporate Capital Tax: Canada's Most Damaging Tax*. Public Policy Sources 56. Vancouver, BC: The Fraser Institute.

Jorgenson, Dale W., and Kun-Young Yun (1991). The Excess Burden of Taxation in the United States. *Journal of Accounting, Auditing, and Finance* 6, 4: 487–509.

Organisation for Economic Cooperation and Development (1997). *OECD Economic Surveys, 1996–1997*. Paris: OECD.

Technical Committee on Business Taxation (1997). *Report of the Technical Committee on Business Taxation*. Ottawa, ON: Department of Finance

Interprovincial fiscal competition in Canada—theory, facts, and options

Finn Poschmann and William B.P. Robson

Fiscal competition among jurisdictions is one of the many subjects in public finance where opinions are firmer than is the evidence. It seems obvious that Canadian provinces compete with each other to attract people, firms, and economic activity. Evidence such as actual tax rates, however, offer little guidance about how, or how strongly, this competition influences their behaviour. And, if the positive issues are difficult to sort out, the normative ones are even more so. Different commentators see fiscal competition as likely to be good or bad in general and those who concede that it has both good and bad elements can disagree profoundly over where to draw the line between the two.

These disagreements are of major policy significance in Canada. Existing practice and many proposals for interprovincial or national fiscal harmonization explicitly or implicitly assume that fiscal competition is problematic. Tax collection agreements and emerging arrangements in the Canada Customs and Revenue Agency (CCRA), for example, derive legitimacy from fears of what unrestricted tax competition among the provinces would produce. Equalization and federal-provincial shared-cost programs are partly responses to a presumed inability of provinces to provide attractive fiscal packages on their own and the social union framework agreement has explicitly been justified with regard to pressures for a "race to the bottom" in provincial social policy.

This paper attempts to sort out some of the key issues in interprovincial fiscal competition. First, it surveys some of the major theoretical inquiries in the area and tries to isolate the formal and informal models likeliest to provide insights for Canada. Second, it presents some of the pertinent data on interprovincial competition in both taxation and program delivery. Finally, it addresses the thorny questions of how to distinguish beneficial from harmful competition. Some final observations on implications for near-term policy coordination close the paper.

Briefly, our principal theme is that the parallels between interprovincial competition within Canada and interfirm competition in a market setting are closer and more powerful in their implications for public policy than is generally appreciated. Provinces do compete on price and there is evidence that lower tax rates yield rewards as measured by local growth in profits and incomes. But, provinces also compete on program quality: the downward ratcheting of spending on government-provided goods and services that is predicted by simple "race to the bottom" views of competition is nowhere to be found.

In view of the prospects for price and quality competition among the provinces to improve the fiscal package citizens throughout the country enjoy, the case for restraining this competition through national or federal agreements on taxation or programs carries a heavy burden of proof.

Views

It is clear at a basic level that jurisdictions compete for individuals, firms, and economic activity. As long as movement across boundaries is possible, the relative attractiveness of one location over another will affect movement and policy makers' choices about taxes and programs—whether or not those choices are conscious responses to competition—will affect relative attractiveness.

What determines movement and how policy makers respond, however, are issues on which there is not much consensus.

"Race to the bottom"

One popular view rests on two assumptions. One assumption is that the strongest, if not the only, force determining mobility is tax burden. Another is that government is necessarily benevolent; policy makers, if not constrained by interprovincial competition, would seek to maximize social welfare calculated in some disinterested way. This view, which has analogues in such areas as safety and environmental standards, sees a tendency for individuals and firms to move to the jurisdiction where the tax burden is lowest, compelling policy makers to cut taxes, and the services they provide, in a multilateral "race to the bottom."

The more formal exposition of the race to the bottom acknowledges the existence of benefits from public services and characterizes under-provision resulting from tax competition as a negative externality. The intuition is that a province might be inclined to provide more public services but would be restrained from doing so by the prospect of capital locating in other provinces, which would benefit those provinces but not the first. Thus, the perceived marginal local benefit of raising taxes is smaller than the local costs. A tax-cutting jurisdiction, in parallel fashion, would benefit from the migration of the tax base from neighbouring jurisdictions, making the marginal benefit of tax-cutting greater than the locally perceived marginal cost. In this view, therefore, policy makers in all provinces have an incentive to set tax rates and public service levels lower than the social optimum.

Not surprisingly, many subscribers to this view see interjurisdictional competition as a bad thing, leading to under-provision of public services, unsafe working conditions, a degraded environment, and so on.[1] Their natural focus when it comes to policy, therefore, is co-ordination of taxes and publicly funded goods and services across jurisdictions, so as to avoid that harmful "race."

While interjurisdictional agreements—or, indeed, mechanisms to restrict movement across subnational borders—could address this problem, the more common approach advocated within a country is that the central government should either directly constrain subnational tax competition or indirectly constrain it by encouraging or mandating generous levels of services and transfer payments, or creating revenue sharing mechanisms: "States might provide higher quality services if they shared some taxes and did not have to worry so much about losing businesses to neighboring states with lower tax rates. They would then have more incentives to compete on the basis of the excellence of their services" (Rivlin 1992: 142).

"Policy makers as monopolist rent-seekers"

Another perspective takes a dimmer view of the prospects for restraint of competition on the revenue side to produce better programs. This view also emphasizes the importance of costs in determining location but adds to the mix an agency problem: policy makers who consider their personal welfare, as well as the interests of citizens, when they make their policy choices. Local residents' natural constraints on policy makers—elections and voting with their feet—may not be sufficient to align policy makers' and voters' utility perfectly, because of several costs: the cost of moving, the cost to voters of obtaining information about policy makers' actions, and the costs involved in actually holding policy makers to account. The result is that policy makers' pursuit of their own welfare drives a wedge between the programs citizens enjoy and the price they pay for them.

From a citizen's standpoint, policy makers' pursuit of their own interests reduces the efficiency with which tax revenue is converted into programs. This view, therefore, sees the downward pressure from interjurisdictional competition on tax rates as a good thing, because it "tames Leviathan"[2]—constraining policy makers from feathering their own nests at the expense of taxpayers and program beneficiaries. The straightforward policy implication of this view is that constraining interjurisdictional competition risks increasing the market power of rent-seeking policy makers, lowering welfare for the population as a whole, and potentially reducing the growth in the efficient provision of public programs over time.

The Tiebout model

Another view brings both costs and program benefits—or, more fully, the utility-enhancing outputs of regional governments—formally into the picture. The classic statement of this view is Tiebout's (1956) allusion to citizens' "voting with their feet." Under some reasonable assumptions, the possibility of movement across borders can be shown to exert a market discipline that induces jurisdictions such as subnational governments to move in the direction of welfare-optimizing equilibria; indeed, they may even do so as effectively as private markets. (See Appendix 1 for a more precise statement of Tiebout's informal hypothesis.)

This more sophisticated view predicts that these equilibria will not be those in which each subnational government adopts the same or similar combinations of taxes and programs. While the population at large is heterogeneous, it will tend to congregate in groups having broadly similar tastes.[3] As like-minded communities elect governments that pursue policies suitable to their collective tastes, the movement of people across borders will tend, through a natural sorting process, to produce communities with different combinations of taxes and public services.[4]

The capacity of the Tiebout model to produce definitive results in a static analysis depends on some key assumptions. One of them is that taxation is not distortionary, so that the level of taxation and the level of programs correspond parsimoniously in all jurisdictions. If taxes are distortionary, a given level of programs could imply a variety of tax levels. Residents might be better off in one community than in another notwithstanding their equal demands for (and receipt of) public services. Another assumption is that each community delivers services at least cost—and that cost must be the same in each community.[5] If not, a given level of taxes would imply a variety of outcomes on the program side. A third assumption—a corollary to the assumption of lump-sum taxation—is that there is no impact of programs on output (and from output back to taxes). Clearly, none of these assumptions holds in real life, which has led to skepticism about the Tiebout model's relevance to real-world policy decisions.

Even some indeterminacy in its static results, however, does not justify dismissing the dynamic forces the model predicts. As Oates points out, even where suboptimal equilibria appear to exist, they

> are not downward spirals "to the bottom"; they are suboptimal equilibria. This raises the obvious and important question of magnitude (which the "race to the bottom" terminology tends to obscure). The real issue here is the magnitude of the deviations (if any) from the efficient outcomes ... Is it a minor distortion or do these equilibria imply significant losses in social welfare? (Oates 1998: 18)

"Federalism as market"

It is finally useful to outline an extension of the Tiebout view that, at least informally, takes the parallel between competition among firms in markets and competition among jurisdictions further (Breton 1985; Robson 1992). This view sees governments of jurisdictions as analogous to owners or managers of firms that compete for customers—individuals and firms—by seeking to provide attractive combinations of programs and taxes. Competitive pressures not only keep agency problems in check but spur innovations as jurisdictions seek to deliver better programs at a given tax cost, lower taxes for a given level of programs, and so on.

Like the analysis of firms in a market setting, this view acknowledges the possibility of externalities that might make interjurisdictional agreements or measures taken by a national government attractive—measures to limit interjurisdictional flows of pollution,[6] for example. Consistent with its foundations in a Tiebout-like view of the world, however, this view tends to put the onus on those who would restrict competition to demonstrate that the benefits from doing so in a particular case would outweigh the costs of creating the opportunity for policy makers to exploit market power.

Central to this view is the dynamism of markets: like competition among firms to produce better products and services to attract customers, competition among jurisdictions to improve their technologies of taxation and program delivery will tend to improve the package residents receive over time.[7] While raising distortionary taxes may discourage local investment, for example, the need to retain tax base will focus expenditure on productive areas, with the possibility that welfare could be higher than would be the case if immobile capital lessened competition. Inter-jurisdictional competition thus raises the possibility of a "double dividend" in productivity: "Not only is the allocation of the private factors improved, there is also a productivity gain in the public sector. None the less, one does not find much about this hypothesis in the literature" (Rauscher 1998: 60).

In a "market" with a limited number of firms, there are many ways in which such competition can play out, many of which produce outcomes different from those of standard microeconomic theory. Mintz and Tulkens (1986) and Mintz and Smart (2001) analyze sales taxes and corporation income taxes in a strategic context; their main result is that it is possible to describe reasonable circumstances[8] where the outcome of the rate-setting game is provincial tax rates that are more divergent than in the absence of competition. In other words, in the presence of competition some provinces are able to improve local welfare by raising taxes rather than lowering them.[9]

More generally, jurisdictions may consider the current menu available to voters—including, implicitly, how capital moves in response to local taxes and benefits—but may also consider how other jurisdictions might change their offerings in response to choices made by the first mover. As in oligopoly situations, it is not difficult to imagine circumstances where such interactions impede the achievement of welfare maximizing outcomes. But, even in oligopoly situations, the pressures of technological change and exogenous shocks tend to undermine anti-competitive behaviour, with the result that productivity growth in more-concentrated sectors is not, over extended periods, systematically lower than in less-concentrated ones.

The important implication for competitive federalism, however, is the following: constraints on tax and expenditure competition seem likely to inhibit the innovation in service delivery that would obtain absent such constraints. And, since all taxes impose some efficiency costs, the competition to produce productivity-enhancing public services, which permit lower tax rates for a given level of services, becomes all the more important.

It is worth emphasizing that while observers concerned about problems arising from specific types of interprovincial competition, such as targeted subsidies or tax breaks intended to attract particular firms or types of business, may be able to make a strong case on the grounds of economic efficiency for limiting them, the test of demonstrating a favourable cost-benefit outcome is not an easy one to pass. The explicit parallel with competition in a dynamic market makes clear why this is so: when retailers, for example, compete with promotions that a central planner would see as distorting, such as loss-leaders, the presumption is that competitive pressure will make such phenomena transitory. Competition is multidimensional, involving numerous taxes, transfers, and services, many of which are multidimensional in their own right. It is far from clear that restricting competition along one dimension will necessarily improve the competitive dynamic in the system as a whole.[10]

There are at least three important differences between firms in a competitive market and governments in a federation that are potentially important for tax and program outcomes. One is that jurisdictions compete both for capital and labour. The lack of perfect alignment between their interests may militate against efficient solutions from labour's point of view.[11] (The analogy in the competitive market would be an agency problem on the consumer side, where the purchaser was not the final user.) This problem has given rise to the extensive literature on the impact of income-shifting on the happy outcomes predicted by the Tiebout model.

The second is that the "refereeing" process is less easy to design where competition among jurisdictions is at issue. Where market failures suggest a need to counteract market power or coordinate among individuals and firms, there are usually disinterested third parties to design and enforce the necessary regulations. When market power or coordination among governments is at issue, these third parties are not so readily found, since the governments themselves cannot be disinterested regulators.

Finally, competition among subnational jurisdictions generally has a "vertical" aspect. Where vertical tax interactions create spillovers—as, for example, when deductibility of a tax imposed by a subnational jurisdiction in calculating a firm's or an individual's tax obligations to a national government has implications for taxes and programs in other subnational jurisdictions—a challenge of either removing the provisions that create the externality or designing a coordination mechanism that limits its effects arises.

These differences between interfirm and intergovernment competition obviously matter for outcomes but they do not in any way undermine the competitive analogy.

Evidence

Although there is a large literature dealing with the theory and evidence on competition in other places and other jurisdictions, systematic evidence that Canadian provinces compete on fiscal offerings is scant.[12] What is currently available is discussed below.

To organize our investigation, we begin by looking at taxes. We first implicitly adopt the "race to the bottom" view that stresses downward pressure on tax rates—and, presumptively, spending—as policy makers respond to individuals' and firms' desires for lower costs. We then turn to look at taxes and spending together and ask about the overall balances of fiscal costs and benefits offered by Canada's provinces and what they tell us about interprovincial competition.

Do provinces compete to lower taxes?

Believers in a race to the bottom might feel that to ask this question is to answer it. Provinces certainly imply that they aim to provide tax rates lower than those of other provinces: comparative tables of provincial tax rates have been featured in budgets for many years.[13] But, evidence on outcomes is mixed.

Two recent papers have undertaken the task of providing an empirical analysis of provincial reactions to tax policy choices made in other provinces (Cavlovic and Jackson 2001; Hayashi and Boadway 2001). These papers focused on corporation taxes.[14] Using the ratio within a province of corporation tax revenue to corporation profits as a measure of corporate tax rates, both found evidence of strategic interactions between Ontario and Alberta, less evidence for Quebec, and little response among the Atlantic provinces.

It is hard, however, to know how much to make of these results. Average tax rates calculated in this way give a partial picture that is hard to interpret.[15] Average rates may reveal something historical about the incentives facing firms with activities in different provinces and which are governed by the profit allocation formula.[16] But, the critical decisions affecting resource allocation—the locations of physical investment (and employment)—will depend on marginal effective tax rates (METRs) on capital investment, which depends not only on corporate income tax rates and base definitions but also on the rates and bases for other taxes, such as taxes on paid-up capital and labour. These problems and other issues such as omitted variables, endogeneity, and difficulty in interpreting time-lags make us doubtful of the capacity of existing models to capture the full range of strategic interactions among provinces.[17]

Actual statutory corporate tax rates can move us a very small step closer to the variable of interest. What do the data on trends in provincial tax rates and firms' investment behaviour suggest?

The first part of our exercise links changes in provincial statutory corporate income tax rates (trends in sector-weighted statutory rates are shown in figure 1) with inter-provincial differences in the growth rate of reported corporation profits expressed in constant dollars per capita. The procedure is a simple bivariate panel of provincial annual data for the period from 1981 to 1999; we find in a simple panel model of provincial differences that falling statutory rates are significantly associated with rising real per-capita corporation profits.[18] This negative relationship, we assert, indicates merely that provinces are indeed under pressure to attract or maintain the corporation tax base or that provinces compete successfully (or not) for the corporation income tax base.[19, 20]

The second part ideally would use a similar procedure to examine the effects of changes in provincial all-in METRs on the growth of provincial constant-dollar net business sector capital stock per working-age resident.[21] Here a negative relationship could indicate provinces competing for shares of tangible capital investment. Absent year-by-year estimates of those METRs, we use the same weighted statutory rates as above, on the assumption that they move in the same direction as would the METRs.[22] We find, for the period from 1976 to 2001, a significantly negative relationship between these rates and the growth of net capital stock per capita (see figure 2 for a plot outlining the historical relationship). We find further reassurance in Mintz and Smart's (2001) result from microdata that shows multijurisdictional entities[23] to report profits in a manner apparently very responsive to local statutory tax rates on corporation income.

We round out the picture with a look at personal income taxes, specifically all-in METRs for employment income (in the hands of adults, weighted by income) by province by year (see figure 3).[24] We use the same bivariate panel approach as above, with changes in METRs "explaining" growth in real per-capita personal income. The relationship is significantly negative over the period from 1984 to 1999 and robust across a variety of specifications. The implication we draw is that tax-cutting provinces do better than others at retaining and attracting the personal income tax base, which we cautiously take to be some evidence of competition occurring.

Figure 1: Trends in "weighted" statutory CIT rates

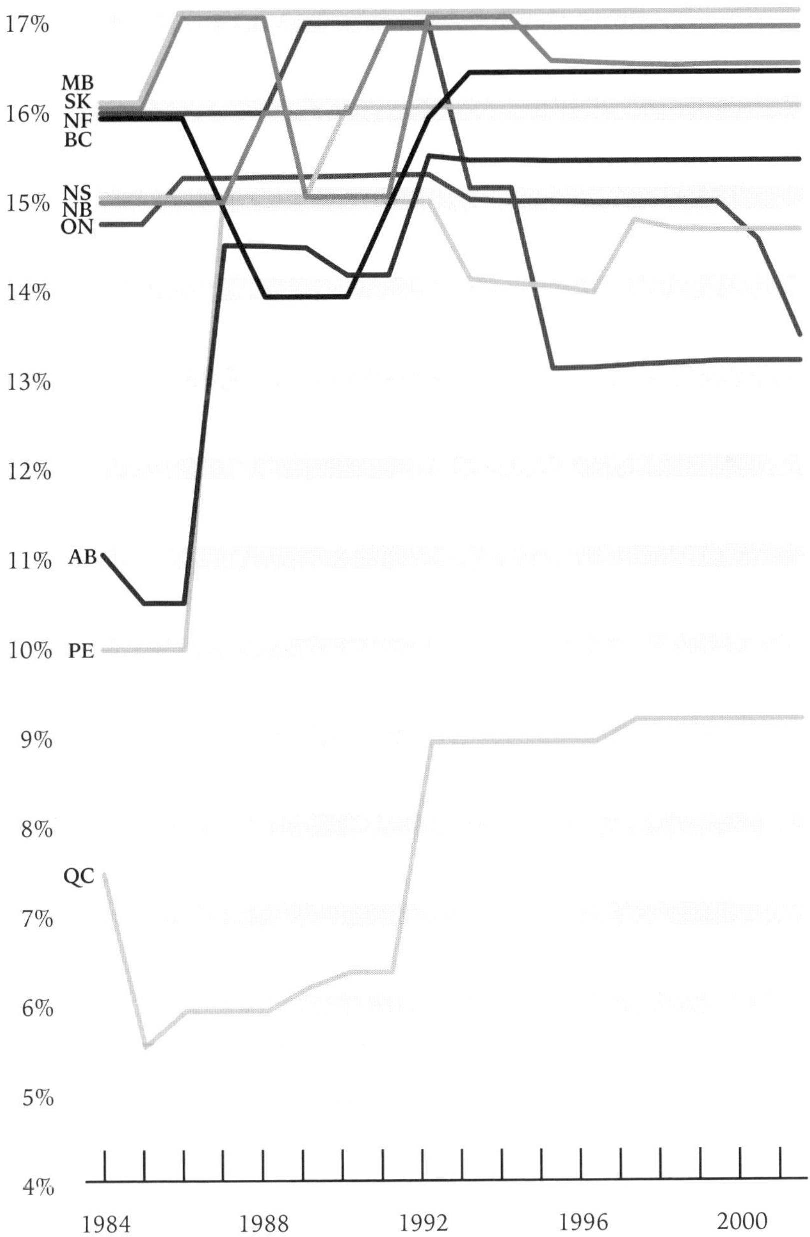

Source: Figures derived from the International Tax Program at the Rotman School of Business, University of Toronto.

Figure 2: Growth in provincial capital stock and historical CIT rates

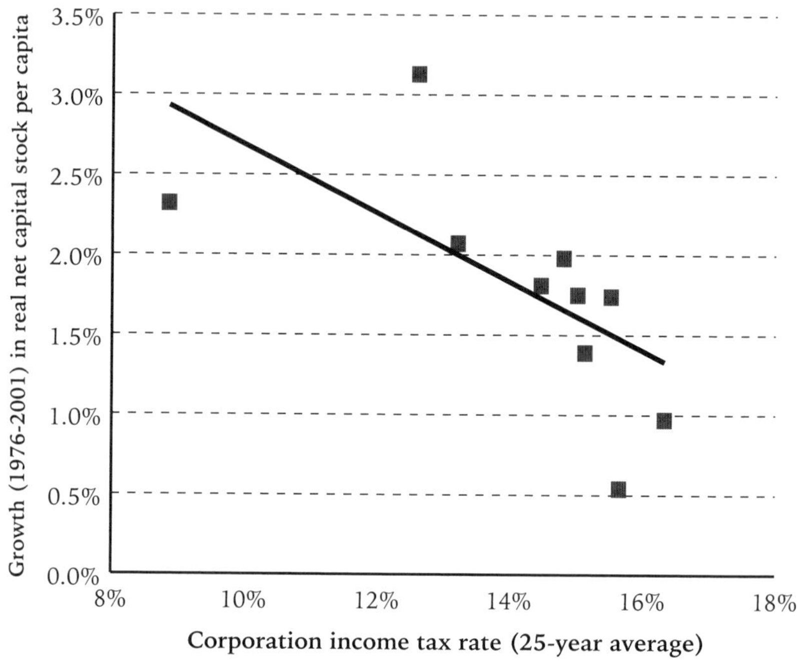

Source: Statistics Canada, CANSIM and the C.D. Howe Institute.

Do provinces compete on the total mix of taxes and programs?

Identifying or empirically specifying fiscal competition is difficult because taxes and spending are clearly jointly determined, leading to problems of endogeneity in the specification of models and likely bias in results. Another point worth emphasizing is that identifying causes of convergence in tax, transfer, or service policy among the provinces is always difficult: in some cases, interprovincial agreements or federal policies are undoubtedly important; in others, competition may be inducing "law of one price" convergence; in others, similarities in the preferences of the population may be the most important factor.

When it comes to overall provincial spending, the first thing the data make obvious is the absence of a race to the bottom. Real per-capita spending has shown no sign of withering away: constant-

Figure 3: Average METRs by province

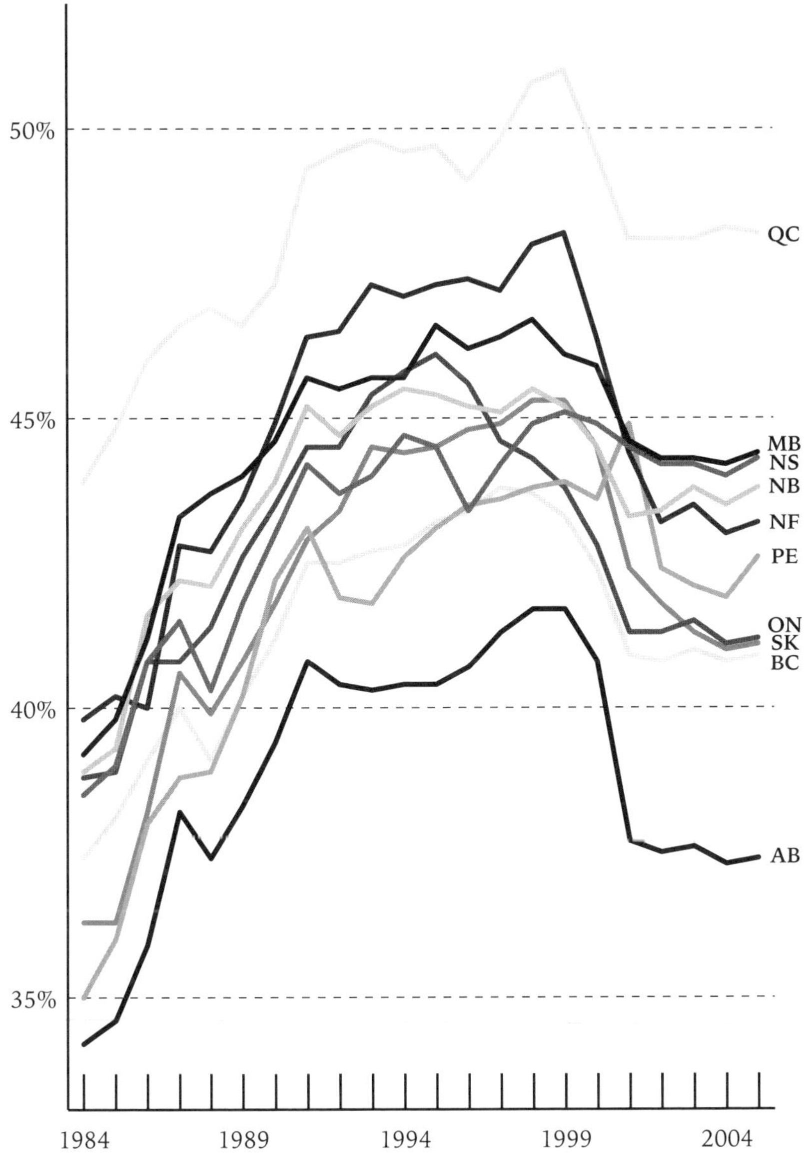

Source: C.D. Howe Institute, via Statistics Canada's Social Policy Simulation Database and Model, Release 8.1. Responsibility for the results and their interpretation lies with the authors.

dollar spending per capita in fiscal 2000 was above the level prevailing in 1989 through 1991 (see figure 4) and stood only modestly below the plateau running from 1992 through 1995. In an illustration of provincial spending on categories that could be defined as in-province public goods and publicly provided private goods (other categories fit less well in the Tiebout framework), a similar overall pattern would stand out: flatness and no downward spiral.

This, we argue, is circumstantial evidence supporting our claim that demand characteristics and institutional factors place a floor under provincial spending. The intuition was given by Tiebout: the import of the fact that the goods and services provided by provincial and local governments are publicly provided private goods is that those governments behave very much like private markets. And, to the extent that collective provision of public goods is considered, interprovincial competition helps deliver market-like quan-

Figure 4: Total provincial revenue and expenditure ($1992 per capita)

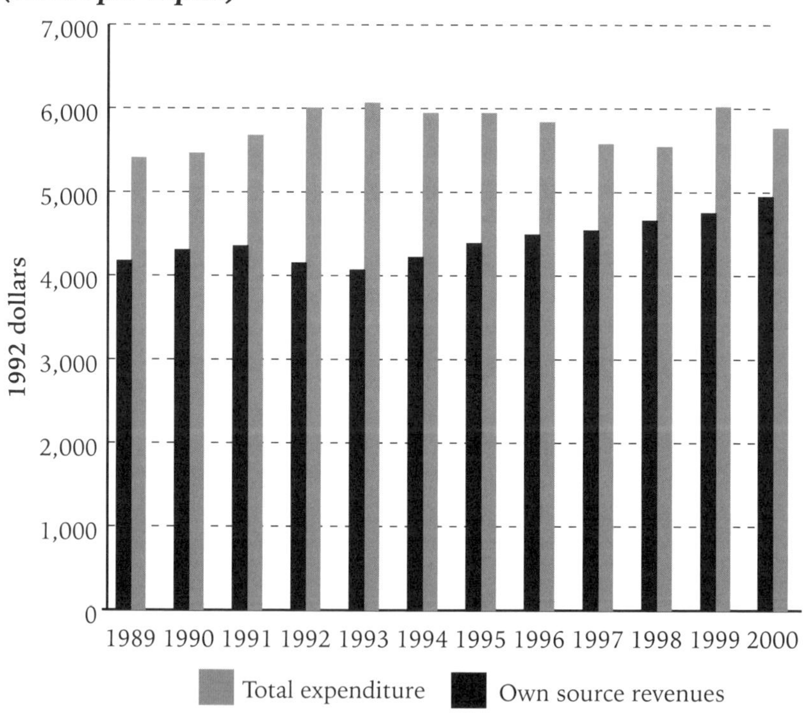

Source: Statistics Canada, CANSIM and the C.D. Howe Institute.

tities and qualities. This is to say that there are key forces encouraging provincial policy makers to deliver services that voters demand and are demonstrably willing to pay for. In the Tiebout framework, what is needed is simply enough different regions and low enough mobility costs for this market discipline to work.

Conundrums

A straightforward observation that follows from the foregoing discussion is that what is not broken does not need fixing: mobile firms and individuals demand a range of services and naturally want them delivered at minimum cost. Actual and potential mobility disciplines governments' spending and taxing behavior. That said, however, there are good and bad aspects of competition, and restraints thereon, that deserve discussion.

Can we distinguish "good" and "bad" competition?

From a normative point of view, "good competition" is whatever is required to deliver market-like outcomes that optimize social welfare. On the other hand, "bad competition" may involve tax arrangements that exploit the non-identity of interest between capital and labour as well as competition that produces externalities such as federally mediated tax spillovers or inadequate investment in areas such as pollution abatement, education, and health.

Among the examples of unhealthy tax competition frequently cited are efforts to "export" taxes through, say, unitary corporate-tax provisions or efforts to draw particular types of investment into a jurisdiction by sector-specific tax breaks. Both of these might be seen as giving rise to an agency problem where the "buyer" of a particular service from a jurisdiction is not the ultimate consumer—though, interestingly, these two examples are opposites in that the former presumes that labour is buying an arrangement that is disadvantageous to capital, whereas the latter presumes the opposite.

These concerns are blunted by consideration of the dynamics of competition. Take, for example, an obvious sector-specific measure: Ontario's research employee stock-option credit, intended to relieve the provincial tax burden on capital gains arising from stock options held by employees of Ontario-based high-tech companies. This is a complex and provincially divisive measure, which arguably would cause interprovincial misallocation of human and financial resources and which would not happen in a fully coordinated system. To the extent that the measure steers resources away from jurisdictions where their exploitation may be more valuable,[25] the distortion could reduce the net welfare of Canada. Generally available tax reductions would be more conducive to welfare maximization, simply because they are less likely to distort resource allocation across sectors and less likely to induce rent seeking.[26]

Yet, these considerations are not enough for a conviction. If Ontario is simply competing for business in the way any commercial entity might, the fact that it wins that business is no evidence of welfare loss and, certainly, there is no net loss if the national supply of capital is fully elastic. Ontario residents may value certain types of activity more than residents of other provinces. Even if a static analysis reveals an interprovincial misallocation of capital as a result such policies (and small open-economy assumptions do not entirely hold), moreover, dynamic considerations may indicate that allowing such competition produces better welfare outcomes in the long run than not allowing it. A federal system cured of presumptively excessive competition may house less happy residents than one suffering from the disease.

Frameworks for tax competition

The case for encouraging, rather than discouraging, competition seems ironclad. Yet, why have there been persistent arguments in the European Union, for example, for tax harmonization and program coordination? The answer must be either that support for tax harmonization in the European Union is based on a crude belief, without solid empirical foundation, in a "race to the bottom" or that it derives much of its impetus from a desire of policy makers (equivalent to the managers of firms in our analogy) to widen their scope for self-serving behaviour.

The Canadian case for further tax harmonization should be informed by Baldwin and Krugman's (2000) critique of the case for tax harmonization within the European Union. Their model sees member countries as constituting a more-industrialized core, with high taxes and high social spending, and a less-industrialized periphery with less of each. Some firms continue to locate in the high-tax core because they benefit there from tightly integrated production arrangements and product markets; other firms locate in the periphery because they do not need the core's facilities but are unlikely to fare well with higher taxes. In this situation, the core would not necessarily benefit from lower taxes and the periphery certainly would not benefit from higher ones.[27]

As to the "bad competition" mentioned above, there exists a framework within the guidelines of the Canada Customs and Revenue Agency (CCRA, formerly Revenue Canada) for administering provincial taxes that, in principle, should avoid the worst cases (see Appendix 2). The CCRA's stated unwillingness to collect taxes, even for a fee, where those taxes run counter to the "economic union criteria," is intended to deal with just this problem.

Our concern with relying on the guidelines lies not only with the problem that deciding what offends the criteria might be unclear; the larger concern is that the newly independent tax collection agency has an incentive to implement every provincial program it is offered. The reason is the usual incentive to build an empire that confronts every regulated monopolist. Our concern is deepened by the fact that the agency's tax collection machinery almost surely has efficiencies from scale: it may be cost effective to collect disparate and disjointed taxes on behalf of a province in situations where it would not be cost-effective for the province to so itself. The presumed and undesired outcome would be a fragmented and distortionary provincial tax base with exorbitant compliance costs. There is no ready solution for this difficulty other than light on the decision making and scrutiny from all sides.

Yet, given the thrust of this chapter, it would be inappropriate to place heavy emphasis on this concern over balkanization of provincial tax codes. The alternative—strong central control or coordination of the tax base—would discourage innovation in tax design and would not necessarily lead to improved welfare outcomes.

This last point seems poignantly clear in the small tempest over capital tax deductibility. It is a commonplace in the literature that tax exportation is one source of externalities and that when taxes paid to one jurisdiction are deductible in determining liability in another, a certain amount of tax exporting will occur. When provincial capital taxes are deducted in determining taxable income, but before the income allocation formula is applied, there is such an interprovincial spillover. Importantly, the tax collection agreements that currently coordinate most corporate and personal taxes in Canada are an obstacle to addressing this problem. Only because Alberta's corporation income tax stands outside the agreements has Alberta been able to contemplate ending provincial capital tax deductibility. Most other provinces have no such freedom. If spillovers are a problem, eliminating the provisions that cause them is likely a more effective response than designing new coordination mechanisms whose benefits in mitigating the spillovers may be small in comparison to their competition-restraining costs.

Frameworks for program competition

The preceding discussion makes plain that Canadians should be skeptical about the need to gird against competition in taxes or spending. Yet, as noted at the outset, it is a matter of federal policy that a "race to the bottom" in taxes and spending exists and necessitates the Social Union Framework Agreement (SUFA). A position paper from federal ministers Stephane Dion and Anne McLellan in February 1999 defended the SUFA's spending incentives—matching grants under federal/provincial shared-cost programs—on the grounds that they would "inhibit any pressures for a 'race to the bottom' in social programs and services for Canadians" (Dion and McLellan 1999). Under the SUFA, Ottawa and the provinces would agree on new programs in areas such as health and education and, if a given province already had programs working in the agreed area, they would still get federal money if they agreed to spend more money in what is called a "related area."

The analogy between competition within a federation and in a market points out problems with this approach. With matching federal dollars, provinces are intended to perceive a marginal cost of public funds that stands at half of the marginal benefit and, therefore, to spend on programs they otherwise would not fund. Likewise, since an extra dollar of spending can be financed with 50 cents in tax revenue, provinces are encouraged to raise taxes where they otherwise would not.[28] In other words, matching funds would sever the link between marginal revenue and marginal spending, a link that is central to the dynamics of competition.

Another way to look at the impact is as a lowered reward for innovation. Provincial technology improvements or innovation in management techniques, in order to avoid 50 cents of provincial spending, would need to deliver a dollar's worth of economies—a provincial initiative that would cut the cost of a program by less than a dollar would save the province less than 50 cents.

All in all, the requirement that money be spent on the federal or similar program undermines competitive federalism in general and, at the risk of repetition, reduces provincial accountability in matching taxes and spending. This seems conclusively to indicate that SUFA-like arrangements to reduce tax competition are hard to justify from a public finance perspective.

Concluding thoughts

A model that treats provinces as analogous to firms competing for customers in a market setting highlights key positive and normative features of interprovincial fiscal competition. At a moment in time, the dynamics of competition for households and business combined with heterogeneous preferences of provincial populations mean that there will be a range of tax rates and spending among the provinces between loose ceilings and loose floors. Over time, the positions of individual provinces within that range will change and the ceilings and floors may move, but the primary driver for those movements is the response of provincial policy makers to changing desires of their actual and potential populations as regards the fiscal mix.

From this perspective, advocacy of measures to restrain fiscal competition carries an onus of proof. Blunting the incentives to compete on tax rates through Equalization or to compete on program offerings through federal mandates and tied-funding arrangements risks exacerbating the agency problem that inhibits the translation of provincial voters' preferences into provincial policy.

Where clear externalities exist, such as would arise from inadequate provincial investment in pollution abatement, education, or disease control, for example, there is a well-grounded case for interprovincial coordination or the involvement of the federal government.

On the other hand, however much a cut in tax rates in one province may inconvenience the government of a neighbouring province, the competitive-market analogy clearly points to the existence of benefits to citizens generally that outweigh the inconvenience—there is no externality and no case for intergovernmental agreement or federal control.

The possibility exists that constraining competition in areas where there may be negative externalities—such as poaching of tax bases—would produce healthy outcomes. Yet, despite the possibility that targeted provincial subsidies and tax breaks might distort the allocation of resources within Canada considered in a static framework, the competitive-market analogy makes clear the difficulty of distinguishing situations that warrant a national response from those that are simply individual steps in a fiscal competition that, over time, produces incremental improvements in the balance of costs and benefits enjoyed by citizens everywhere.

Appendix 1: The Tiebout hypothesis

Myrna H. Wooders gives succinctly the hypothesis and the fiscal implication:

> The Tiebout Hypothesis asserts that, in economic situations where it is optimal to have many jurisdictions offering competing packages of public goods, the movement of consumers to jurisdictions where their wants are best satisfied and competition between jurisdictions for residents will lead to near-optimal, "market-like" outcomes. A jurisdiction (or club) is a group of individuals who collectively provide public goods for themselves exclusively (the public goods are local). Tiebout also suggested that individuals would sort into taste-homogeneous jurisdictions ... [T]he fiscal externality problem appears to be that, in Tiebout economies, it is optimal to tax players, including firms, for their external effects. If jurisdictions try to tax players in excess of the external effects they impose, there is a potential for profitable secession or opting out. Because of the assumed mobility of players in Tiebout economies, the redistribution implicit in such taxation cannot be sustained. (Wooders 1999: 10585)

The assumptions (mainly from Blankart and Borck 2000)

1 Consumers are completely mobile and move to the jurisdiction that best satisfies their preferences.

2 Consumers are fully informed about communities' taxes and supply of public goods and move in response to differences in taxes or spending levels.

3 There are a large number of communities among which consumers may choose.

4 Individuals live on dividend income, so there is no requirement that individuals live and work in the same jurisdiction.

5 Governments use lump-sum taxes or user charges to finance public services.

6 There are no interjurisdictional spillovers; that is, public goods are purely local public goods.

7 The average cost per person of providing public goods to the population is a U-shaped function of the number of residents.

8 Communities attract residents exactly until the optimal city size—i.e., the minimum per-capita cost—is reached.

Relaxing assumption 5, given that taxes in practice are distortionary, is the most common exercise in Tiebout-type analysis and yields some interesting results. One is that that high demanders of public goods should be especially careful to choose tax mixes that are likely to be relatively efficient: this point is sometimes used to explain heavy use of consumption taxes in many European countries, wherein economic performance has been reasonable notwithstanding high overall tax burdens relative to countries that rely more heavily on income taxes. Another example, offered by Brueckner (2000), takes the preceding point to its logical end: high demanders of public services, given distortionary capital taxation, will live in communities whose high tax rates inhibit growth of the tax base (put another way, a persistently low tax base necessitates high rates to finance a given level of services). In this example, heavy demanders of public services would be better off if their jurisdiction were financed through head (poll) taxes. One extension to the provincial case is that provinces should rely more on relatively non-distorting consumption taxes than on the other available bases.

Appendix 2: The guidelines of the Canada Customs and Revenue Agency for administering provincial tax measures

The guidelines below are quoted from Canada Customs and Revenue Agency 2002.

> ***Minimum criteria***
> The Agency will administer provincial/territorial taxes if:
>
> - they are legally valid;
> - they adhere to basic principles such as those that do not jeopardize the system of self-assessment, do not involve double taxation, and that contain generally accepted standards for fairness; and
> - the Agency and the province/territory can arrive at mutually acceptable contractual arrangements.
>
> ***Economic union criteria***
> The economic union criteria establish conditions under which provincial/territorial tax programs will **not** be administered by the Agency, even if they meet the above minimum criteria. They also determine whether or not provinces/territories will be charged for the administration of a provincial/ territorial tax measure.
>
> - Discriminatory locational incentives—The Agency will not administer measures that provide a locational incentive, which discriminates between provincial and territorial residents and non-residents. However, the Agency may administer locational tax incentives available to all taxpayers on a non-discriminatory basis.
> - Non-harmonized measures The Agency may administer these on a full cost-recovered basis.[29] They would include non-harmonized income tax credits or other alterations (*e.g.*, tax on income)[30] related to taxes administered under tax collection agreements. They also include other taxes, such as corpo-

rate income taxes or provincial and territorial retail sales taxes that are not harmonized with the counterpart federal tax.

- Fully harmonized taxes—The Agency would administer these at no cost to the province/territory (based on agreements between the Minister of Finance and the province/territory). They are defined as taxes that fully replicate the federal tax and include income taxes now under tax collection agreements (the existing tax-on-tax system) and harmonized sales tax. They also include certain income tax credits that the federal government now ad-ministers on a fee basis but which are fully harmonized, such as the political contribution tax credit.

Notes

1 When it is competition among jurisdictions within a country that is at issue, the view that such competition needs to be restrained often draws additional force from fears that subnational jurisdictions will be more responsive to business pressures than national governments or from an expansive view of entitlements to government benefits attendant to citizenship that only strong central governments can defend. Noel 1999: 197–98 provides a useful survey of such views.

2 See Edwards and Keen 1996.

3 In this respect, the Tiebout model contrasts with much of the tax competition literature, which has tended to focus on mobility of tax bases rather than mobility of individuals (Brueckner 2000) and typically assumes identical tastes among individuals. Taking both aspects together has been an important extension of the fiscal competition literature (Henderson 1994, Wilson 1997) and below we draw on this work.

4 An implication of this view is that the separate communities ought to be more homogenous than the overall population. Given the multitude of dimensions along which individuals can differ, this implication is hard to test empirically. For an unfavourable judgment, see Rhode and Strumpf 2000.

5 The specific Tiebout assumptions are that the average cost per person of providing public goods is a U-shaped function of the number of residents and that communities attract residents until the minimum per-capita cost is reached. If there were scale economies to be had, the optimal size of a jurisdiction would become infinitely large, with diseconomies of scale leading to the opposite result.

6 Such as observed in interstate agreements on Chesapeake Bay and international agreements on the Great Lakes basin.

7 This aspect of competition is too little explored in the literature. Wilson 2000 is a notable, if partial, exception.

8 Such as where the demand for local public goods is highly inelastic; another likely possibility is where governments are able to tax inframarginal locational rents.

9 And, the implication of this is that in a Nash model of provincial tax competition, finding a positive slope on a given reaction function is not necessarily evidence that there is tax competition among the provinces; the slope might be negative or indeterminate and yet "competition," broadly writ, would still be the appropriate description of the continuing dynamic. It follows, therefore, that we might not recognize tax competition when we see it or might claim to see it when it is not necessarily there.

10 Huber 1999 makes the point that depending, for example, on the wealth distribution within states, coordinating capital tax levels among states may leave overall welfare higher, the same, or lower than without such coordination.

11 As would be the case if revenue-maximizing or rent-seeking policy makers focused on productivity-enhancing public expenditures, to the detriment of spending that benefitted labour as opposed to capital. The possibility of "too much" spending in support of capital investment is raised in Keen and Marchand 1996; the outcome is easy to enough to picture in the context of revenue-maximizing public policy makers.

12 An important (related) paper is the analysis of municipal behaviour by Brett and Pinkse 2000 .

13 A recent instance: *Province of Alberta Budget 2000*: 98–102.

14 The former paper also looked for competition on personal income taxes but the data suggested few conclusions.

15 Among the numerous difficulties is loss carry-forwards that can produce fluctuations in effective average rates while having nothing to do with provincial tax policy choices or current economic conditions. See Mintz 2000 for a more complete list of complications.

16 See Mintz and Smart 2001. The allocation of corporate taxes on multiprovince firms among provinces is governed by a formula making reference to shares of sales and employment, which limits, though it does not eliminate, opportunities for income-shifting.

17 While there has been some theoretical work on commitment (time-consistent policy choices), there have been no empirical studies dealing with announcement effects. For example, Nash and Stackelberg models that have been tested have used one-year lags as indicative of the action horizon; but it seems very unlikely that recent choices in Alberta and Ontario have not been affected by their own and others' announced plans for future years.

18 The relationship holds across a number of specifications.

19 This result is consistent with the finding in Bird and Mintz 2000 that Quebec, among all provinces, has an extremely high ratio of corporation taxable income to assets, which is also consistent with the notion that in Quebec, labour is relatively less mobile than capital, as compared with other provinces.

20 If Canada and, therefore, the provinces are governed by the usual small open-economy assumptions, this is clearly welfare-enhancing, as capital (or, at least, corporate profit) is drawn in from the world at large. If there is a fixed amount of capital available over the relevant time scale, the gain in activity is not necessarily net welfare-enhancing—we need to know what is happening on the expenditure side.

21 We use the measure assuming straight-line depreciation (i.e., unpublished Statistics Canada data for constant dollar net capital stock by province).

22 The assumption is reasonable to the extent, for example, that inter-provincial differences between corporation income tax bases are small.

23 Where those firms are not required to allocate income according to formula.

24 Derived via Statistics Canada's Social Policy Simulation Database and Model, Release 8.1; responsibility for the results and interpretation lies with the authors.

25 Again, assuming Canada's economy is not fully open or the national supply of capital is somehow fixed.

26 Indeed, rent-seeking is a generic problem for regimes with high tax rates and exemption mechanisms (like Ontario's credit) that shrink the base. When rates are low and the base broad, there is less return to lobbying for exemptions for any particular activity.

27 It may be useful to contemplate this model in the context of congestion. If these external costs increase with density—say, as roadways approach capacity—a higher-than-otherwise tax rate may be necessary in the core region, so that firms do not locate there rather than the periphery. But, this analysis does not force any conclusion other than that provinces should not lower tax rates beyond what is commensurate with the capital investment (density) they wish to build up. On the other hand, constraints on tax competition should not force tax rates higher than commensurate with province's desired growth target. Ludema and Wooton 2000 shows the link between agglomeration forces, economic integration, reduced tax competition, and higher tax rates.

28 This is an apt point at which to observe that provinces that receive Equalization may not engage in tax competition in same way that non-recipients do. One reason may be that provinces that do not compete (do not protect or enhance their tax bases) are compensated for their action or inaction by way of grants under that program, which are explicitly tied to differences in tax bases; see Smart 1998. If provincial policy makers are relieved of full responsibility for raising the revenue they spend, moreover, the equalization program is another wedge creating room for provincial policy makers to seek rents.

29 Supplementary materials attempt to distinguish between nearly harmonized measures, for which the CCRA would charge the incremental cost of administration, and nonharmonized measures, which would be billed at the average or full cost of administration.

30 In fact, tax on income may fall in the nearly or fully harmonized category, and thus be charged at a lesser rate.

References

Baldwin, Richard E., and Paul Krugman (2000). Agglomeration, Integration and Tax Harmonization. CEPR *Discussion Paper* 2630 (November). London: Centre for Economic Policy Research.

Bird, Richard, and Jack M. Mintz (2000). Tax Assignment in Canada: A Modest Proposal. In Harvey Lazar (ed.), *Toward a New Mission Statement for Canadian Fiscal Federalism* (Kingston: Institute for Intergovernmental Relations): 263–92.

Blankart, Charles B., and Rainald Borck (2000). Local Public Finance. Unpublished paper (January 31). Humboldt-Universität zu Berlin.

Breton, Albert (1985). Supplementary Statement. In Canada, Royal Commission on the Economic Union and Development Prospects for Canada, *Report,* vol. 3 (Ottawa: Supply and Services Canada): 486–526.

Brett, Craig and Joris Pinkse (2000). The Determinants of Municipal Tax Rates in British Columbia. *Canadian Journal of Economics* 33, 3 (August): 695–714.

Brueckner, Jan K. (2000). A Tiebout/Tax-Competition Model. *Journal of Public Economics* 77: 285–306.

Canada Customs and Revenue Agency (2002). *Provincial/Territorial Participation.* Digital document available at: http://www.ccra-adrc.gc.ca/agency/toc-4000-e.html (updated: 2002-01-04).

Cavlovic, Ann, and Harriet Jackson (2001). Bother Thy Neighbour? Intergovernmental Tax Interactions in the Canadian Federation. Working paper. Ottawa: Department of Finance.

Dion, Stéphane, and Anne McLellan (1999). *Collaborative Use of the Spending Power for Intergovernmental Tranfers* [sic]: *The Race to the Top Model.* Ottawa: Privy Council Office, Gov't of Canada. Digital document available at http://198.103.111.55/aia/.

Edwards, Jeremy, and Michael Keen (1996). Tax Competition and Leviathan. *European Economic Review* 40: 113–34.

Hayashi, Masayoshi, and Robin Boadway (2001). An Empirical Analysis of Intergovernmental Tax Interaction: The Case of Business Income Tax in Canada. *Canadian Journal of Economics* 34, 2 (May): 481–503.

Henderson, J. Vernon (1994). Community Choice of Revenue Instruments. *Regional Science and Urban Economics* 24: 159–83.

Huber, Bernd (1999). Tax Competition and Tax Coordination in an Optimum Income Tax Model. *Journal of Public Economics* 71: 441–58.

Keen, Michael, and Maurice Marchand (1997). Fiscal Competition and the Pattern of Public Spending. *Journal of Public Economics* 66: 33–53.

Ludema, Rodney D., and Ian Wooton (2000). Economic Geography and Fiscal Effects of Regional Integration. *Journal of International Economics* 52, 2 (December): 331–57.

Mintz, Jack M. (2000). A Eulogy for the Use of Average Tax Rates in Investment Equations. In J. Hines (ed.), *Studies in International Taxation* (Chicago: University of Chicago Press).

Mintz, Jack M., and Michael Smart (2001). Income Shifting, Investment and Tax Competition: Theory and Evidence from Provincial Taxation in Canada. 2001 Working Paper prepared for the conference on World Tax Competittion sponsored by the Office of Tax Policy Research and the Institute of Fiscal Studies (May 24/25, 2001). Toronto, ON: University of Toronto.

Mintz, Jack M., and Henry Tulkens (1986). Commodity Tax Competition between Member States of a Federation: Equilibrium and Efficiency. *Journal of Public Economics* 29: 133–72.

Noel, Alain (1999). Is Decentralization Conservative? Federalism and the Contemporary Debate on the Canadian Welfare State." In robert Young (ed.), *Stretching the Federation: The Art of the State in Canada* (Kingston: Institute for Intergovernmental Relations): 195–219.

Oates, Wallace E. (1998). Environmental Federalism in the United States: Principles, Problems, and Prospects. Unpublished paper (January). Department of Economics, University of Maryland.

Rauscher, Michael (1998). Leviathan and Competition among Jurisdictions: The Case of Benefit Taxation. *Journal of Urban Economics* 44: 59–67.

Rhode, Paul W., and Koleman S. Strumpf (2000). A Historical Test of the Tiebout Hypothesis: Local Heterogeneity from 1850 to 1990. NBER *Working Paper* No. 7946 (October). Cambridge, MA: National Bureau of Economic Research.

Rivlin, Alice (1992). *Reviving the American Dream: The Economy, the States, and the Federal Government.* Washington, DC: Brookings Institution.

Robson, William (1992). *Dynamic Tensions: Markets, Federalism, and Canada's Economic Future.* Toronto: CD Howe Institute.

Smart, Michael (1998). Taxation and Deadweight Loss in a System of Intergovernmental Transfers. *Canadian Journal of Economics* 31, 1 (February): 189–206.

Tiebout, Charles M. (1956). A Pure Theory of Local Expenditures. *Journal of Political Economy* 64: 416–24.

Wilson, John D. (1997). Property Taxation, Congestion, and Local Public Goods. *Journal of Public Economics* 64: 207–17.

Wilson, John D. (2000). Welfare-improving Competition for Mobile Capital. Unpublished paper (March). Department of Economics, Michigan State University.

Wooders, Myrna H. (1999). Multijurisdictional Economies, the Tiebout Hypothesis, and Sorting. *Proceedings of the National Academy of Sciences of the United States of America (PNAS)* 96 (September): 10585–88.

Taxation and foreign direct investment in Ireland

Brendan Walsh

During the 1990s, the Irish economy boomed. Rapid output and employment growth resulted in a sharp rise in the ratio of employment to population, which played a major role in closing the gap in living standards between Ireland and the rest of the European Union (EU). Substantial inflow of foreign direct investment (FDI)—mainly from the United States—reduced the economy's dependence on agriculture and low-productivity industries. The Irish economic success story has attracted considerable international interest. Even though the economy slowed dramatically in 2001, the transformation of the 1990s is still worthy of scrutiny to see what lessons can be learned. The focus of this paper is on the contributions of tax policies to the Irish economic renaissance.[1]

The record

Figure 1 shows the growth rates of GDP in Ireland and the EU since 1979. Since 1989, Ireland has consistently out-performed Europe. While Gross Domestic Product may overstate the economy's performance (see below), the growth rate has been unambiguously spectacular since 1994. This exceptional growth moved the coun-

Figure 1: Growth in Ireland and the EU since 1986

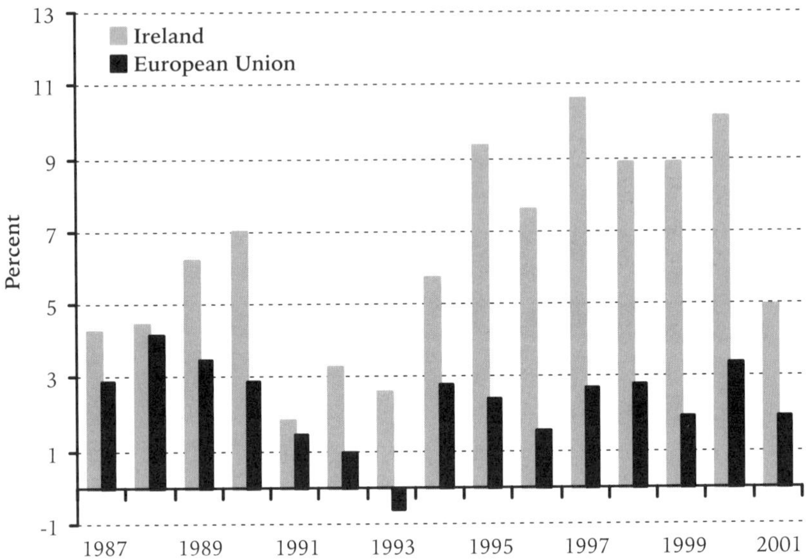

Source: Eurostat; Irish Central Statistics Office.

try quickly up in the EU living-standards league. Whereas in the mid-1980s Ireland was in much the same relative position as when the country joined the European Economic Community in 1973, by 1999 it was above the European average (figure 2). On a global basis, Ireland moved from about twenty-fourth among the major nations to ninth in 1999.

In view of Ireland's traditional concern with emigration and unemployment, the performance of the labour market deserves special attention. In fact, it is here that developments have been most dramatic. Figure 3 shows how the decline in employment in the early 1980s gave way to an extraordinary employment boom in the 1990s, when unparalleled rates of job creation were recorded. The number at work has risen by more than 40% since the mid-1980s, while there has been little net employment growth in the EU as a whole. Figure 4 shows how sharply the unemployment rate declined during the second half of the 1990s. The unemployment rate fell below 4% in 2001, leading to concerns that labour shortages would lead to a wage explosion. The reduction in the last half of 2001 in the growth rate eased these strains.

Figure 2: Real convergence

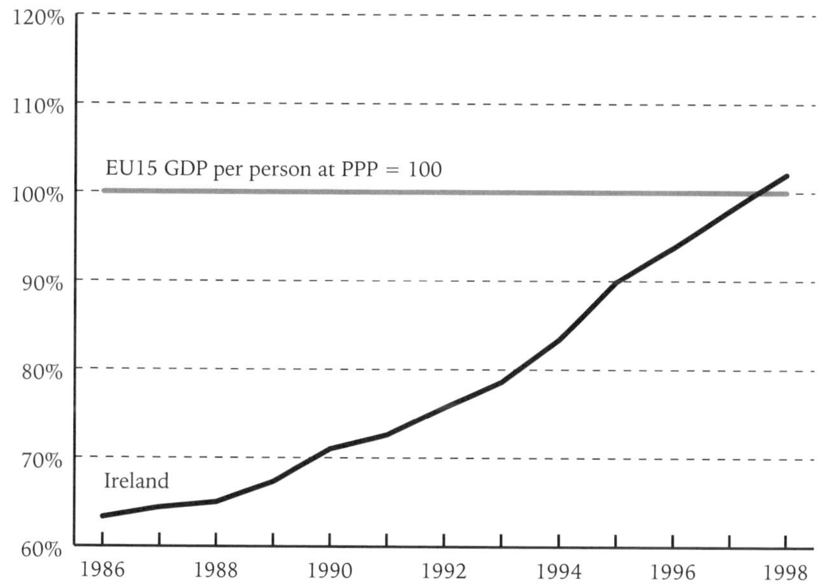

Source: Eurostat; Irish Central Statistics Office.

Figure 3: Employment growth

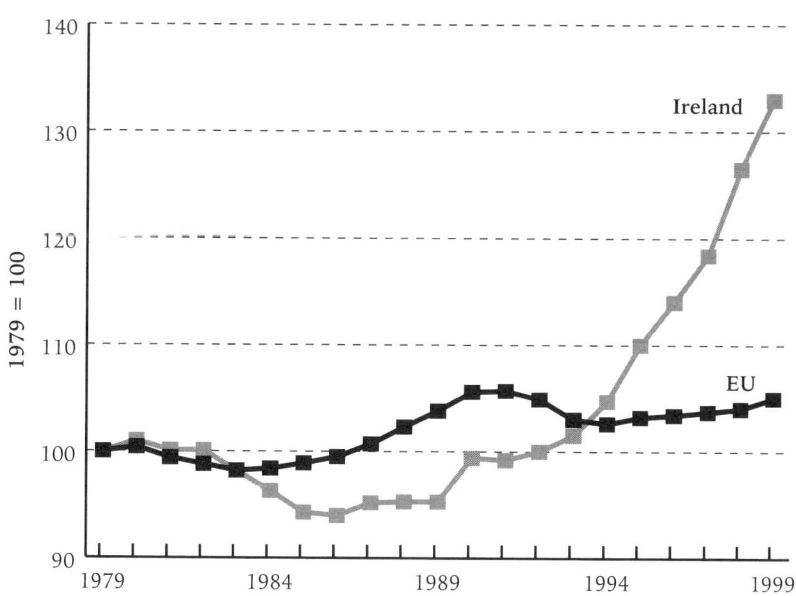

Source: Eurostat; Irish Central Statistics Office.

Figure 4: Unemployment rates in Ireland and the EU

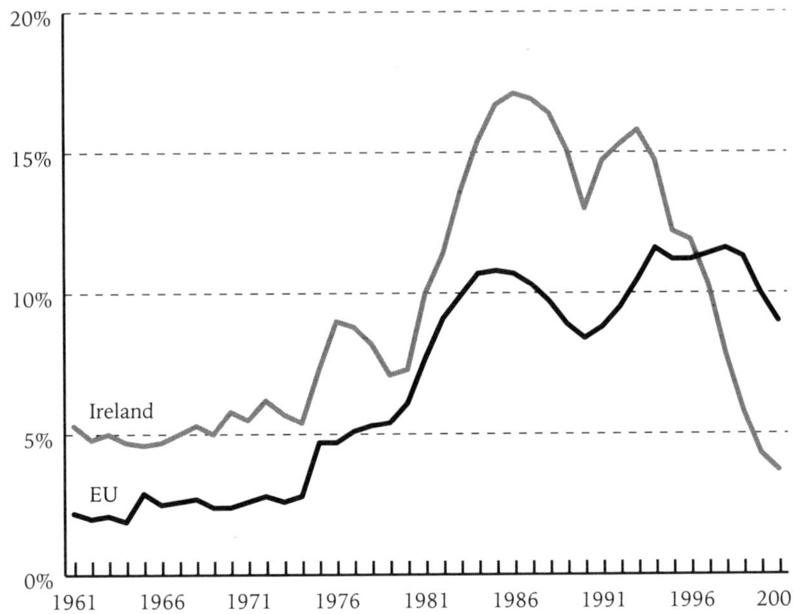

Source: Eurostat; Irish Central Statistics Office.

The most dramatic symbol of the change in the Irish labour market is replacement of the traditional stream of emigration by the highest net immigration rate in the EU (figure 5). Worries about emigration have been replaced by controversies over policies towards immigrants and asylum seekers from non-EU countries. Finally, the belated convergence of Ireland's birth rate to the European norm reduce the proportion of the population aged under 15 years from 33% in 1970 to 21% in 2001, while the share of the elderly in the population remained unchanged. The outcome of these developments was that the proportion of the total population in non-agricultural employment rose from 26% in 1971 to 42% in 2002.

To complete this glowing picture, the rapid growth has not been by achieved through fiscal irresponsibility or at the cost of high inflation. As the Irish growth rate rose above that of the rest of Europe, the inflation rate fell and the public finances improved steadily. The country easily met the criteria laid down in the Maastricht Treaty to adopt the new single currency—the euro—in Janu-

Figure 5: Net migration rate

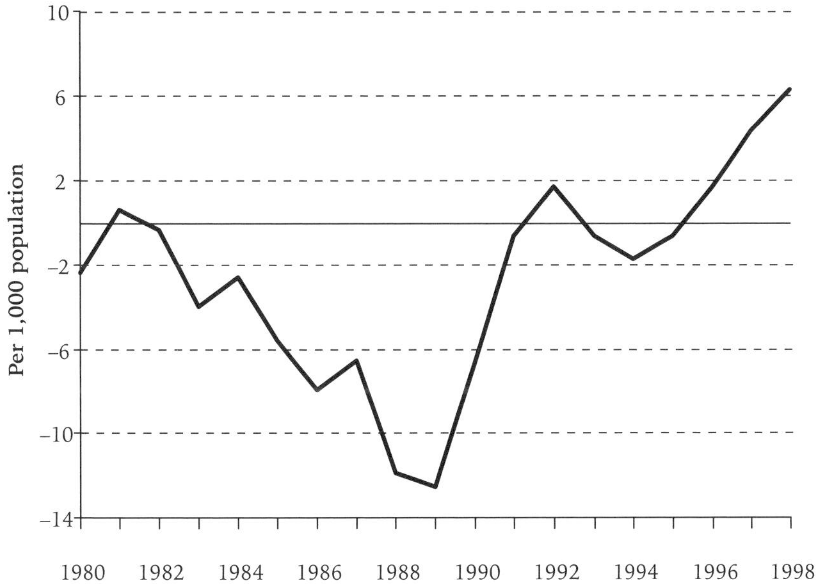

Source: Eurostat; Irish Central Statistics Office.

ary 1999. In fact, there was a greater need to fudge the criteria to allow countries such as Belgium, France, and Italy to join than there was for Ireland to be admitted. The speed with which the ratio of national debt to GDP fell during the 1990s confounded those who were so understandably depressed by its rapid rise in the first half of the 1980s (figure 6). True, Ireland has recorded relatively high inflation since 2000 due to the effects of a lower real interest rate and the weak euro as well as the rise in wages in the service sectors of the economy. A relatively relaxed view has been taken of the surprisingly high inflation rate in the belief that it is part of the country's adjustment to its new-found prosperity.

Macroeconomic preconditions

Irish commentators are agreed that the following broad developments should be included in the list of those that contributed to the recent success of the economy (Walsh 2000).

Figure 6: Ratio of debt to GDP

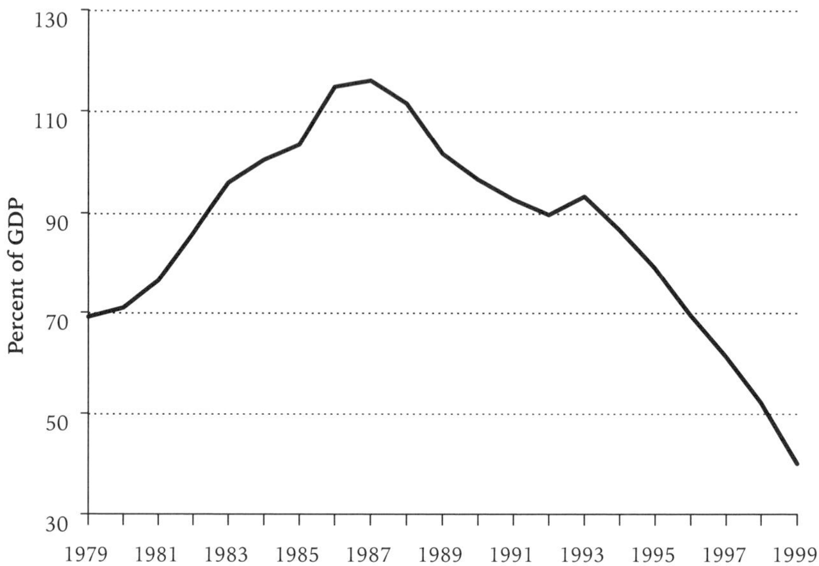

Source: Eurostat; Irish Central Statistics Office.

Fiscal stabilization

In the course of the 1980s, the country struggled to correct the major imbalances in the public finances inherited from the recklessness of the late 1970s, which required a major shift in resources from domestic absorption to net exports (see Walsh 1996). This painful adjustment process was largely completed by the late 1980s. (For a review of these developments, see Honohan 1999.)

During the first half of the 1980s, attempts to stabilize the public finances relied heavily on higher taxation. These met with only limited success as the tax based shrank due to soaring unemployment, higher emigration, increased cross-border shopping, and flight of capital. The economy seemed to be sinking under the stabilization effort. After 1987, the emphasis shifted. Public expenditure was pruned. Both current and capital spending by the government fell in nominal terms. The economy responded positively, entering a virtuous cycle as faster growth facilitated reductions in the burden of taxation. Some commentators have taken this as an illustration of economic expansion during fiscal austerity by government, with the positive effects of increased confidence on private spending more than offsetting any negative effects of the reduction in pubic spending. Although confidence did return as it became clear that the public finances were coming under control, favourable external developments and a competitive exchange rate were probably more important. At the end of the 1980s, the "Lawson boom" in the United Kingdom provided a stimulus to Irish exports. The employment boom it generated attracted large numbers of Irish emigrants to Britain, relieving pressure on the labour market. During the 1990s, as the American boom gathered pace, Ireland benefited from increased inflows of investment by sophisticated industrial and financial firms.

Aid from the European Union

Funds from the European Union (EU) have been proportionately more important in Ireland than in any other member state. One reason for this is that Ireland has benefited disproportionately from the Common Agricultural Policy since joining the EU in the 1970s. In addition, the country received special aid on joining the European Monetary System in 1979 and more money flowed in from the Cohesion, Regional, and Social Funds in the early 1990s. This last infusion helped to insulate Ireland from the global recession of the early 1990s.

It is generally believed that Ireland used aid from the EU effectively. Indeed, the process of applying for funding led to a marked improvement in the overall planning of Irish public spending. Net inflows from the EU peaked at about 5% of GDP in the early 1990s and are now declining steadily. After the next reapportionment of the EU aid budget, Ireland is likely to become a net contributor rather than one of the largest net recipients on a per-capita basis.

Exchange rate policy

In 1979, Ireland indicated its desire to join the new exchange rate arrangements in Europe even if this entailed breaking the link with sterling, as quickly proved necessary. In 1999, the new single European currency was adopted, thereby ending the life of the independent Irish pound introduced in 1927. It may be no coincidence that the boom really got underway shortly after the 10% devaluation of the Irish pound in the exchange rate mechanism of the European Monetary System in January 1993. The currency had fallen to a very a competitive level, especially relative to sterling, before it was finally converted to the euro in 1999.

The inflow of foreign direct investment

Although reliable data on flows and stocks of foreign direct investment (FDI) are not readily available, it seems that Ireland's share of the flow of FDI from the United States to the EU rose from 2% in 1987 to over 7% in 1993 (Barry 1999: figure 3.10). Several factors contributed to the increased inflow of FDI but from the perspective of the present publication it is important to note that no significant changes in the corporation tax (CT) regime occurred over this period.

The role of FDI in the growth of the Irish economy is illustrated by the fact that foreign-owned firms now account for about 47% of Ireland's industrial employment, 77% of net industrial output, and 83% of merchandise exports (figures 7 and 8). Foreign firms predominate in the International Financial Services Centre (IFSC), where over 7,000 people are now employed in back-office activities like routine data entry and processing and record keeping, and in higher value-added activities like treasury management, fund mamagement, and risk analysis in a designated area of Dublin. While output and employment in indigenous industrial and banking firms have grown in recent years, their relative importance in the total economy has declined. Several of the larger overseas companies employed over 3,000 people in Ireland. Virtually every major microelectronics and pharmaceutical firm in the world now has an Irish affiliate. Employment in these firms held up well during the American recession of 2001/2002. The resilience of the new industrial sectors is evidence of the profitability of Ireland as a location.

Explaining the success in attracting FDI

In view of the contribution made by foreign firms to the Irish boom, it is important to try to account for the country's attractiveness to FDI.

A European export platform

Since the completion of the EU's single market in the early 1990s, Ireland offered US firms a convenient platform from which to supply their European customers. While its peripheral island location added to transport costs, this disadvantage was not important for

Figure 7: Emploment in manufacturing

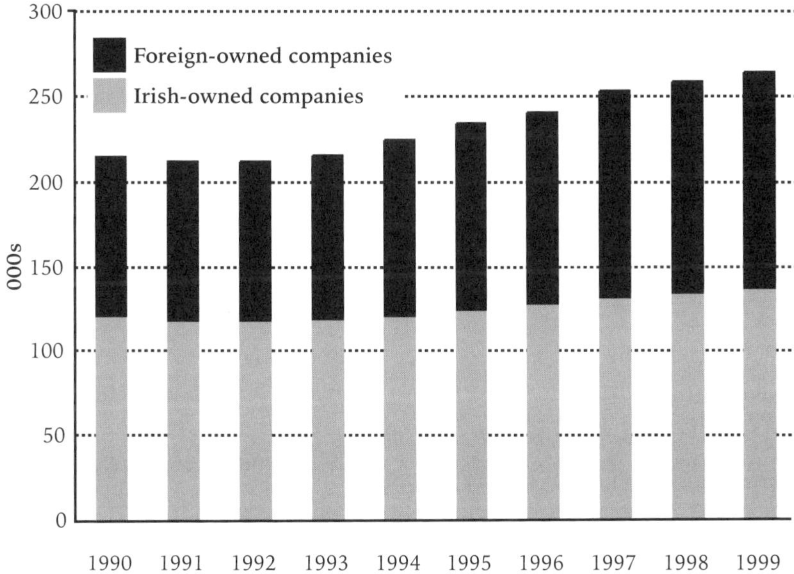

Source: Eurostat; Irish Central Statistics Office.

Figure 8: Employment in international services

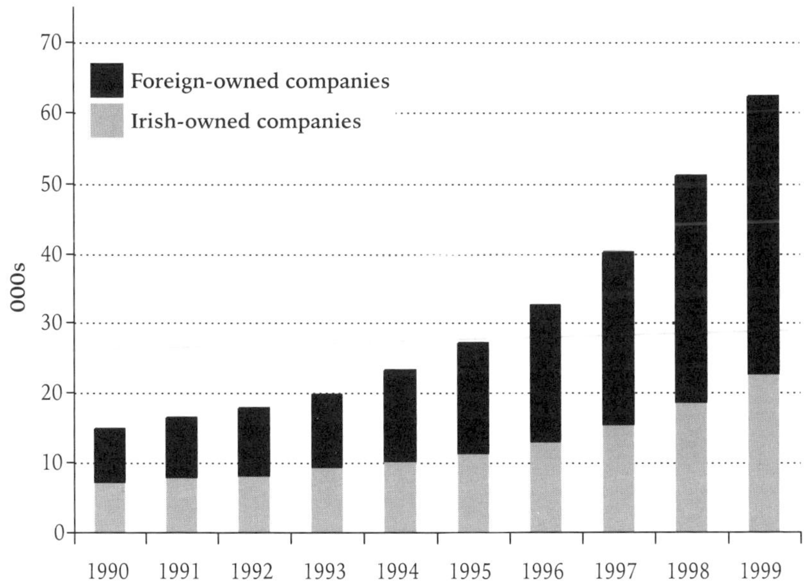

Source: Eurostat; Irish Central Statistics Office.

the very high value-added products in the electronics, pharmaceutical and financial services sectors where inward investment has been concentrated.

Favourable climate for FDI

Ireland has shown a consistently favourable attitude towards overseas investment since the 1960s. Among the inducements to firms to choose Ireland as their European location, the low rate of CT and liberal grants for fixed assets and training have been paramount. Ireland has the lowest rates of CT in the EU. This is true whether the comparison is based on the statutory rates or the effective rates (Nicodème 2001)—see figures 9 and 10. But, there were no changes in the tax system in the late 1980s that could be given credit for triggering the boom. Indeed, the effective CT rate actually increased in the 1980s (see below) so is not possible to invoke it as

Figure 9: Statuory corporation tax rates, 1990 and 2003

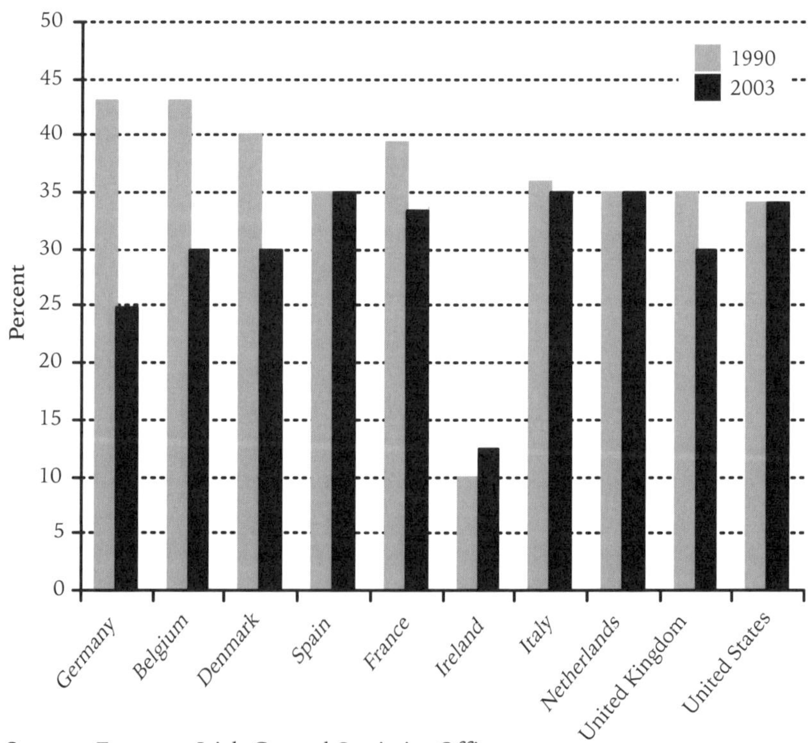

Source: Eurostat; Irish Central Statistics Office.

Figure 10: Effective corporation tax rates, 1995

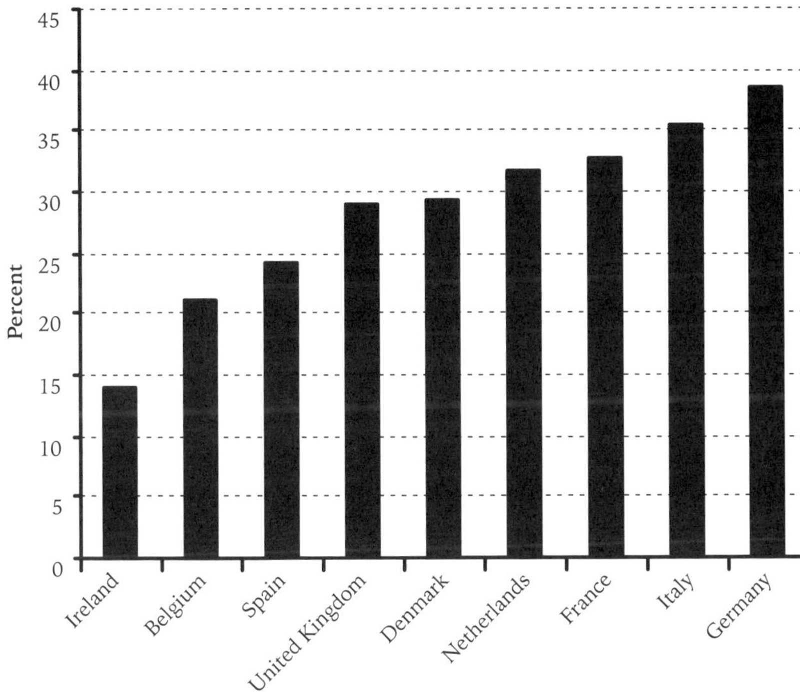

Source: Eurostat; Irish Central Statistics Office.

an explanation for the timing of the boom, even though its importance in the economy's longer-term success is not disputed. In fact, it is noticeable that previous studies do not explicitly mention the CT regime as an explanation for the increase in Ireland's share of American investment in the EU in the late 1980s (Barry, Bradley, and O'Malley 1999).

Industrial promotion

The main Irish industrial promotion agency—the Industrial Development Authority—has a long history of active encouragement of inward FDI. A gradual refinement of these policies led to more sophisticated targeting of overseas investment in the 1980s and 1990s. By trial and error, those industries were identified that were most likely to be attracted by the advantages that Ireland has to offer. Over time, the emphasis switched to subsidiaries of "high tech" industries with a focus on electronic engineering, pharmaceuticals, medical instrumentation, computer software, and some food processing sectors. The industries that came to Ireland appear to share a need for a ready supply of well-educated, flexible workers, and are structured so that they can reap maximum benefit from the low CT rate applied to manufacturing industry. As the former insistence on regional decentralisation was tacitly relaxed, cities like Dublin, Cork and Galway attracted significant clusters of firms in these industries.

Supply of low-cost labour

When asked about the key attraction of locating in Ireland, the "correct" answer for an industrialist to give should stress the importance of Ireland's plentiful supply of English-speaking, skilled labour. It is true that by the 1980s the majority of those leaving the educational system were well-qualified young people with second- and third-level qualifications. They were eager to work in Ireland at wage rates that were relatively low by comparison with those prevailing on the European mainland. Subsidiaries of multinationals employing these young people in Ireland were able to achieve high productivity levels here.

Corporatism

Much of the credit for maintaining the supply price of labour at a competitive level during the 1990s has been given to the return to centralized wage bargaining in the late 1980s. In the 1990s, a series of National Wage Agreements was negotiated between the "social partners"—employers, unions and the government. The promise of steady reductions in income tax rates helped gain acceptance for moderate rates of pre-tax pay increases over three-year intervals and there was a marked drop in the incidence of industrial disputes. This arrangement has proved difficult to maintain in recent years, as the labour market grew tighter. None the less, early in 2000 another three-year wage agreement was negotiated, labelled the Partnership for Prosperity and Fairness. It is interesting to note that American firms thrived in a setting of centralized pay bargaining that is completely alien to their domestic industrial relations environment. Many also combined this corporatist approach with a union-free work place.

One of the consequences of the policy of buying pay moderation through reductions in income taxes and other taxes has been that

Ireland went from being a country with relatively high taxes in the mid-1980s to one of the least heavily taxed countries in the EU by the end of the 1990s (figure 11). In addition to their contribution to moderating pay demands, income tax reductions were justified on supply-side arguments and concentrated on situations where excessively high marginal tax rates prevailed in the past. In particular, the tax code has been restructured to increase the rewards to two-earner households and there has been a marked increase in the labour-force participation rate among married women. The falling tax burden may also have played some part in attracting former emigrants back to work in Ireland.

By 2000, however, public opinion became increasingly critical of the growing deficiencies in the availability and quality of public services, especially in the health sector. In the debate on the appropriate level of spending on public goods and services, the low burden of taxation is frequently invoked to persuade politicians that the priority should shift from further tax reductions to increased public

Figure 11: Tax revenue as a percentage of GDP

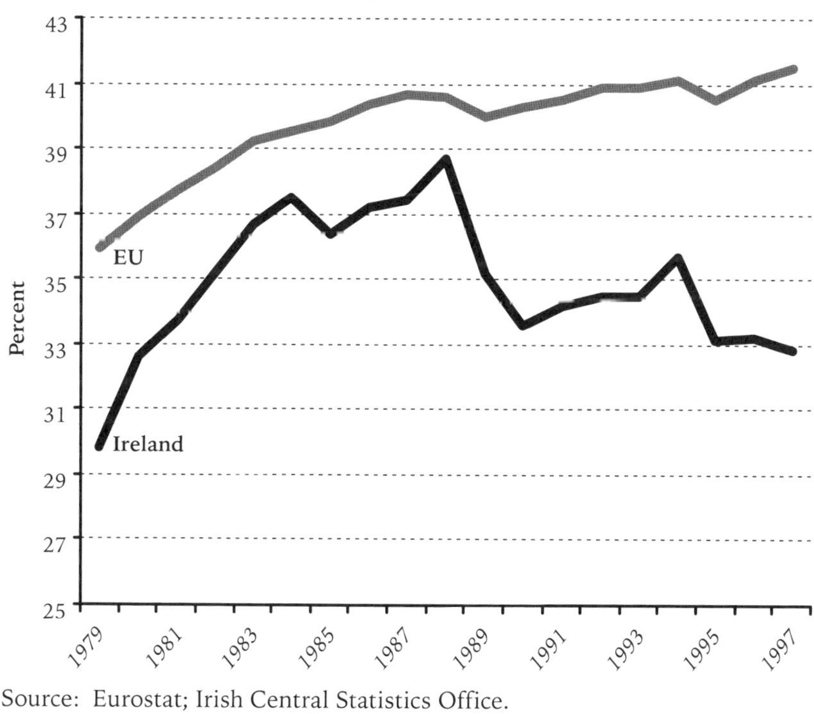

Source: Eurostat; Irish Central Statistics Office.

spending. Unfortunately this shift in attitude occurred just as the economy lost momentum in 2001 and the buoyancy of tax revenue enjoyed over the preceding five years was drying up. Commitments to large increases in public sector spending combined with stagnant tax receipts made large inroads on fiscal surplus in 2002.

Other advantages

In addition to the attractions listed above, Ireland is, of course, English speaking, enjoys reasonably easy access to the United States and has close cultural ties with North America. The legal and accountancy professions are "Anglo-Saxon." American firms have found it relatively easy to recruit managers familiar with their business culture: in fact, many were able to identify Irish people working in their American branches who were keen to return to Ireland to head up new projects there.

Tax policy

I have emphasised the prominence of a favourable CT regime among the attractions Ireland offers to inward investors. It is time to look at this topic in more detail.

To understand the present Irish CT regime we need to recall that, from the 1930s to the 1960s, the country relied heavily on protectionist measures to promote industrial development. The result was a growth of employment in small, inefficient firms oriented almost exclusively towards the tiny domestic market. During the 1950s, there was a growing awareness of the limitations of this policy, heightened by the prospect of economic integration in Europe. This prompted a switch to other measures to promote industrialization, in particular attempts to attract inward FDI. Initially, foreign investment was encouraged only in areas where it would not represent a threat to established domestic firms. However, this consideration declined in importance as the prospect of dismantling tariffs and the almost inevitable collapse of employment in "infant industries" loomed. It was hoped that new, outward-oriented firms would offset the loss of employment in the older firms and, as we have seen, this goal was realized in the 1990s.

The switch to outward orientation was gradual. In 1947, a customs-free zone was created at Shannon Airport. The Industrial Development Authority was established in 1949 and, during the 1950s, given increasing powers and resources to aid manufacturing industries with grants. In 1956, a 100% tax remission, known as Export Profit Tax Relief (EPTR), was applied to profits from manufacturing exports. Any remaining restrictions on inward foreign investment were removed by the repeal of the Control of Manufactures Act in 1958. Thus, by the 1960s, the former hostility to FDI had been completely transformed to active encouragement. Foreign investors were offered the attractions of a low CT rate and grant-aid to come to Ireland. No restrictions were placed on their freedom to remit profits from the country. Few other developing countries exercised as liberal a regime towards FDI at this time. The completion of the change to outward-looking policies came with the passage of the Anglo-Irish Free Trade Area Agreement (1965), entry into the European Economic Community (EEC) in 1973, the completion of the EU single market in the early 1990s, and the adoption of the euro in 1999.

It was inevitable that the EEC and the EU should raise the question of the compatibility of the Irish CT structure with obligations under the Treaty of Rome. Because the EPTR was targeted on exports, it was deemed discriminatory and was phased out over the period from 1981 to 1990. In its place, a 10% "preferential" CT rate was applied to profits from the manufacturing industry and internationally traded services.[2] In the late 1980s, the 10% preferential CT was extended to activities located in the International Financial Services Centre (IFSC) in Dublin. But, in the course of the 1990s Ireland's success in attracting FDI in the "high-tech" and financial sectors provoked claims of "unfair tax competition" from countries such as Germany and Belgium that were not pleased to see some relocation of activity to Ireland.

The CT tax system in place in Ireland in the 1990s was dualistic, with low rates applicable to export sales (up to 1981) or manufacturing and internationally traded services (after 1981), on the one hand, and a high "standard" rate applicable to the remainder of the corporate sector, on the other. In the early 1980s, the standard rate was 50% but this has been reduced to 20% by 2001 (see below). Such has been the growth of manufacturing in the 1980s and 1990s that tax payments at the "preferential" rate quickly grew to more than half of the total take from CT. However, the only major taxpayers of the "standard" CT rate have been the non-IFSC banks. The anomalous situation in which the lowest rate of profit tax in the EU applied to one set of businesses and one of the highest rates applied to all the rest was not acceptable to the EU. The preferential rate was originally introduced as a temporary measure, to be phased out in 1990 but it was subsequently extended to 2010 (2005 in the IFSC). Some features of the tax system, in particular the application of the special inducements to attract activity to the IFSC, have been viewed as "unfair tax competition" in some European circles. In negotiations between the Irish government and the EU Commission, the following compromise was approved.

- The preferential rate of tax will continue to apply to manufacturing firms until 2010.
- The preferential IFSC tax will continue to apply to qualifying firms until 2005.
- Remission of local taxes and special capital allowances in the IFSC to cease immediately.
- A uniform CT rate of 12½% will apply to all firms by the year 2010 at the latest.

The 1999 Finance Act set out the schedule for achieving a single CT rate of 12½% by 2003. The 2002 Budget lowered the CT rate to 16%.

These changes in the Irish tax regime should be viewed in the context of a general tendency towards lower tax rates across the EU. To the degree that these cuts reflect a desire to attract foreign firms at the expense of other countries, they are part of a non-cooperative game. If FDI is highly sensitive to tax differentials and, bearing in mind that corporation taxes account for relatively small proportion of total government revenue, there are grounds for fearing that a "race to the bottom" will develop as countries use lower tax rates to try to raise domestic employment. Following the introduction of the single European currency in 1999 and the removal of the exchange rate as an instrument of national policy, the belief has grown that competitive tax cuts will replace competitive devaluations. This has led to demands for tax harmonisation: "... tax cooperation can be viewed as the next step after the creation of the euro for reducing both impediments to the completion of the Single Market and the scope for non-cooperative behaviour in this highly integrated area" (European Parliament 2001: 13). However, this claim would not command wide support among European finance ministers, who cherish their freedom of manoeuvre in the fiscal area.

It is important to try to assess the sensitivity of FDI to tax differentials. While firms may be attracted to, and anchored in, locations by agglomeration economies—that is, the advantages of operating in an area where a concentration of similar firms has created deep labour, capital and sub-supply markets—and by the reluctance of firms to relocate, it seems that flows of FDI are to tax differentials and, perhaps, have become more so as markets become increasingly integrated. A recent study concluded that "taxes appear to be an important consideration for firms' decisions whether or not to invest abroad, as well as where to invest abroad" (Gropp and Kostial 2000: 19).

How important has Ireland's low CT rate been in attracting FDI to the country? It has been estimated that the increase in the Irish statutory CT rate from 10% to 12.5% will reduce the inflow of FDI to the country by about 7% (European Parliament 2001). But, the effects of this would be minor compared with those of a more thorough harmonization of EU CT rates. Gropp and Kostial estimate that, if CT rates had been harmonised on the EU average over the period from 1990 to 1997, Ireland would have experienced a fall of more than 1.3% of GDP per annum in its net FDI flows. There would also have been a fall of about 0.8% of GDP in revenue from this tax. It is therefore clear that Ireland's strategy of using a low CT regime to attract inward FDI is vulnerable to the growing concerns about "unfair tax competition" and the drive to harmonise EU tax rates.

Side effects of the low CT rate

We should acknowledge some of the peculiar consequences of the low CT rate that has been the centrepiece of the Irish incentives package. In the first place, it is easy to exaggerate the "high tech" nature of the new industries that have been attracted. The end products produced and sold by the Irish subsidiaries of MNCs tend to be technologically sophisticated, ranging from state-of-the-art computer chips to the latest pharmaceutical and medical care products, but few of these firms have located a full range of functions in Ireland. While most Irish operations involve processes that are considerably more advanced than routine assembly, the highest corporate functions—managerial, financial, R&D, and marketing—are usually performed at home by the parent company. The average skill levels in the "high tech" sectors is significantly but not dramatically above the average for all Irish industries: 19% of the employees in foreign-dominated sectors are "administrative and technical" personnel compared with an average of 14% for all manufacturing. Despite the relative importance of manufacturing to the Irish economy, business expenditure on R&D as a proportion of GDP is below the EU average (Barry, Bradley, and O'Malley 1999). However, these criticisms may have lost some of their force in recent years as the Irish subsidiaries of multinational corporations (MNCs) increase in sophistication and the range of their functions and as more indigenous firms start up to profit from the opportunities offered in the booming economy. The spin-off effects of the microelectronics industry in the software sectors is a notable example.

A more important consequence of the role of low CT in the Irish success story is the extent to which the economy—or at least its statistical representation—has been distorted through "transfer pricing." The low CT rate encourages MNCs to use various internal pricing stratagems to inflate the profits attributable to their Irish subsidiary. The industrial sectors that have boomed in Ireland are those that are particularly well able to avail of the advantages offered by transfer pricing in minimizing their global tax liabilities. They are "patent intensive" rather than capital or technology intensive. Four sectors in particular exhibit characteristics that can only be explained as a response to the global tax-planning incentives provided by the low Irish CT rate: cola concentrates, software reproduction, certain organic base chemicals, and computers. The difference between Ireland and Europe in net output per employee in the cola-concentrates industry was over £½ million in 1995. This difference has been taken as an estimate of "entrepôt activity" in Irish industry, akin to the passage of vast amounts of goods through ports such as Hong Kong or Singapore. In aggregate, this activity has been estimated to equal over 15% of GDP (Honohan, Maître, and Conroy 1998; Honohan and Walsh 2002).

The location in Ireland of enormously profitable subsidiaries of MNCs has inflated the figures for output and exports in certain sectors of the economy and led to a growing outflow of profits and other payments from the country. This is reflected in the exceptionally large gap between Irish Gross *National* Product and Gross *Domestic* Product. In 1998, GDP exceeded GNP by 14.3%, easily the largest gap in the OECD. Interest payable to non-residents on the national debt accounts for a declining proportion of this outflow, the bulk of which is attributable to "dividends, distributions of branch profits and inter-affiliate interest."[3] The very high value added per employee in these sectors also exaggerates the apparent productivity of the Irish labour force and its growth rate.

Nevertheless, the effects of transfer pricing on the measurement of economic growth should not be exaggerated. A minimalist calculation of the contribution of MNCs to the Irish economy that included only their labour costs reduced the estimated growth rate of national output in the 1990s by less than one half of one percentage point (Keating 1995). Moreover, it is now generally recognized within the country, if not always internationally, that GNP provides a better guide than GDP to the "true" performance of the Irish economy. In fact, the more arcane concept of National Disposable Income is an ever better yardstick because it takes account of the importance of net international transfers. While these measures have been growing by about one half of one percentage point per year less than GDP, it is obvious that this correction does little to dent the record of the "Celtic tiger" when this is taken to refer to the rapid growth of income per person. However, it does put a bigger dent in the rosy view of the rate of productivity growth that emerges from the official statistics.

Finally, we should not lose sight of the fact that revenue from the 10% CT rate on the inflated profits of the Irish subsidiaries of MNCs has swelled the Irish exchequer's coffers, creating head room for lower taxes on labour and expenditure. However, it is true that a low tax rate on one type of income erodes the tax base and increases the rate of other taxes required to finance a given level of public expenditure. This argument was very relevant in Ireland in the 1980s when the low CT rate contrasted starkly with the very high marginal tax rates paid by individuals. Employees of a company that paid less than 10% of profits in tax would have faced a marginal income (including social security) tax rate of almost 75% as well as very high rates of VAT and excise taxes on drink, tobacco, electrical goods, and cars. Forward shifting of these high taxes offset some of the attraction of the low CT rate. A more even spread of the tax burden would have resulted in lower aggregate deadweight losses. This case was made as long ago as 1984 by the Irish Commission on Taxation, which argued for a thoroughgoing simplification of the tax system and against excessive reliance on targeted tax incentives.[4] The same points were reiterated in a review of Irish industrial promotion published in 1992.[5] Thus the EU's emphasis on standardization of tax rates and reduction in special tax incentives accorded with domestic advice on tax policy. But, it is unlikely that this advice would have been acted on in the absence of the threat of sanctions from Europe.

It is striking that the burden of taxation in Ireland fell sharply after the watershed year of 1989, while it continued to grow in the EU. As a consequence, the gap between Ireland and EU widened markedly during the 1990s. Measured relative to GDP, Ireland now has one of the lowest tax burdens in the OECD (see figure 11).[6] Disentangling cause and effect is extremely difficult in this area. Did the accelerated growth rate lead to a fall in the tax burden or was the faster growth due to lower tax rates? It is true that towards the end of the 1980s the emphasis of policy shifted to tax cuts and especially to lowering the high marginal rate payable on wages and salaries. But, no dramatic changes in tax rates or in the structure of taxation occurred in the late 1980s that can be identified as the factor that triggered the boom. And, it is obvious that the rapid decline in the ratio of tax to GDP during the 1990s was primarily a reflection of the large inflow of FDI and exceptional growth of GDP rather than *vice versa*.

It is not implausible to give some credit for the drive to reform European tax structures to the role of the low CT rate in the Irish success story. The Irish example seems to have played a part in converting European governments to the belief that the heavy burden of CT had contributed to the problems of slow growth and high unemployment labelled Eurosclerosis. In the late 1990s, Germany, Denmark, France, the United Kingdom, and Italy have implemented or announced CT rate cuts. (As we have seen, at the same time Ireland announced an increase in its low statutory rate from 10% to 12.5%.) The most important development was the German government's announcement that it was reducing the corporation tax rate from 40% in 2000 to 25% in 2001, leading to a significant decrease in the effective tax rate as well. As the movement to reduce CT rates gathers momentum in Europe, Ireland's competitive advantage in this area is being eroded. But, this is not necessarily a zero sum game: the aggregate performance of the European economy may be improved by learning from the role of a favourable tax regime in the Irish success.

Conclusion

Simplistic conclusions about the contribution of tax policy to Ireland's economic boom are not warranted. The recent success of the economy has been due to variety of factors whose relative importance is difficult to establish. Taking a long view, the rapid growth of the 1990s could be regarded as a belated catch-up with the leaders that was postponed by the policy errors of the 1970s and the painful correction of these during the 1980s. However, it cannot be doubted that the timing of the boom in the late 1980s points to the contribution of several policies put in place towards the end of the decade: the successful fiscal adjustment, the reversal of the upward trend in the tax burden, the competitive level of the exchange rate, and wage moderation achieved through "social partnership." Ireland's commitment to the EU project, the ratification of the Single European Act (1986), and the adoption of the single European currency should also be acknowledged while, in the longer run, Ireland's location, use of the English language, familiar business culture, and general openness to American influences have helped make the country an attractive location for FDI. Further, comparative research is required to establish the relative importance of each of these factors. But, after all these caveats, it cannot be doubted that a favourable climate for FDI and especially a low CT rate have been crucial to the recent boom and the form that it took.

The Irish tax system has evolved towards greater uniformity and less reliance on targeted (i.e. distortionary) incentives. From the

1960s through the 1980s, a zero tax rate on export profits was used to promote outward orientation in manufacturing. In the 1990s, in response to pressure for a less discriminatory tax regime, a 10% rate was applied to all profits from manufacturing and "internationally traded services." The commitment now is to apply a 12½% rate to all corporate profits.

A low corporate tax rate did contribute to raising the country's share of the flow of FDI into the EU and continues to be an important component of Ireland's favourable business environment. This inflow played a very significant role in the boom of the 1990s. In recent years, Ireland has raised the statutory CT rate while it was being reduced in other member states, so that the country's competitive advantage is being eroded. In the future, Ireland shall have to rely increasingly on other factors, especially relatively low unit labour costs, to maintain its attractiveness as a location for manufacturing industry and internationally traded services.

Notes

1 This paper updates and extends the material in Walsh 2000b.

2 A plethora of additional tax incentives were also introduced such as accelerated depreciation allowances and tax breaks linked to preference share financing and leasing.

3 Royalties and license fees paid abroad were formerly included in GDP but are now treated as a cost of production and excluded.

4 See Commission on Taxation 1984: para. 6.13–36.

5 The "Culliton Report" (Ireland, The Department of Industry and Commerce 1992).

6 A caveat is required because this comparison uses GDP in the denominator and Irish GDP exceeds GNP by about 15%. Adjusting for this would still leave Ireland with a relatively low tax burden.

References

Barry, F., ed. (1999). *Understanding Ireland's Economic Growth.* Basingstoke: Macmillan.

Barry, F., J. Bradley, and E. O'Malley (1999). Indigenous and Foreign Industry. In F. Barry (ed.), *Understanding Ireland's Economic Growth* (Basingstoke: Macmillan): 45–74.

Commission on Taxation (1984). *Direct Taxation: The Role of Incentives* (Second Report). Dublin: The Stationary Office.

Dornbusch, R. (1989). Credibility, Debt and Unemployment: Ireland's Failed Stabilization. *Economic Policy* 8: 173–209.

European Parliament, Directorate-General for Research (2001). The Reform of Taxation in EU Member States. *Economic Affairs Series* Econ 127 EN.

Gropp, R., and Kostial, K. (2000). The Disappearing Tax Base: Is Foreign Direct Investment Eroding Corporate Income Taxes? Working Paper No. 31. Frankfurt: European Central Bank.

Honohan, P. (1999) Fiscal Adjustment and Disinflation in Ireland: Setting the Macro Basis of Economic Recovery and Expansion. In F. Barry (ed.), *Understanding Ireland's Economic Growth* (Basingstoke: Macmillan): 75–98.

Honohan, P., B. Maître, and C. Conroy (1998). Invisible Entrepôt Activity in Irish Manufacturing. *Irish Banking Review* (Summer): 38–52.

Honohan, P., and B. Walsh (2002). Catching Up with the Leaders: The Irish Hare. *Brookings Panel on Economic Activity* April 4–5. Washington, DC: Brooking Institution.

Ireland, The Department of Industry and Commerce (1992). *A Time for Change: Industrial Policy for the 1990s.* "Culliton Report." Dublin: The Stationery Office.

Keating, W. (1995). Measuring Growth. In *Proceedings of Conference on Measuring Economic Growth* (Novermber 9) (Dublin: Central Statistics Office and Irish Economic Association).

Leddin, A., and B. Walsh (1998). *The Macroeocnomy of Ireland.* Fourth edition. Dublin: Gill and Macmillan.

Nicodème, G. (2001). *Computing Effective Corporation Rates: Comparisons and Results.* Economic Papers 153. Brussels: European Commission Directorate-General for Economic and Financial Affairs.

Walsh, B. (1996). Stabilisation and Adjustment in a Small, Open Economy: Ireland, 1979–95. *Oxford Review of Economic Policy* 12, 3 (October): 74–86.

——— (2000a). From Rages to Riches: Ireland's Economic Boom. *World Economics* 1, 4 (October-December): 113–33.

——— (2000b). The Role of Tax Policy in Ireland's Economic Renaissance. *Canadian Tax Journal* 48, 3: 658–73.

A tale of two provinces—tax policy in Alberta and Ontario

Kenneth J. McKenzie

Provincial governments in Canada account for roughly half of total taxes levied in the country and they have been rather more aggressive, and innovative, in the area of fiscal policy than the federal government. Therefore, it is useful to study the tax policies of provinces that have been successful in stimulating economic prosperity. Such a study can provide important input into changes in federal tax policies that can result in greater prosperity for all of Canada.

While all provinces have instituted fiscal reforms over the past several years, the governments of Alberta and Ontario have led the country in terms of both the timing and scope of fiscal reforms, particularly in the area of tax policy. The genesis of these reforms coincided with the election of Alberta premier Ralph Klein in 1993 and Ontario premier Mike Harris in 1995. Although the approaches to tax reform followed in the two provinces share some common characteristics, in some important and fundamental ways they are also very different. The purpose of this chapter is to compare and contrast the approaches to fiscal reform followed in these two provinces, with an emphasis on tax policy.

I begin by looking at the "big picture" in the two provinces. I then turn to an analysis of specific initiatives in the areas of personal and corporate taxation. The approach I take is to analyze the tax policy initiatives in the two provinces in terms of their impact on labour markets and capital markets separately. This is, I think, a natural way to think about the implications of the tax initiatives in the two provinces, and a way that yields several important insights.

The big picture

My starting point for the comparison of tax policies in the two provinces is the election of Ralph Klein as premier of Alberta in 1993 and the election of Mike Harris as premier of Ontario in 1995. Even those with a casual awareness of the political scene in Canada recognize the election of Progressive Conservative governments under their leadership as a watershed in the provincial fiscal environment in this country.

Prior to the election of Klein and Harris, the government finances of Alberta and Ontario were in dismal shape: Ontario had a run of five consecutive deficits in excess of $10 billion prior to 1995, which caused the net ration of debt to GDP in the province to rise from 22% in 1991/1992 to over 30% in 1994/1995. Prior to 1993, Alberta ran eight consecutive deficits, ranging from $1.3 billion to over $4 billion, which caused the net ratio of debt to GDP to rise a staggering thirteen percentage points, from 2% in 1986/1987 to 15% by 1992/1993. In both provinces, these were the high-water mark for their ratios of debt to GDP. Under the Klein government, Alberta moved into a net asset position of over 3% of GDP by 1999/2000, which represents a remarkable eighteen-percentage point turnaround in just seven years. Harris's government oversaw a somewhat less dramatic, but still significant, five-percentage point reduction in the net debt-to-GDP ratio to 25% by 1999/2000.

How were these lower ratios of debt to GDP achieved? There are several ways to answer this question. One is to pore over the budget documents of provincial governments before and after the fiscal turnaround to document the various change in spending and revenue. Since this approach is very time consuming, I take a simpler approach and consider changes made at a more aggregate level. For this purpose, I trace the evolution of the net ratio of debt to GDP through time to establish the extent to which the improvements occurred through tax and spending changes. Thus, consider the government budget identity:

$$\Delta b_t = b_{t+1} - b_t = (g_t - t_\tau - f_t + (r - \alpha)\, b_t) \;/\; (1 + \alpha) \qquad (1)$$

where b is the net debt/GDP ratio, g is government program spending as a percentage of GDP, τ is provincial own-source tax revenue as a percentage of GDP, f is federal transfers as a percentage of GDP, r is the interest rate on government debt and α is the growth rate in GDP.

This equation shows that there are three key sources of change in a provincial government's debt/GDP ratio. One is the primary deficit $(g - \tau - f)$. A positive value for the primary deficit indicates that program spending exceeds tax and transfer revenue, which results in a net addition to debt while a negative value implies a net reduction in debt. The second key variable is the interest rate payable on outstanding debt. The higher the interest rate, the higher is the debt servicing cost and therefore the larger is the annual deficit and growth in the debt. The third key variable is the rate of growth in GDP. The more quickly the economy grows, the smaller will be the ratio of debt to GDP. As the equation indicates, it is the relative magnitudes of the interest rate payable on government debt (r) and the underlying rate of growth in GDP (α) that is key. Intuitively, this condition shows that, if the interest rate exceeds the rate of growth in the economy, the ratio of debt to GDP rises because the effect of the higher cost of servicing the debt exceeds the benefits due to the growth in GDP.

I employ this simple budgetary equation in several ways. The first is to use it to obtain an expression for what is known as the *sustainable tax rate* (Blanchard 1993). The sustainable tax rate is the tax rate (tax revenues as a percentage of GDP) required to finance a given level of program spending (as a percentage of GDP) so that the existing debt/GDP ratio is maintained at its existing level. It is obtained by setting $\Delta b_t = 0$ in the above expression and solving for τ_t, which gives:

$$\tau^*_t = g_t - f_t + (r - \alpha)\, b_t \qquad (2)$$

This equation says that to maintain existing program spending as a proportion of GDP (gt) and keep the net debt/GDP ratio from changing, the provincial government's own-source revenues as a percentage of GDP (the sustainable tax rate τ^*t) must cover program spending not financed by transfers from the national government (the amount gt – ft) plus the excess of debt service costs over economic growth ((r – α) bt). Thus, the higher the program spending not financed by transfers and the higher the cost of debt service relative to the economy's growth rate, the higher will be the sustainable tax rate.

Given the definition of the sustainable tax rate, we can then determine whether existing fiscal policy is sustainable in this sense by comparing the sustainable tax rate, τ^*_t, to the actual tax rate, τ_t (the actual ratio of own-source tax revenue to GDP). If the resulting *tax gap*, $\tau^*_t - \tau_t$, is positive; that is, the sustainable tax rate exceeds the actual tax rate, and the net debt/GDP ratio will increase. If the tax gap is negative, the current fiscal policy reduces net debt/GDP. If they persist indefinitely, neither positive nor negative tax gaps are sustainable in the longer run. An indefinitely persistent positive tax gap means that the debt/GDP ratio will eventually approach infinity, which would lead to an ultimately unbearable tax burden just to finance the debt. An indefinitely persistent negative gap means that the debt/GDP ratio eventually approaches negative infinity, as the government accumulates private assets (rather than debt) in its own portfolio. Of course, neither of these limiting cases will occur in practice, as government policies must necessarily change in response to indefinitely growing debt or assets (relative to GDP). Thus, the existence of either gap for a prolonged period of time implies the need for the government to change its tax policies or its spending policies, or both. Of course, if the tax gap is zero, the current debt/GDP ratio is maintained. The analysis of the tax gap over time thus provides information about the changes in tax and spending policies needed to attain any desired change in the ratio of debt to GDP.

It is important to understand two things from the definition of the sustainable tax rate. The first is that there is no presumption that setting the actual tax rate equal to the sustainable tax rate and, therefore, eliminating the tax gap and maintaining the existing debt/GDP ratio, is in any way an optimal economic policy. For example, it may well be desirable to run negative tax gaps over a period of time in order to reduce the debt/GDP ratio. Indeed, and as we shall see, fiscal policy in Ontario and Alberta throughout the period studied was geared toward doing precisely this. Second, there is also no presumption that positive or negative tax gaps should be eliminated by adjusting tax policy rather than spending policy. The focus on the sustainable tax rate is arbitrary; one could just as easily determine the sustainable spending rate by rearranging the formula. The purpose of the expression is to identify current pressures, tendencies, and directions in fiscal policy, not to determine an optimal configuration of fiscal policy.

Figures 1 and 2 show the net debt/GDP ratio and the tax gap in Ontario and Alberta respectively, from 1988/1989 to 1999/2000. The "Klein Effect" in 1993 and the "Harris Effect" in 1995 are very evident. Prior to 1993, Alberta ran a series of sizable positive tax gaps and, as a result, the debt/GDP ratio rose accordingly. The Klein

Figure 1: Tax Gap and Ratio of Net Debt to GDP, Ontario

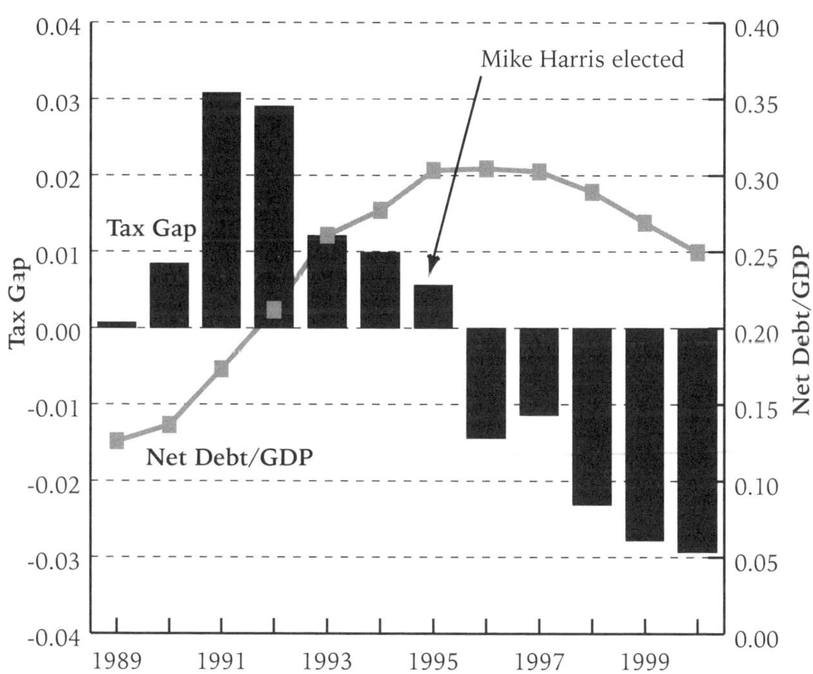

Sources: Author's calculations; Financial Management System data, several years.

Figure 2: Tax Gap and Ratio of Net Debt to GDP, Alberta

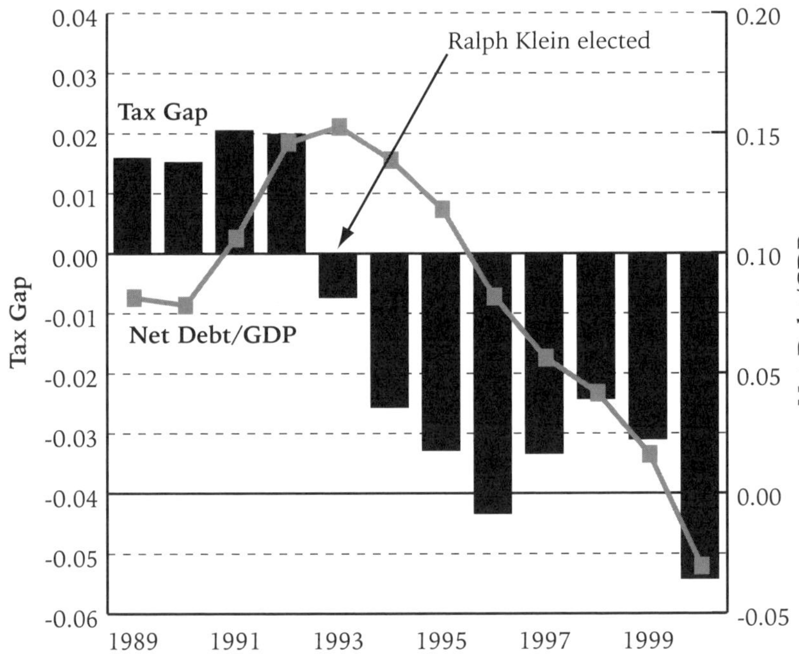

Sources: Author's calculations; Financial Management System data, several years.

government moved quickly to turn things around, as we see a modest negative tax gap in 1993 followed by substantial negative gaps thereafter. As indicated above, the result was a turn-around of 18 percentage points in the debt/GDP ratio by 1999/2000. The Harris government also moved quickly to a negative tax gap, which resulted in a five-point reduction in debt/GDP over the five-year period.

Figure 3 shows the extent to which the turn-around in the tax gap was caused by reductions in program spending (total spending net of debt service) as a percentage of GDP. In Alberta, spending fell from 17.2% in 1992/1993 to 12.7% in 2000. In Ontario, the ratio of program spending to GDP fell from 14.8% in 1994/1994 to 11.8% in 2000. The size of the cut in Alberta is particularly noteworthy.

Figure 4 reflects in part the fact that Alberta chose to forgo tax cuts early in the Klein government's first mandate in favour of paying down the debt and instead implemented significant cuts to personal taxes and, to a lesser extent, corporate taxes in 2001, only

Figure 3: Program Spending as Percentage of GDP, Ontario and Alberta

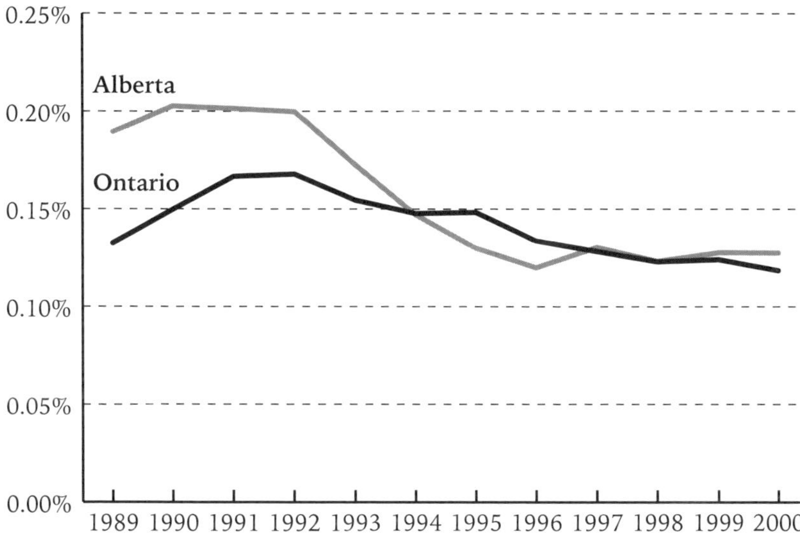

Source: Financial Management System data, several years.

Figure 4: Own Revenue as Percentage of GDP, Ontario and Alberta

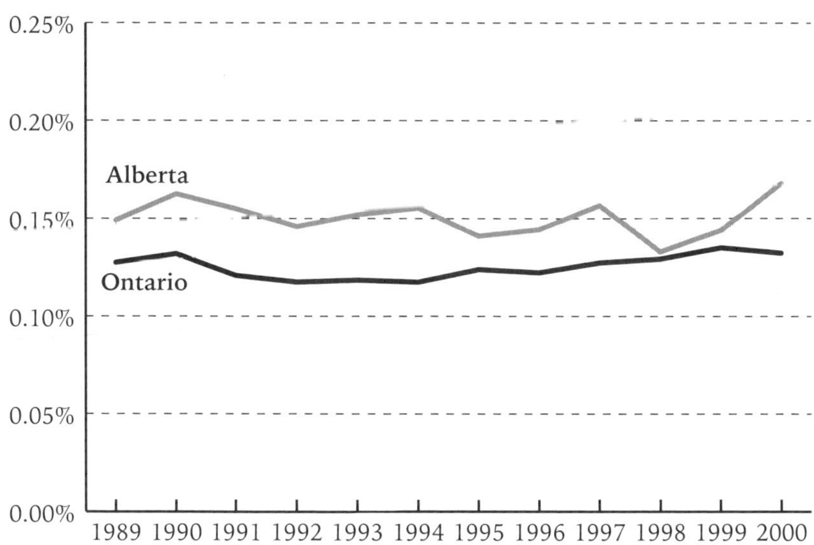

Source: Financial Management System data, several years.

after having moved to a net asset position in 2001. Ontario followed a different approach, choosing to implement tax cuts first, primarily for low- and middle-income earners (more on this below). This, of course, delayed paying down the debt and partly accounts for the more modest reduction of the debt/GDP ratio in Ontario.

Recalling that the actual tax rate is given by actual own-source revenues as a percentage of GDP, figure 4 shows that the actual tax rate has been relatively constant under both the Klein and the Harris governments. Indeed, there has been a modest rise in tax revenue as a percentage of GDP in Ontario, despite tax reductions. This rise is due to strong overall economic growth, fueled largely by the lengthy economic expansion in the United States over this period. In Alberta, the fairly large increase in the ratio of revenue to GDP in 1999/2000 was due largely to the rise in oil prices.

Fiscal policy, economic growth, and the debt/GDP ratio

Until recently, the Klein and Harris governments have been fortunate to implement their fiscal reforms in an environment of relatively robust economic growth. An interesting question, then, concerns the extent to which the reduction in the debt/GDP ratio in the two provinces can be attributed to this normal economic growth throughout the period rather than to the discretionary fiscal policies of the government. This issue is of particular interest in the study of the success of the Klein and Harris governments in lowering the ratio of debt to GDP.

To consider this issue, we can look at two ways in which growth can affect the debt/GDP ratio. First, equation (1) implies quite simply that economic growth decreases the ratio directly simply by increasing the denominator. Second, it is important to establish the extent to which the growth in GDP has been caused by the changes in tax and spending policies themselves. This analysis can be undertaken by using an approach suggested by Pierre Fortin (1996) and refined by Ron Kneebone and Jack Leach (2001) and which uses equation (1) to decompose the change in the ratio into its various constituent parts. To do this, we must come up with an estimate of potential GDP for the two provinces over the periods in question and determine the extent to which actual exceeded potential GDP. This figure reflects the extent to which GDP growth was above "normal." There are several complicated ways of estimating potential GDP. Kneebone (forthcoming), however, points out that running a Hodrick-Prescott filter through the GDP series yields an estimate of potential GDP that is very similar to that which arises under more sophisticated approaches.

Figure 5 shows actual and potential GDP for Ontario from 1980/1981 through to 1999/2000 using a Hodrick-Prescott filter. Particularly noteworthy is the fact that Ontario GDP was actually lower than potential from 1990/1991 to 1997/1998. Only in the last two years of the Harris regime has Ontario's growth rate been high enough to close the gap so that actual GDP exceeded potential. Alberta's experience throughout the Klein regime has been similar. As shown in figure 6, the province grew roughly at potential from 1992/1993 through 1996/1997, slightly below potential from 1996/1997 to 1998/1999 and above potential thereafter.

Table 1 decomposes the change in the net debt/GDP ratios in Alberta from 1993/1994 to 1999/2000 and in Ontario from 1996/1997 to 1999/2000. The first row shows the actual percent-

Figure 5: Actual and Potential GDP for Ontario

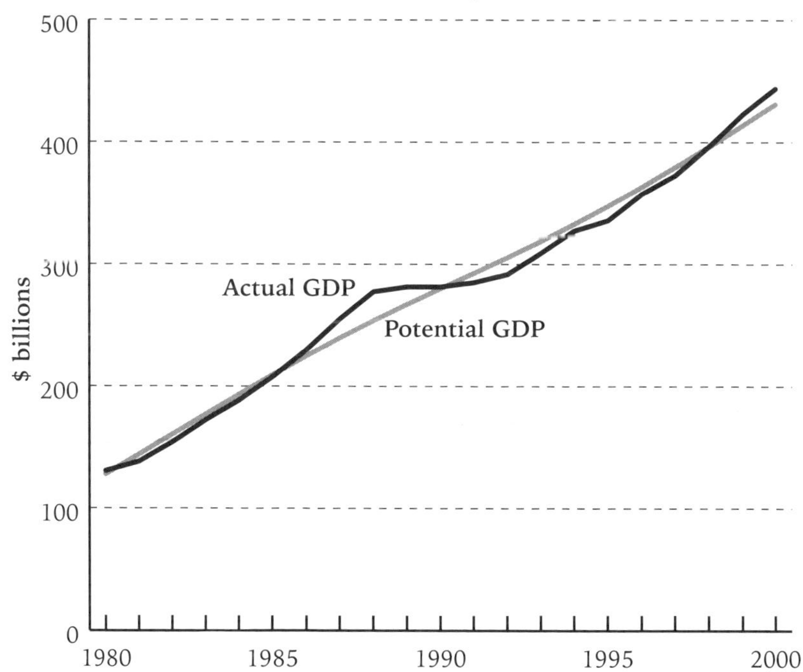

Source: Author's calculations.

Figure 6: Actual and Potential GDP for Alberta

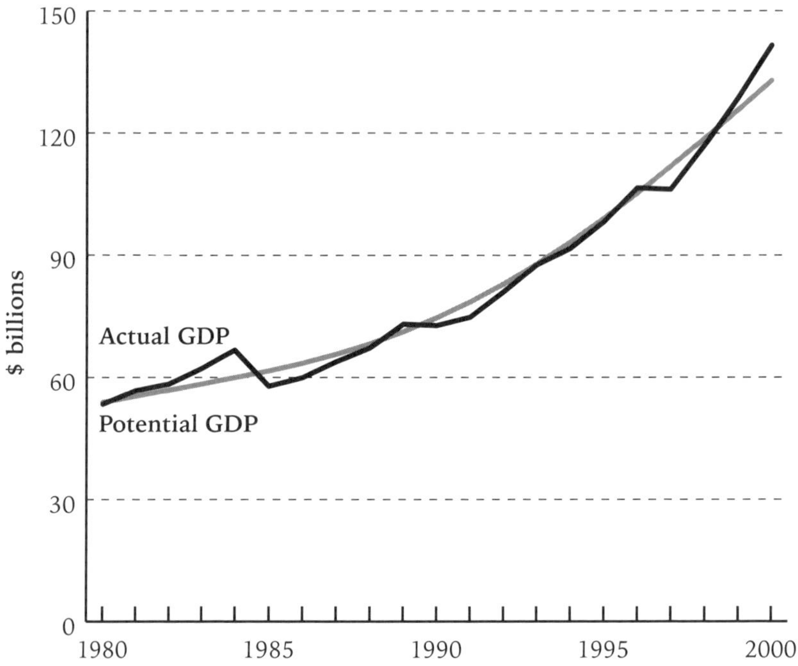

Source: Author's calculations.

age change in the ratio. The second row shows the change due to discretionary fiscal policy, which is measured by the difference between cyclically adjusted program spending and own-source revenues expressed as a percentage of GDP $(g - \tau)$. The third row shows the change due to the difference between the interest rate and economic growth $(r - \alpha)\ b$.

As can be seen from table 1, of the 18.30 percentage-point improvement in net debt/GDP in Alberta over the Klein years, fully 13.67 percentage points, or 75%, was due to discretionary fiscal policy, as measured by the primary deficit $(g - \tau)$. As indicated above, the bulk of this was due to expenditure reductions. The remainder was due to economic growth and lower interest rates.

Of the 5.49 percentage point turn-around in net debt/GDP ratio in Ontario, 3.03 percentage points, or 55%, was due to improvements in fiscal policy. The remainder was due to economic growth and lower interest rates on government debt.

Table 1: Change in Ration of Net Debt to GDP in Alberta under Klein and Ontario under Harris

	Alberta (1993/94–1999/00)	Ontario (1996/97–1999/00)
Change in Net Debt/GDP (Δb)	–18.30	–5.49
Due to Fiscal Policy (g–τ)	–13.67	–3.03
Due to Growth (r–α)b	–4.63	–2.46

Source: Author's calculations.

Of course, all of this leaves unanswered the role that fiscal policy itself plays in actually stimulating provincial growth. The approach reflected in table 1 presumes that potential GDP is itself unaffected by fiscal policy. In small, open economies such as Alberta and Ontario and over the short period of time considered here, this is a reasonable assumption. In the longer term, one might expect fiscal policy in general, and tax policy in particular, to feed through to affect both the level and growth of potential GDP. Regardless, the calculations show that Alberta relied to a significantly greater extent on discretionary fiscal policy, in particular expenditure cuts, to lower their debt/GDP ratio over this period than did Ontario.

The labour market—labour supply and migration

Taxation affects the labour market in two ways. First, according to the argument from *standard labour-market efficiency,* taxation affects the incentive to work. Second, the tax system creates incentives for individuals to move across borders, a phenomenon commonly called the "brain drain" in the popular press though economists usually talk of *fiscally induced migration*. While these two issues are obviously related, for expository purposes I will deal with them separately.

Standard labour-market efficiency

Discussion of tax policy at the provincial level in both Alberta and Ontario has focused not so much on the level of taxes but on the degree of progressivity in the personal income tax, which has important implications for the efficiency of labour markets. A well-established proposition in public finance states that the more progressive the rate structure associated with raising a given amount of revenue, the greater the disincentive to work and the lower the amount of labour income produced in the economy. These tax-induced inefficiencies directly reduce the standard of living in the two provinces. The argument from standard labour-market efficiency thus implies that the choice of the appropriate degree of progression in the tax system involves, to a large extent, the classic trade-off between equity and efficiency. How much income, or standard of living, is the public prepared to sacrifice in order to pursue distributional objectives and tax high-income earners proportionately more than the low-income earners?

Fiscally induced migration

The effects on migration stemming from taxation and other differences in the fiscal environment are widely debated but no consensus has emerged. Recently, most of the discussion in the popular press has focused on the "brain drain" from Canada to the United States, even though labour is much more mobile intranationally, within Canada and between provinces, than internationally. Indeed, Tanis Day and Stan Winer (1994) provide evidence that Canadians—particularly anglophone Canadians—are quite responsive to differences in net fiscal benefits—the value of government services less taxes—across provinces. Thus, the "brain drain" induced by taxation and other fiscal factors is likely to be a much bigger factor at the provincial than the federal level.

The importance of the international "brain drain" has been the subject of considerable debate. Without entering that discussion directly, I conclude from this debate that the federal personal income tax can be somewhat progressive, though perhaps less than currently, without inducing much international brain drain. On the other hand, fiscally induced migration among provinces is much more sensitive to the progressivity of the income tax. This implies importantly that the use of the personal tax system as a redistributive mechanism should be confined largely to the federal government and that provincial governments should not rely heavily on the tax system to redistribute income. Thus, although the federal government can, and arguably should, impose a progressive rate structure, the provinces should not.

This insight has been put forward before by Jon Kesselman (2000) for Canada and Martin Feldstein and Marian Wrobel (1998) for the United States. The latter authors' empirical results suggest that the high degree of interstate mobility in the United States essentially rules out the use of redistributive tax policy at the state level and that there is in fact no trade-off at the state level between distribution goals and economic efficiency. In addition, changes in the progressivity of personal income taxes at the state level alter the structure of employment and distort the mix of labour inputs used by firms in the state. Thus, changes in such tax progressivity in individual states create efficiency losses without achieving any redistribution.

It is interesting to consider the structure of the tax systems in Alberta and Ontario in this context. As shown in table 2, Alberta has an initial exemption of $12,900 and taxes all income above this level at a single 10% rate. Ontario uses a lower initial exemption but has marginal tax rates up to just over $61,000 in taxable income that are less than 10% and therefore lower than Alberta's. For taxable income in excess of roughly $61,000 Ontario's marginal tax rate is higher, at 11.16%. (Note that all of the following tables are for single, working-age individuals).

But table 2 does not tell the whole story. Unlike Alberta, Ontario levies surtaxes on "high income" individuals. A surtax is a "tax on a tax." Ontario levies two surtaxes, one at 20% on basic provincial

Table 2: Basic Provincial Personal Income Tax Rates in Alberta and Ontario, 2001

	Exemption	Tax Rates	Brackets
Alberta	$12,900	10.0%	All income
Ontario	$7,368	6.20%	$0–$30,814
		9.24%	$30,815–$61,629
		11.16%	$61,630 and over

Source: Canadian Tax Foundation 2002.

taxes greater than $3,569, and one at 36% on basic provincial taxes greater than $4,491. These surtaxes have the impact of increasing the top marginal rate for Ontario from the 11.16% indicated in table 2, to over 17.4%. Table 3 shows the combined federal and provincial marginal tax rates in Alberta and Ontario taking into account basic taxes and the Ontario surtaxes.

The biggest differences emerge in the "upper income" ranges, in excess of approximately $63,000 in taxable income. For taxable income in excess of $100,000, the marginal tax rates in Ontario are substantially higher—almost 7.5 percentage points—than in Alberta.

While marginal tax rates are important for the overall efficiency of the tax system, average tax rates are important both for distributional reasons and for location decisions, which are inframarginal

Table 3: Federal and Provincial Income Tax Rates in Alberta and Ontario, 2001

	Taxable Income	Tax Rates		
		Federal	Provincial	Total
Alberta	$0–$7,368	0	0	0
	$7,369–$12,900	16.0%	0	16.0%
	$12,901–$30,754	16.0%	10.0%	26.0%
	$30,755–$61,509	22.0%	10.0%	32.0%
	$61,510–$99,999	26.0%	10.0%	36.0%
	$100,000–Max	29.0%	10.0%	39.0%
Ontario	$0–$7,368	0	0	0
	$7,369–$30,754	16.0%	6.2%	22.2%
	$30,755–$53,600	22.0%	9.24%	31.24%
	$53,601–$61,509	22.0%	11.088%	33.088%
	$61,510–$63,200	26.0%	13.92%	39.92%
	$63,201–$99,999	26.0%	17.4096%	43.4096%
	$100,000–Max	29.0%	17.4096%	46.4096%

Sources: Author's calculations; Canadian Tax Foundation 2002.

in nature. Under the residence principle of personal income taxation followed in Canada, individuals cannot allocate a portion of their personal income across jurisdictions—it is an all or nothing proposition.[1] Thus, in assessing the "competitiveness" of the tax system in, say, Ontario vis-à-vis Alberta from this perspective, it is the *average* effective tax rate that matters, not the *marginal* tax rate. While the marginal rate structure obviously affects the average tax rate, so too do various other things, most particularly the income exemptions.

Figure 7 shows the average tax rates in Alberta and Ontario for various household income levels. These calculations are based on Statistics Canada's SPSD/M model and, therefore, incorporate several aspects of the tax/transfer system other than the personal income tax rates discussed above. As the figure shows, for lower income households the average tax rate in Alberta is lower than Ontario, for middle and upper-middle income households average tax rates are about the same, while for upper-income households the average tax rates in Alberta are again lower.

Studies of the brain drain from Canada to the United States have generally concluded that the net loss of Canadians to the United States is rather small in relation to the Canadian population and labour force. However, of those Canadians who do move to the United States, a disproportionally large number are skilled workers in the higher income ranges—the "best and the brightest." Some analysts have suggested, therefore, that reductions in the brain drain can be achieved most effectively and cheaply by the use of lower marginal tax rates on high-income earners rather than of across-the-board tax cuts (see Finnie 2001). Given the evidence suggesting that skilled, high-income individuals are the most mobile internationally, we may assume that such individuals are also the most mobile nationally. If this is true, then Ontario's approach of focusing cuts on lower-income earners is rather curious. As documented above, relative to Alberta at least, high-income earners in Ontario face high marginal and average tax rates, which promote, so the argument goes, both the national and international brain drain.

The discussion of labour markets to this point has focused on the ways these markets are affected by the personal income tax. But corporate income taxes can also affect labour markets in two important ways. First, as will be discussed in more detail below, the

Figure 7: Average Tax Rates, Ontario and Alberta (2001)

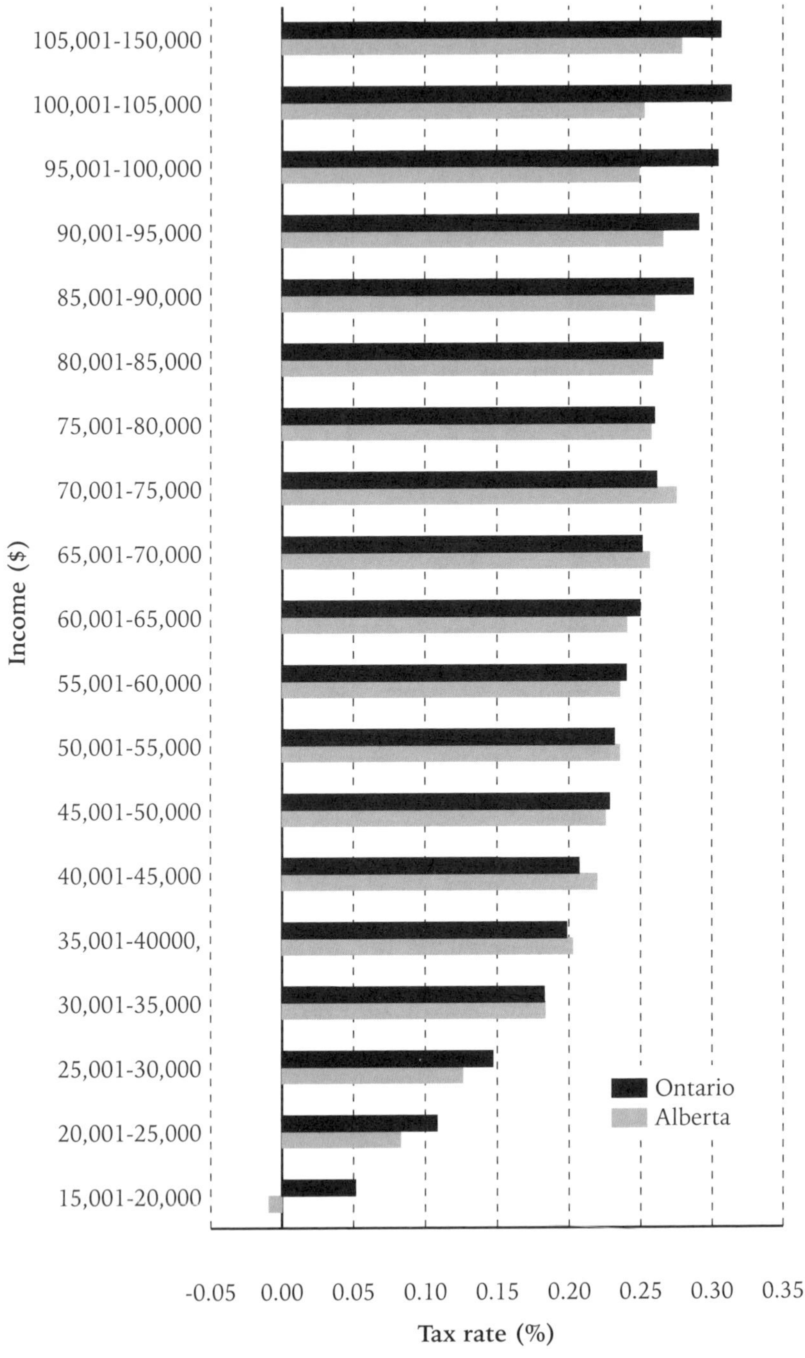

Source: Author's calculations based on Statistics Canada, SPSD/M Model.

long-run incidence of provincial corporate income taxes is likely to fall to a large extent on workers and, in particular, on low-skilled workers. This conclusion is based on the notion that in the long run capital is quite mobile across provinces so that if corporation taxes in one province are higher than elsewhere, capital will leave the high-tax province until after tax incomes are equalized. As a result of the lower capital stock in that province, the demand for labour and wages is lowered so that, in effect, the higher corporation tax rate is paid in part by workers through their lower income.

Second, what is perhaps less widely appreciated is that under the Canadian CIT allocation formula there are some important interactions between labour markets and CIT differentials among provinces. When a company has operations in more than one province, there must be some way to allocate the profits across the provinces in order to apply provincial corporate income taxes. In Canada, we use a formula allocation approach. Under the allocation formula, a corporation with operations in more than one province has to report income for tax purposes in each province according to the corporation's share of sales and wages in each province. Specifically, the allocation formula requires that the share of corporate taxable income allocated to a province is equal to 50% of that province's share of sales plus 50% of its share of the corporate payroll.

In 2000, Ontario announced its intention to lower its CIT rate on larger corporations to 8% over five years (from a general rate of 14% and a manufacturing rate of 12%). Given Ontario's status as the biggest province in the country and the province's disproportionate share of industrial activity, this put tremendous pressure on the other provinces. Alberta responded in 2001 by announcing its intention to lower its CIT rate to 8% as well (from a rate of 13.5% on all large corporations). Alberta's announced cut in the CIT rate was justified in part by the fact that the reduction in the CIT rate in Ontario would act effectively as a tax on new workers employed in Alberta due to the way that the CIT allocation formula works.[2]

The reason for this is that, if a corporation has activities and, especially, employees, in both Ontario and Alberta, and if the CIT rate in Ontario is significantly lower than Alberta, there is a disincentive for the company to hire new workers in Alberta. This is because the allocation of corporate profits for tax purposes is based, in part, upon the share of the company's payroll in each province. If new workers are hired in Alberta, this increases the share of profits allocated to Alberta, which means that a greater share of corporate profits will be taxed at the higher Alberta tax rate. This increases the cost of hiring new workers in Alberta relative to Ontario. Because of the way the allocation formula works, if the Ontario CIT rate is lower than the Alberta CIT rate, the result is akin to imposing a tax on new workers hired in Alberta. Moreover, this effective taxation of labour in Alberta is imposed immediately, prior to any outflow of capital from Alberta to Ontario that might be expected to occur in the long run. While Alberta was the first province to react to Ontario's CIT rate cut, no doubt other provinces will follow, to the extent that they can.

The capital market—savings and investment

Provincial taxes also have implications for the savings decisions of individuals and the investment decisions of firms. To address these implications, it is necessary to deal with two issues. One stems from the fact that the existing personal *income* tax structure in Canada makes it very similar to a *consumption* tax. The second concerns the relationship between savings and investment in a small, open economy like that in Canada, which is affected by the relationship between the personal and corporate income taxes

The personal income tax system in Canada is designed to mimic the taxation of consumption in several ways. The most important is the tax-sheltered treatment of RRSP/RPP contributions. Satya Poddar and Morley English (1999) estimate that, because of various tax shelters, most particularly the treatment of RRSPs, as much as 75% of investment income in Canada goes untaxed at the time that it is earned. The deferment of taxes on income from savings due to tax shelters such as RRSPs means that the effective tax rate on this income is zero, as would be the case under a consumption tax.

This does not mean, however, that the personal income tax system does not impinge upon the savings decisions of Canadians. The 75% figure referred to above is an average while economic theory suggests that efficiency costs and distortions should be measured at the margin. In this case, the relevant margin is the effective rate of tax on an additional, or marginal, unit of saving. While the data studied by Poddar and English imply that the *average* effective tax rate on income from savings is likely very low due to tax shelters, the *marginal* effective tax rate may actually be quite high. Poddar and English also report that over half of taxable dividends and two thirds of taxable capital gains are reported by individuals with assessed incomes in excess of $100,000, and that the vast bulk of investment income is earned by individuals with income in excess of $50,000. These high-income earners are most likely to have exhausted the "easy" ways of tax sheltering their investment income as they reach their RRSP/RRP limits. Increases in income from saving are, therefore, quite likely to be subject to taxation and, at the margin, cannot be considered subject to the consumption-tax treatment.

Recent empirical support for this view comes indirectly from a paper by Michael Veall (1999), who investigates whether the flattening of the Canadian personal tax structure in the 1988 tax reform had any effect on RRSP contributions. He found "no convincing evidence that these changes affect RRSP contributions" (Veall 1999: 21). While it is important to emphasize that he examined only the impact on RRSP rather than all savings, Veall's empirical result is consistent with the interpretation that any increase in savings in Canada in response to reduced taxes on investment income, if it takes place at all, tends to take place in non-RRSP vehicles at the margin.

Table 4 presents marginal effective tax rates on the real return to saving an additional dollar for income in the form of interest, dividends, and capital gains received by individuals in the highest tax brackets in Alberta and Ontario. The rates were calculated under the assumption that the income is fully taxed at the highest marginal tax rate in each province and take into account the

Table 4: Real Marginal Effective Tax Rates on Savings, 2001

	Alberta	Ontario
Interest	54.6%	65.0%
Dividends	33.3%	46.2%
Capital Gains	21.5%	25.7%

Source: Author's calculations.
Note: Assumes a nominal rate of return of 7%, inflation of 2%, and (for capital gains) a holding period of 10 years.

taxation of the inflationary component of the return to savings, the presence of the dividend tax credit, and the deferral effect of taxing capital gains on realization rather than upon accrual.[3] Table 4 shows that the marginal effective tax rate on savings in 2001 was substantially higher in Ontario than in Alberta. The difference in the rates is due mainly to the surtaxes charged on personal income taxes in Ontario, which result in very high marginal tax rates, as discussed earlier. The obvious conclusion is that the more progressive rate structure in Ontario, which generates very high marginal tax rates from those who earn higher income, tends to discourage savings and distort savings decisions much more than the flatter rate structure in Alberta.

Let me now turn to the implications for capital markets of the fact that Canada is a "small, open" economy. This attribute of Canada arises from the fact that savings and investment in the country are only a small share of the world capital market so that they do not influence world interest rates and borrowing costs. These conditions, combined with the absence of severe restrictions[4] on the ability of Canadians to invest savings or finance domestic investment by borrowing abroad, result in a "disconnect" between the supply (savings) and demand (business investment) sides of the capital market. For this reason, there is no necessary relationship in Canada between domestic business investment and domestic savings that exists in large countries or small countries with severe restrictions on international capital mobility.

It is extremely important to understand the implications of this "disconnect" for tax policy—in particular, for provincial tax policy. If capital is in fact perfectly mobile, it means that on the supply (savings) side of the capital market the before-tax rate of return earned by savers in Canada is fixed from our perspective, determined by the international financial market. On the demand (business investment) side of the market, it means that the after-corporate-tax rate of return that businesses must pay investors in order to attract their savings is also fixed, determined by the international financial market. What this implies is that, unlike a closed economy, or an economy with immobile capital, the savings of Canadians do not necessarily end up being invested in Canadian companies and, even when they do, an increase or decrease in the supply of those savings has no impact on the after-corporate-tax rate of return that businesses must provide to their investors. Rather, decreases or increases in Canadian savings show up simply as a change in the proportion of domestic business investment financed by Canadians, the remainder being financed by foreign savings. As such, while taxes imposed on the return to savings at the personal level will distort the supply of savings by Canadians, and generate the usual type of efficiency costs associated with these distortions, when capital is perfectly mobile there is no impact on business investment in Canada, and the efficiency costs are confined to the supply side of the capital market. Similarly, changes in the taxation of business investment in Canada will distort capital investment in the country, and generate the associated efficiency costs, but these effects will be confined to the demand side of the capital market and will have no impact on the saving decisions of Canadians.

Importantly, as alluded to previously, perfect capital mobility also suggests that the *burden* of taxes levied on the investment (demand) side of the market will eventually be borne completely by less mobile factors within Canada, such as labour. This is because the after-corporate-tax rate of return on domestic investments is fixed by the international market. An increase in the corporate tax rate on domestic capital will simply drive capital out of the country, in order to keep the after-tax rate of return the same, which will lower the demand for less mobile factors such as labour, which will in turn lower wages. This is particularly true for low-skilled workers, who are less mobile than high-skilled workers. Perfect capital mobility in a small, open economy thus has stark implications for the analysis of the taxation of capital.

Canada—a small, open economy?

The validity of the preceding analysis depends crucially on the assumption that Canadian capital is perfectly mobile. The existence of perfect capital mobility is a matter of some debate. John Helliwell and Ross McKitrick (1999) provide a summary of the issues and argue that, if capital in Canada is perfectly mobile, then there need be no correlation between national savings and investment rates because of the "disconnect" noted above. However, empirical investigations of OECD countries, including Canada, consistently reveal a strong *positive* correlation between domestic saving and investment. Helliwell and McKitrick, for example, estimate a national savings retention rate of around 0.60 for Canada, which is significantly different than zero. This suggests that Canadian savings do tend to manifest themselves largely in domestic investment, and that Canada is not a completely open, small economy facing perfect international capital mobility. Instead, Canada may be best viewed as a small, open economy with "fairly" high capital mobility. The implications of this characterization have not been fully explored in the literature about public finance, though they suggest to me that domestic taxation of savings and investment have at least some of the unintended consequences on labour income and net foreign indebtedness noted above.

While Canada as a whole may not be a small, open economy with perfect capital mobility, individual provinces within the most certainly country are. This proposition is documented and supported strongly by Helliwell and McKitrick, who show that the correlation between savings and investment in individual provinces is statistically indistinguishable from zero. This finding has important implications for provincial tax policies. In particular, it suggests that individual provinces cannot increase provincial business investment by lowering personal taxes on saving but that they can increase investment through the lowering of taxes on business. Changes to provincial income taxes designed to encourage both savings *and* investment require lower personal income taxes *and* lower corporate income taxes.

Recent studies suggest that corporate taxes have a significant impact on business investment decisions, particularly those of multinational corporations.[5] Since provincial corporate taxes currently add from 9 to 17 percentage points to the overall basic income tax rate facing corporations in Canada, lower provincial taxes are able to enhance Canada's competitive position internationally and increase the rate of investment. This is particularly important in light of evidence that technological advances tend to be embodied in new capital (see Cummins 1998).

Competitiveness, the tax base and the marginal effective tax rate

The preceding analysis focused on the rate of taxation of business profits. However, there are two other important differences between Alberta's and Ontario's tax policy for business that affect investment. First, Ontario levies a capital tax on large corporations equal to 0.30% of paid-up capital; Alberta does not levy such a capital tax. Second, Ontario has several special corporate-tax incentives targeted to different sectors; Alberta does not. Examples of such targeted investment incentives in Ontario are for research and development and for the movie industry.

When thinking about the competitiveness of corporate tax systems across jurisdictions, most people focus on *statutory corporate income tax (CIT) rates*. These are the tax rates set out in the Income Tax Act. While important, the statutory CIT rate is only one part of the corporate tax system. Equally important is the *tax base*, which is determined by the various rules that govern the rate and nature of various deductions and write-offs against corporate revenue. There may also be tax credits associated with certain types of investments that further reduce corporate tax liability directly. Generous write-offs and credits can negate the impact of a high statutory tax rate. Moreover, many jurisdictions impose *other taxes* on capital, such as explicit capital taxes, that are not taken into account in a simple comparison of statutory CIT rates. As suggested above, both of these considerations are important in a comparison of corporate taxes in Alberta and Ontario.

Economists have developed a measure designed to reflect the effect of tax rates and the tax base. This measure is called the *marginal effective tax rate* (METR) on corporate capital. It reflects the overall competitiveness of a province's business tax regime. The METR may be considered to measure the rate of return on investment needed to compensate investors for their forgone investment opportunities.

The following numerical example illustrates the concept of the METR and the method for computing it. Consider that a company requires a return of 5% on its assets after taxes to place money into a given project. This rate is commonly called the "after-corporate-tax-hurdle" rate of return. Now consider that the corporate income and capital taxes on that project, at the given statutory rates and after taking into account the various write-offs, deductions and credits allowed under the CIT, amount to 5% of invested assets. Under these assumptions, the firm requires a pre-tax rate of return of 10% to meet its target after-corporate-tax rate of return of 5%. The difference of 5 percentage points between the rate of return before and after the tax hurdle is called the "marginal tax wedge." The METR on capital in this example is calculated by dividing this tax wedge by the before-tax-hurdle rate of return, which gives a METR of 50% ((10% – 5%)/10%). The METR thus measures the effective rate of tax levied on a marginal investment project that just earns the required hurdle rate of return after the payment of corporate taxes.

It follows from the definition that a positive METR indicates that the tax system discourages investment and that a negative METR encourages investment. In either case, the tax system introduces distortions and consequent inefficiencies into the economy by causing investment to be either lower or higher than it would be in the absence of taxation. A METR of zero means that the tax system has a neutral effect on investment.

The calculation of METRs is useful in assessing the relative competitiveness of the business tax regime across jurisdictions using a single and sensible summary measure. This measure accounts for differences in statutory CIT rates, types of investment, in tax bases due to write-offs and credits, and in direct capital tax rates.

Table 5 shows some METR calculations for Ontario and Alberta for manufacturing and non-manufacturing capital in the light of existing federal and provincial tax regimes and after pending reductions in federal and provincial corporate taxes.

Recall that both before and after the proposed rate cuts, the statutory CIT rates in Alberta and Ontario are very similar. Yet the calculations in table 5 show that the METR on capital in Ontario is substantially higher than it is in Alberta. This reflects the very important role played by capital taxes in the determination of METRs.

Table 5: Federal and Provincial METRs on Capital, Alberta and Ontario

	Alberta	Ontario
Manufacturing—Current	21.0%	25.3%
Manufacturing—Rate Cuts	17.3%	23.1%
Non-manufacturing—Current	29.0%	33.8%
Non-manufacturing—Rate Cuts	19.8%	25.8%

Source: Author's calculations.

In particular, the presence of Ontario's capital tax adds from four to five percentage points to the overall METR on capital in that province vis-à-vis Alberta.

The METRs illustrated in table 5 are calculated on an aggregation of capital in the two provinces, specifically machinery and equipment, buildings and structures, land, and inventory. As mentioned above, corporate tax policy in Ontario is also characterized by a tendency to offer special incentives for particular sectors. This is evident in the current system in the lower tax rate levied on non-manufacturing corporations (though this will disappear when the rate cuts are fully phased-in). It is also evident in its treatment of R&D expenditures, which receive very generous investment allowances over and above the federal tax credit for R&D. By way of contrast, the approach in Alberta has been to offer a level playing field, with no sector-specific tax rates and no incentives for R&D.

The implications of this in the case of R&D are illustrated in table 6, which presents calculations of the marginal tax wedges (the difference between the pre-tax and post-tax required rates of return on marginal investments) on R&D capital for Ontario and Alberta. The calculations are presented under the assumption that cuts in the provincial corporate income tax rates at both the federal and provincial level are fully phased-in (yielding a combined federal-provincial corporate income tax rate in each province of 29%, consisting of the 21% federal rate and 8% provincial rate).[6]

Table 6 indicates that the marginal tax wedges are negative in both provinces, as expected since generous federal R&D incentives result in lower tax obligations. As a result, the before-tax-hurdle rates of return are 4.6% and 3.2% lower than the required after-tax rate of return for Ontario and Alberta respectively. The gap between the two provinces is due to the fact that Ontario offers substantial incentives for R&D while Alberta does not. The R&D tax incen-

Table 6: Federal and Provincial Tax Wedges on R&D Capital, Alberta and Ontario (percentage points)

	Alberta	Ontario
Tax Wedge on R&D Capital	–3.2	–4.6

Source: Author's calculations.

tives in Ontario no doubt have a positive effect on investment in the province. However, as noted above and in many other studies,[7] such targeted incentives are distortionary and cause inefficiencies. The problems would be eliminated if the provincial governments discontinued R&D subsidies, lowered overall taxes on corporations correspondingly and relied on federal subsidies to compensate investors for any positive spillover effects created by R&D spending.

Sales taxes

While Alberta and Ontario have in many ways blazed the trail for tax reform in Canada, both provinces have displayed a decided lack of initiative on the issue of sales taxes. Ontario levies a single-stage retail sales tax while Alberta is the only province in the country that has no sales tax at all. These policies fly in the face of much economic theory and empirical evidence that sales and other consumption taxes promote efficiency and growth better than income and other direct taxes.

In some recent studies, McKenzie (2000a) and Dahlby (2000) show that Alberta can completely eliminate its existing personal income tax and replace the lost revenue with a sales tax levied on the federal GST base at a rate roughly comparable to existing sales tax rates in the other provinces. These studies estimate that introducing a sales tax in Alberta in this way—by eliminating the personal income tax—would add about a tenth of a percentage point to the long-run growth rate in Alberta. A similar policy has been recommended for the federal government by Don Drummond of the Toronto Dominion Bank who argued that revenue lost through lower income tax rates should be replaced by an increase in the GST rate.[8] He estimates that a reduction in personal income taxes by $10 billion and an increase in the federal GST rate from 7% to 10% would increase the long-run rate of growth in Canada by as much as a half of a percentage point.

While seemingly modest, these estimated increases in the growth rate can compound over time to yield substantial increases in Canadian living standards. For example, the work by Dahlby (2000) and McKenzie (2000a) suggests that the present value of the growth stimulus due to replacing the provincial personal income tax in Alberta with a sales tax is equivalent to each household receiving an extra year's income (about $40,000). Despite studies such as these, the government of Alberta has steadfastly refused even to consider the possibility of introducing a sales tax to replace (or reduce) the income tax.

Ontario has also resisted reforms to its system of sales tax. Of particular concern is the failure to replace the existing retail sales tax with a GST style value-added tax. Economists believe that for a number of reasons, not the least of which is the removal of taxes on business inputs, value-added taxes are much more efficient than sales taxes. Politically, the adoption of a value-added tax does not mean the loss of Ontario's sovereignty over the details of the tax system and the base to which the tax is to be applied. The experience of Quebec supports this contention.

Conclusion

This paper has presented a comparative analysis of the tax policies in two provinces, Alberta and Ontario. Each province has implemented fairly substantial fiscal reforms over the past several years on both the tax and expenditure fronts. In Alberta, these reforms coincided with the election of Ralph Klein in 1993 and, in Ontario, with the election of Mike Harris in 1995.

The two provinces have followed very different approaches in carrying out the reforms. Ontario cut expenditures and at the same time implemented cuts in personal income tax very early on in the process. As a result, there was very little reduction in the absolute level of the debt, as the province relied on economic growth and low interest rates to improve its net debt/GDP ratio over time. I calculate that three quarters of the five-percentage-point improvement in the debt/GDP ratio in Ontario during the 5 years following the election of the Harris government was due to economic conditions as opposed to discretionary fiscal policy.

Alberta, on the other hand, made expenditure cuts and used the resulting surplus to pay down the debt for seven years and only then implemented tax cuts. As a result, over half of the 18-percentage-point improvement in the debt/GDP ratio in Alberta that took place since the election of the Klein government was due to discretionary fiscal policy.

In my view, Alberta's approach is superior to that of Ontario, which left a large amount of debt that will cause interest costs to soar when interest rates rise and increase the burden when economic growth falters. Alberta does not face these risks, at least to the same extent.

The two provinces also followed markedly different approaches to the implementation of cuts in the personal income tax. Ontario opted to focus the cuts for low- and middle-income earners, maintaining a highly progressive rate structure with high marginal rates on higher income earners. Alberta opted for cuts across the board, implementing a single rate tax with a high initial exemption. Again, I believe that Alberta's approach is superior. The high personal exemption in Alberta benefits low-income earners directly and results in low average rates for high- as well as low-income earners. Importantly, the much lower average tax rates on high-income earners in Alberta substantially reduces national and international brain-drain pressures and encourages savings. The personal income tax structure in Ontario, by contrast, imposes much higher taxes on high-income earners and thus encourages the brain drain and discourages savings.

Both provinces also implemented significant reductions in their corporate income tax rates. But again, Ontario and Alberta used different approaches. Ontario continues to levy a tax on the stock of corporate capital, in the form of the corporate capital tax. Alberta never had such a tax. The Ontario capital tax increases the effective tax rate on capital in Ontario significantly. Ontario also offers substantial tax incentives targeted to specific industries and types of expenditures, especially with respect to expenditures on R&D. Alberta eschews such targeted treatment, pursuing instead a policy of across-the-board tax relief. I believe that Alberta's strategy is superior to that of Ontario. Targeted tax incentives distort the economic environment and cause businesses to alter the basis upon which they make investments. This departure from tax neutrality generates significant economic costs.

Disappointingly, neither government has shown any initiative in its use of the sales tax. Alberta refuses to levy a sales tax to reduce, or even eliminate, the personal income tax, despite evidence that such a move would significantly increase growth and living standards in the province. Ontario refuses to change its retail sales tax to a GST-style value-added tax despite evidence that such a tax is more efficient and can be imposed at the provincial level without loss of political sovereignty.

Acknowledgments

I thank Jon Kesselman and Herbert Grubel for useful comments on an earlier draft.

Notes

1 Legal stratagems do exist that allow individuals to shift capital gains to other provinces but these are not widely accessible and can be quite costly.

2 See Government of Alberta 2000.

3 For the methodology behind these calculations, see McKenzie 2000 a, b.

4 An obvious exception is the foreign content limitation for RRSPs.

5 See Chirinko and Meyer 1997, Wasylenko 1997, Altshuler and Cummins 1997, and Cummins, Hassett, and Hubbard 2000.

6 The approach to calculating marginal effective tax wedges for R&D in the table is based on McKenzie 2002.

7 See Government of Canada 1997.

8 See Beauchesne 2001.

References

Altshuler, Rosanne, and Jason Cummins (1997). *Tax Policy and Dynamic Demand for Domestic and Foreign Capital by Multinational Corporations.* Technical Committee on Business Taxation Working Paper 97-4. Ottawa: Department of Finance.

Beauchesne, Eric (2001). Raise GST to 10 percent: TD Bank: Income Taxes, Not Sales Taxes Drive Away Workers: Expert Says. *The Ottawa Citizen* (November 22), Final Edition: D1.

Blanchard, O. (1993). Suggestions for a New Set of Fiscal Indicators. In H.A.A. Verbon and F.A.A.M van Winden (eds.), *The Political Economy of Government Debt* (North-Holland): 25–40.

Canadian Tax Foundation (2002). *Finances of the Nation.* Toronto, ON: Canadian Tax Foundation

Chirinko, Robert, and Andrew Meyer (1997). The User Cost of Capital and Investment Spending: Implications for Canadian Firms. In P. Halpern (ed.), *Financing Growth in Canada* (Calgary, AB: University of Calgary Press): 116–43.

Cummins, Jason (1998). *Taxation and the Sources of Growth: Estimates from United States Multinational Corporations.* NBER Working Paper No. W6533. Cambridge, MA: National Bureau of Economic Research.

Cummins, Jason, Kevin Hassett, and Glenn Hubbard (2000). Tax Reforms and Investment: A Cross-Country Comparison. *Journal of Public Economics* 62, 1-2: 237–73.

Dahlby, Bev (2000). *Tax Reform and Economic Growth in Alberta.* Calgary, AB: Canada West Foundation.

Day, Tanis, and Stan Winer (1994). Internal Migration and Public Policy. In A. Maslove (ed.), *Issues in the Taxation of Individuals* (Toronto, ON: University of Toronto Press): 3–61.

Feldstein, Martin, and Marian Wrobel (1998). Can State Taxes Redistribute Income? *Journal of Public Economics* 68, 3 (June) 369–96.

Finnie, Ross (2001). *The Brain Drain: Myth and Reality, What It Is and What Should Be Done.* Choices (November). Montreal, QC: Institute for Research on Public Policy.

Fortin, Pierre (1996). The Canadian Fiscal Problem: The Macroeconomic Connection. In Pierre Fortin and Lars Osberg (eds.), *Unnecessary Debts* (Toronto: Lorimer): 53–63.

Government of Alberta (2000). *Report of the Alberta Business Tax Review Committee.* Edmonton, AB: Alberta Treasury.

Government of Canada (1997). Report of the Technical Committee on Business Taxation. Ottawa: Department of Finance.

Helliwell, John, and Ross McKitrick (1999). Comparing Capital Mobility across Provincial and National Borders. *Canadian Journal of Economics* 32, 5 (November): 1164–73.

Kesselman, Jon (2000). *Flat Taxes, Dual Taxes, Smart Taxes: Making the Best Choices.* Policy Matters (November). Montreal, QC: Institute for Research on Public Policy.

Kneebone, Ron (forthcoming). Recent and Not So Recent Trends in Provincial Government Spending in Alberta. In L.S. Wilson (ed.), Managing in an Era of Fiscal Surpluses (Edmonton, AB: Institute for Public Economics).

Kneebone, Ron, and John Leach (2001). The Accumulation of Public Debt in Canada. *Canadian Public Policy* 27, 3 (September): 320–35.

McKenzie, Ken (2000a). Inflation Indexing of Capital Gains Taxes: An Examination of the Economic Implications. *Tax Forum* (Spring): 4–11.

McKenzie, Ken (2000b). *Replacing the Alberta Income Tax with a Sales Tax: Not Heresy but Good Economic Sense.* Calgary, AB: Canada West Foundation.

McKenzie, Ken (2002). Measuring Tax Incentives for R&D. Unpublished paper. Department of Economics, University of Calgary.

Poddar, Satya, and Morley English (1999). Canadian Taxation of Personal Investment Income. *Canadian Tax Journal* 47, 5: 1270–304.

Veall, Michael (1999). *Did Tax Flattening Affect RRSP Contributions?*. Social and Economic Dimensions of an Aging Population Working Papers. Department of Economics, McMaster University.

Wasylenko, Michael (1997). Taxation and Economic Development: The State of the Economic Literature. *New England Economic Review* (March/April): 49–52.